WHEN THE TIME COMES

Conversations with
Acharya Chandranath Kumar

By The Same Author

Felicitavia
The Ashram
Anandamurti: The Jamalpur Years
Devi
Song of the Taino

WHEN THE TIME COMES

Conversations with
Acharya Chandranath Kumar

Devashish Donald Acosta

InnerWorld Publications
San Germán, Puerto Rico
www.innerworldpublications.com

 Published in the United States by InnerWorld Publications, PO Box 1613, San Germán, Puerto Rico, 00683.

Library of Congress Catalog Card Number: 98-85902

ISBN 978-1-881717-01-0

When the urge for liberation arises,
the sadguru appears.

— Shrii Shrii Anandamurti

PREFACE

THE ANCIENT DISCIPLINE KNOWN as Yoga encompasses a wide variety of different paths and traditions. The essentials of this discipline are common to them all, but there are differences in vocabulary and approach that can cause confusion or make the differences seem greater than they actually are. Acharya Chandranath is the oldest living disciple of Shrii Shrii Anandamurti, the guru of Ananda Marga, whom he affectionately refers to as Baba.[1] While most of Dada's teachings will be familiar to readers from other spiritual traditions,[2] others are best understood in the context of his relationship with his guru. Hence, wherever necessary I have added footnotes in order to clear up any possible confusion, not only for practitioners from other yogic or meditative traditions, but also for those to whom the basic concepts of yogic practice may appear somewhat alien or unfamiliar.

Because the use of certain Sanskrit terms are fundamental to yogic practice, I have retained these words where Dada has used them and either given a translation in square brackets the first time they appear or footnoted them where a translation would have been unwieldy. As a general

1 Acharya means "teacher" (literally: one who teaches by example). It is a title given in Ananda Marga to those who are trained and authorized to teach the various meditation lessons and other practices. Ananda Marga (the path of bliss) is the name of the organization founded in January 1955 by Shrii Shrii Anandamurti (1922-1990) for the purposes of propagating his spiritual teachings and establishing service projects. Ananda Marga now has yoga centers and service projects in over 180 countries.

2 Dada means "elder brother." It is a common form of address in northern India and is commonly used to address acharyas in Ananda Marga.

rule, those Sanskrit words that appear in only one place are italicized and defined only where they appear. All other Sanskrit terms are non-italicized and are included in the glossary at the end of the text.

I would like to emphasize to the reader that the conversations recorded here are directed to those who are actively practicing spirituality. In both the yogic and Tantric traditions, it is primarily practice that counts, not philosophy; hence the conversations recorded here, with an adept who has made it to the end of the path that we are all walking, should be of great value to anyone with a sincere interest in spiritual practice.

INTRODUCTION

THERE IS A SAYING in India that if you want to see God, then look for him in his realized saints.[1] Of course, God is everywhere, and nowhere is he closer to us than within our own sense of existence, but the pathways that lead to that realization are long and steep, and there is nothing more helpful to us in our journey toward the Divine than the company of one who has reached there and can show us the way.

In the fall of 1993 I moved from California to the Anandanagar Ashram in West Bengal, India,[2] and over the next four years I was fortunate enough to be able to pay regular visits to such a man. Whenever I would return home to Anandanagar after one of those visits I would feel that my meditation had somehow been raised to another level. Things that had never been clear to me became clear. The Divine Presence was stronger. I would return convinced that the experiences Dada Chandranath talked about, as

1 Throughout these conversations Dada uses the masculine singular pronoun (he) to refer to the Divine. This is traditional practice in Indian English, and I have preserved his original usage rather than attempting to find a usage more in keeping with contemporary efforts to eliminate sexist language from modern English. In Sanskrit and its modern descendants, such as Bengali, a single pronoun is used for both male and female, thus this problem doesn't arise.

2 Anandanagar is the central headquarters of Ananda Marga. It is a sprawling complex of over two thousand acres located in one of the most backward and undeveloped areas in India — Purulia District in West Bengal. The residents of Anandanagar run over fifty developmental projects, including a hospital, alternative medicine clinic, several orphanages, reforestation center, infrastructure development, agricultural research institute, and numerous educational institutions. Apart from working in the projects, all the residents of Anandanagar are active practitioners of meditation and yoga, making it one of the largest spiritual communities in the world.

if they were the most natural thing imaginable, were tangible and within reach. Most of all, I found in him someone whom I could emulate in every sphere of life. When I saw his humility, his nobility of mind and character, his moral steadfastness, his human warmth, and the light than came from eyes that were always fixed on God, I felt an unbidden desire spring up inside me to mold myself after him. The path is subtle, so subtle sometimes that we easily lose sight of it beneath our feet. The most important things cannot be learned through words and are difficult to understand even through our own practice. But see them alive in another human being and what was unfathomable and inexplicable becomes an image painted into memory, always there to instruct us where words fail.

Whenever I could, I would bring visitors to see Dada. They would bring their questions and with each answer I would learn something new about the spiritual path. One day I was sitting listening to Dada answer a question and I felt a sudden dismay that I didn't have a tape recorder to preserve what my memory was incapable of preserving. I still remember the question. A friend of mine from England was explaining that whenever she would do intense *sadhana* for some time it would always be followed by a period of intense clash.[3] She would often get overwhelmed or discouraged at these times and stop doing such intense practice. Then she asked, "Dada, how to manage?"

"There is nothing to manage," he replied. "You will have to accept the suffering." He paused and looked at her with a compassionate smile. Then he went on to explain that if one does intense sadhana over a period of time, then strong clash is bound to follow because when one's speed is increased the resistance will always be greater. It is a simple law of nature. But what happens, he said, is that if you can maintain the intensity of your practice, then eventually you get used to that level of resistance and you no longer experience it as suffering. It is like when someone starts running or lifting weights for the first time. After the first workout, their muscles will ache and they will suffer physically for several days. But if they can keep up with their exercise and not be put off by the difficulties it entails, then eventually their muscles get used to that level of strain and they no longer experience it as pain. Rather, after some time they learn to enjoy the effort in itself. But if they give up and abandon the exercise, and then pick it up again after a gap of several weeks, they will have to go through the same process again and suffer the same aches and pains.

3 *Sadhana* literally means "effort to complete." It is the most commonly used term for spiritual practice, or more simply, for meditation.

By the time Dada had finished talking I had resolved to get hold of a tape recorder and record his answers for the benefit of all the people who would like to come to India and talk to him but who would never get the chance. Soon afterward I prepared a list of questions with the help of a few friends and paid him a visit at his village home in Gadopur. My next visit was couple of months later at the home of his eldest son in Patna, and between the two visits I had enough material for a book.

I have a couple of regrets concerning the scope of this book. The first is that the conversations themselves don't give the reader much of an idea of what it is like to have a chance to spend so much time with such a being. The real communication between a saint and those who go to them to learn about spirituality doesn't take place at the verbal level. The better part of the teaching lies in a transmission that cannot be seen or heard, much less captured on the written page. It can only be felt and experienced in the spark that travels unseen from the mind that is one with God to the mind that hungers for that same experience. I have added a few excerpts from my diary to try to give the reader some sense of the spiritual climate that these conversations took place in, but they barely begin to do it justice. And I will add one anecdote here from a different visit, earlier in the same year. Hopefully it will give the reader an initial glimpse into Dada's personality, although I must point out that Dada is fond of saying that it is not the personality that counts, it is the ideology.

On that occasion I had brought a group of westerners to see Dada, including a senior American monk of Ananda Marga. On the trip up to Patna I mentioned that Dada sat in *nirvikalpa samadhi* four times a day.[4] On the second day of our visit, Dada, myself, and this American monk went out to the porch to do our noon meditation while the women who had accompanied us remained inside to meditate. As we were sitting down, the monk turned to Dada and said, "Dada, Devashish tells me that you sit in nirvikalpa samadhi four times a day. Is it true?"

Dada smiled broadly and said, "Devashish knows, I don't know."

4 *Samadhi* means "yogic trance", or the state of union with God. There are two primary types of samadhi — *savikalpa* samadhi, where the mind of the spiritual aspirant merges into the Cosmic Mind, and *nirvikalpa*, where the mind dissolves into pure Consciousness and even the sense of "I" disappears. It is said that nirvikalpa cannot be described because the mind itself, the experiencer, does not remain, thus Dada's tongue-in-cheek comment a few lines later. This nirvikalpa state is the ultimate goal of yogic practice.

Again the monk pressed him. "But Dada, does that mean that yesterday, when we were doing our noon meditation together, you went into nirvikalpa samadhi?"

Then Dada said, "You see, when you come out of nirvikalpa samadhi your mind is abnormal. You cannot immediately eat your meal or talk to people. You need some time for your mind to come back into normal consciousness. Baba always used to tell us that whenever you have to be in public you should remain normal. Let us say you have to go to the ashram for group meditation and afterward you have to give a talk. You should not go into samadhi then. You should remain normal. Or say some people have come to meet you and you have to sit and talk to them and answer their questions. You should not go into samadhi. But in the morning, when you wake up and sit up on your bed for some meditation, then it is okay. After you take bath and sit for your full practice, it is okay. In the evening, when you sit again for full practice, it is okay. And at night, before you go to sleep, it is okay. But Baba always used to say that you must remain normal in public."

Then the monk asked him how he knew how long he would go into samadhi for. Dada replied that you take a *samkalpa*, a determination or resolve, before you go into samadhi that I will come out after ten minutes or twenty minutes or one hour, depending on the time one has at one's disposal. Satisfied, we closed our eyes and did some noon meditation.

There were eight or nine guests for lunch that day. During the meal different people were asking Dada questions about spirituality and devotion. After we finished, the monk was asking some general questions about sadhana and then he mentioned that he sometimes liked to do some Dhyana first,[5] before doing the other lessons, and he wondered what Dada thought about that. Dada arched his eyebrows and said, "No, no, nirvikalpa samadhi must always be last. After you come out of nirvikalpa samadhi you won't want to do the other lessons. You won't want to bring your mind down to the lower chakras. Nirvikalpa should always be last."

"But Dada," the monk replied, "I don't go into nirvikalpa samadhi when I do Dhyana."

"Yes, yes," Dada said, "but you will, you will."

The other regret I have is that I was there alone to ask the questions.

5 *Dhyana* literally means "meditation." In the Ananda Marga system of sadhana it refers to a type of meditation on Consciousness that leads to nirvikalpa samadhi. It is taught as the sixth lesson.

These conversations would have sparked questions in other's minds that never occurred to me. I also wish our conversations could have been more conversation and less of list of questions that often had little to connect them, but for this a little patience is required. The art of spiritual conversation with someone like Dada Chandranathjii takes time to master,[6] and I only felt like I was beginning to get the hang of it at the tail end of the last interview.

Other than this, I wish the reader a happy journey through these pages. May they bring you some measure of the joy they gave me in their creation.

6 *Jii* is a suffix commonly added to the end of a person's name in north India. It denotes respect.

Part One

Gadopur

June 3, 1997

IT WAS MID-MORNING WHEN I arrived in Mahua and hired a rickshaw to take me to Dada's farmhouse in the small village of Gadopur. Dada was waiting for me in the courtyard when the rickshaw pulled up, and after a quick bath I joined him on the veranda to enjoy a late breakfast of litchis and mango from his orchards and yogurt from his dairy. While I ate, Dada explained to me about the different farm activities that were going on at that time of year, and in the meantime I watched a pair of farmhands in the courtyard practice the age-old art of separating the *dal* from the chaff. They were squatting by the side of a huge mound of mung pods with towels wrapped around their heads, Egyptian-style, seemingly impervious to the heat and the glare. Each of them had a flat wicker basket, open at one end, in which they would place a handful of mung pods and then flip them up in the air and catch them as one might flip a pancake and catch it in a pan. With each toss a few more beans would separate from their pods and move back toward the closed end of the basket. When the chaff was fully separated they would toss the separated beans into a second pile and grab another handful.

By the time the meal was over I found myself feeling as much at home there as I did anywhere else in the world. The closest I had ever gotten to being a farmer was watching my garden grow in Anandanagar, and occasionally giving instructions to my gardener about what to plant, but after listening to Dada talk about what was happening on the farm it felt like the most natural life in the world. Perhaps I have some farming history buried in the forgotten memories of past lives, but I'd rather think it was Dada, transmitting the farmer's love for the nature he lives with, that made me feel that way. We spent the rest of the morning talking about the farm and farming, and I felt as happy as I knew how to feel.

When it was time to break for noon meditation and lunch, I pulled out my list of questions and showed it to him, asking him if he remembered that I had once said that I wanted to do a book of questions and answers with him. He looked it over for a minute or two, smiled, and then said, "Yes, but it is better if you get the answers from within. It's not very difficult. With a little thinking and concentration it is very easy to get the answer from within oneself. And that answer is the real answer."

"But Dada," I said, "these answers aren't for me. They're so other people can get a chance to read what you have to say."

There was a bright gleam in his eye. "Yes, we will answer your questions, no doubt, but still, it is better if the answer comes from within. One day, when you get time, you come here for a longer period. Come for fifteen days, twenty days, one month, and enjoy the spiritual environment. After that you won't have any more questions."

I spent the afternoon with Dada's grandson, Hrishikesh, who took me to visit the cottage of a local mahatma, or saint, who had died more than forty years earlier. The cottage and the garden that surrounds it have been preserved as a shrine that people still come to visit from different parts of India. The caretaker is the great-grandson of that mahatma, a devout Brahmin who performs all the daily rituals but doesn't meditate. While I could feel the spiritual vibration of the cottage and the grounds, I felt a little strange seeing how little interest the caretaker had in spiritual matters apart from his daily offices. Still, I was glad that I had seen the place. It added a visual context to the story that Dada had once told me about his initiation. He had begun searching for a guru in earnest in 1950 or 51 but had not been able to find anyone that satisfied him.[1] In 1952 he returned to Gadopur on leave and went to meet this mahatma who had by then become a well-known saint with disciples from all over India. He was greatly impressed and ended up asking him for initiation. The mahatma, however, declined to initiate him and told him in Bhojpuri, *Samay aya ta mili.*—"You will get it when the time comes." A year later he heard about Baba from a fellow employee and went to visit him for the first time. When Chandranathjii arrived at Baba's house, Baba's brother, who was sitting out front, ushered Dada into the front room and then went into the back room through a curtained doorway to get Baba. Just before Baba passed

1 Spiritual teacher. *Guru* literally means "dispeller of darkness."

through the curtain to enter the room, Chandranathjii heard him say in Bengali: *Ki, samay hala?*—"Has the time come?"

After we got back I went for a walk with Dada. He took me to the field where DMC had been held in 1982,[2] and then on to the mango orchard. When we got back to the house we sat down under a huge mango tree, heavy with fruit, that stands directly across from the courtyard. For some reason, Dada said, he enjoyed sitting beneath this particular tree very much. He found it quite cool. A few meters away there was a small thatch shed where a carpenter was busy making chairs from Dada's *sesam* trees. We sat there watching the carpenter practice his craft and enjoying the shade of the towering mango at the end of a hot Indian summer day. Dada began talking about how the pleasure that one gets from artificial things cannot compare with the pleasure one gets from nature. He mentioned the city festivals, all that noise and revelry that makes it hard to even think sometimes. But when a person learns to get pleasure from nature they find a pleasure these festivals cannot begin to give. "Look at that tree," he said, "how straight and tall it is. How it points to the sky, as if it were pointing to the Infinite, reminding you of the presence of God. Can you get this from any artificial thing? Even a pop song describing God cannot give you the thrill that you get from looking at this tree."

While we were sitting there, two local Margis arrived on scooter from a nearby town to visit Dada.[3] He gave a few last-minute instructions to the workers and then asked Ram Pirit, a village boy in Dada's employ, to pull up some chairs from the veranda and set them up in the courtyard. By that time the sun had fallen behind the house and the two towering mango trees that rise above it on either side, and the entire courtyard was out of the sun's reach. I gathered up my tape recorder and my papers and went to sit with them, feeling a tingle of anticipation. Dada began talking in Maethili, the local language, inquiring after their welfare and discussing whatever it was they had come to discuss, but after some time he began singing a few lines from a Prabhat Samgita.[4] His eyes were half-closed and

2 *Dharmamahacakra* — "the great circle of Dharma." This was a spiritual program held at certain times during the year. It would generally last several days and during the program Baba would give spiritual discourses twice a day.

3 Practitioners of Ananda Marga sadhana.

4 Shrii Shrii Anandamurti composed 5018 devotional songs between the years 1982 and 1990. They are collectively known as Prabhat Samgita. Samgita means "song"; Prabhat was Baba's first name. Traditionally in India, the songs of a particular composer are known by his or her first name followed by samgita.

I swore I could see a certain light coming from his face.

When he opened his eyes, he looked at his two visitors and started explaining the song, but inexplicably he was now speaking English. I wasn't even sure that they understood, but they were as quiet and as attentive as I was. Puzzled but thankful for my good fortune, I reached over to the small table in front of us where I had set my Walkman and pushed the record button. Dada continued talking to them but he didn't switch back to Maethili until it was time for them to go and the conversation turned to more mundane topics.

C: *Nirava* means "no sound." When nobody is there, there can be no sound. So *nirava rate*. I am alone. There is no sound. No one is there.

Tomari sathe—But I am with you. Is there any sound when you go into samadhi? Is there anybody else with you? Is there anything around you? No. *Nirava rate*. But you are there, God is there. When a sadhaka, a devotee, goes into samadhi there is nobody there, there is no thought, there is no sound. But he is with them. So the devotee sings *nirava rate tomari sathe, na bala katha anek rayegecche*—In the silent night, alone with you, so much was left unsaid. Why? When there is nobody to disturb us and you are with me, then why did these talks remain unspoken? Because the mind is not there. Who will talk? When you come out of samadhi, and your mind starts working again, you feel this—Oh, so much remained unsaid. There is so much you wanted to ask him. But again, when you go into samadhi, you cannot talk. *Nirava rate tomari sathe, na bala katha anek rayegecche*. The devotee wants to ask these questions, but how can they when they have no mind? The mind is lost in him, the mind is merged in him. There is no one there to ask the questions.

Sing Prabhat Samgita and try to understand the real meaning—not the literal meaning, but the real meaning. You will feel very happy. You will enjoy it.

There is one song: *Ami base achi nadir tiire tahari ashay, he karnadhar kathay? Karnadhar* means "one who takes you across the river in a boat", "helmsman." Now who is *karnadhar* in this universe? He alone. *Kathay*—where are you? O my Lord, where are you? I am sitting by the riverbank waiting for you. The devotee, the spiritual practitioner, is waiting for him to come, feeling his absence. Before you reach samadhi, when you are struggling to enter into samadhi but not getting it, you feel like this.

For example, Rabindranath Samgita refers to the songs of Rabindranath Tagore.

Base achi nadi tiire tahari ashay he karnadhar kathay? Where are you, my Lord? I am waiting for you at the bank of the river, waiting and waiting.

So when I hear these songs, when I go through these songs, I feel so much happiness, so much joy, such a deep satisfaction. I feel like reading them over and over again.

Imagine the state of mind of a devotee, when they feel *base achi nadi tiire tahari ashay he karnadhar kathay*. Oh my Lord, where are you? I am sitting here, waiting for you at the bank of the river. You might have heard about Lord Krishna who told Arjuna: *Daevyesha gunamayi mamamaya duratyaya, mameva je prapadyante maya metam tarantite*. This *maya*—this universe with all its attractions is *maya*—this *maya* is very difficult to cross. It is like a turbulent river or ocean. It's very difficult to cross. But one who submits to me, who surrenders to me, *mameva ye prapadyante*—who seeks shelter in me—they cross it successfully. That is the idea here. *Base achi nadi tire tahari ashay, he karnadhar kathay?* I am waiting for you, because you are the only person, rather the only existence who can take me across this turbulent river.

If you can understand the real meaning and feel the happiness that this brings with it, it is very helpful in sadhana. There is another song. *Priya amar, priyatama tumi mor, ghana tamasay jhainjha jhatikay, sathe acho Cita-chor*. You are dear to me. Oh, you are dearest to me, not only dear. You are dear to me, you are dearest to me. *Priya amar, priyatama tumi mor. Ghana tamasay*—even in the darkest night. *Jainjha jhatikay*—in the storm and rain, lightning and rain. *Sathe acho Cita-cor*—you are with me, O Cita-cor. *Cita-cor* means "one who has stolen my mind." My mind is lost in you, so you have stolen my mind.

You are dear to me, you are dearest to me, and you are always with me, even in the darkest night, even when there is cyclone and rain. Cyclone and rain and darkest night are symbols for our worst days, our most troublesome days. So even when I am passing through the darkest of times, passing through the most troublesome of periods, you are with me. O my dear, O my dearest one, you are always with me.

These are the songs of a devotee. They help to elevate their mind.

At this point Dada started singing a song in Sanskrit, an old chant of Shankaracharya — Bhaja Govindam. Again his eyes half-closed and I could feel my own ideation soaring, carried away by the vibrations coming from the saint and his song. After he finished singing, he remained silent for a minute or two and then opened his eyes as he had done before and started explaining the meaning of the song in English to his visitors while I kept the tape recorder running and listened, completely enchanted by the mood and the devotional feeling behind his words.

Nobody has come to this earth to stay forever; everybody has come here for a certain period, a limited period. And what can you do within this limited period? You can't do many things. You can't do much. You can do something.

You are not all-powerful, you can't do everything and anything. You can do something.

And what should that something be? That something should always be *bhaja Govindam, bhaja Govindam, bhaja Govindam, mor*—O fool, remember him, remember him, remember him.

Always keep in mind that you have to leave this earth someday. Don't forget him and don't become enmeshed in the pleasures of this earth. Remember him, keep him always in your mind, and then work. And what should your work be? *Atma moksartham, jagat hitayaca.* For your salvation do sadhana, and for the good of the people, for the good of the world—not only human beings, but birds, animals, plants also—for everybody, everywhere, do such work that benefits them. Feed the plant. Don't allow the plant to dry out. Water the seedling so that it can grow into a healthy tree. Help everybody and everything. That should be the motto of life. Sadhana, or spiritual practice, for yourself, for your salvation, but not only sadhana. Do good to others also.

Baba told a story once during DMC at Bhagalpur in July 1955. The topic was *Dharmatattva*. Do you know the definition of Dharma in Ananda Marga?[5] It does not mean religion. It doesn't mean Hinduism or Christianity or Sikhism or Islam. Dharma means the constant desire of the human being to achieve something infinite. If you get a certain amount of money you will not be completely satisfied; you will want more. If you get a good house you will eventually want a better house. There is no end to our desires. Today we eat something tasty; tomorrow we again have the desire to eat something tasty. It's endless. We want everything in infinite form. But nothing is infinite in this universe except him, except the Lord, except God. So, unknowingly, the human mind is always aspiring toward God, because it is always aspiring toward something infinite. And he is the only infinite existence. Whether we are aware of it or not, we all aspire for

5 Dharma is used colloquially to mean "religion" in the north Indian languages. Its etymological meaning is "the essential or true nature of any entity."

him. So, when we have to stay here for a certain period, the motto of life should be "sadhana and good deeds." *Atma moksartham, jagat hitayaca.*

The story Baba told was about a man called Dhruva. Dhruva was the son of a king in ancient times. When Dhruva was very young he began devoting himself to spiritual practice. When the sage Narada Muni heard about this, he approached Dhruva and said, "Dhruva, you are the son of the king. Why are you doing such rigorous spiritual practice? Why don't you go and enjoy the comforts of the palace. Be a king and rule for many years. Enjoy this world as king, and then in your old age you can devote yourself to spiritual practice."

When Dhruva heard this he asked Narada, "Can you give me the guarantee that everyone"—this is a principle we are talking about and this principle is for everybody—"can you give me the guarantee that everyone will live to old age, that no one will die prematurely?"

"No, how can I give you this guarantee?" Narada replied.

"Then let me practice while I'm young," Dhruva said.

After narrating this story, Baba went on to say that one's *shaeshyavastha,* that is, one's childhood or youth, is meant for education and dharma sadhana. Not only education. Even when you are a student you should do spiritual practice. So, study and spiritual practice in your *shaeshyavastha.*

Then you become a young adult, *jubavastha.* What should you do in that period of your life? *Arthoparjan* [earning] and dharma sadhana. You have to earn a living in order to provide yourself and your dependents with food, clothes and shelter. But not only earning. Earn your living and do your spiritual practice.

The third stage is *prodhavastha.* Now you are neither old nor young. You have become mature, let us say above forty, above forty-five, above fifty. You are moving from young adulthood to old age. During that period you should do *samajik prathistha* and dharma sadhana, that is, social service and spiritual practice. You have learned many things in the course of your life and developed your capabilities. Use that capacity and knowledge to help others through social service and do your spiritual practice.

And then comes *Barddhatva. Barddhatva* means "old age." When you become very old, say seventy-five, eighty, eighty-five, then your limbs become weak. You no longer have the capacity to move about and work. In that stage one should do only dharma sadhana, only spiritual practice. A man like me can be said to be in his *barddhatvavastha.*

So a person should work according to their age, but at no stage in their life should they neglect their spiritual practice. Study and spiritual practice.

Earning and spiritual practice. Social service and spiritual practice. And then, in the last stage, in the last lap of your life, only dharma sadhana, only spiritual practice.

And everybody should remember that a person should begin doing spiritual practice in their childhood. Nobody should wait for old age to begin their spiritual practice. That is why Baba has said in *Caryacarya* that when a child attains the age of five they should be initiated into meditation.[6] Let them practice Namah Mantra [a introductory meditation technique], because this is as much as they can understand at this point. This will create an impression in their mind. Their mind will be trained for further, more rigorous spiritual practices later on.

So the children should not be neglected. They should start spiritual practice at the age of five, and this is the guardian's responsibility. A child of five does not know what they have to do. They only know that they are a student, that they have been sent to school, that they have to study. Yes, study, but do some spiritual practice also. Suppose the child begins their studies at seven o'clock. Then prepare them for spiritual practice at six-thirty or quarter-to-seven. Ten to fifteen minutes is sufficient to begin with.

Here Dada switched back to Maethili but before we broke for evening meditation he switched back to English one more time.

Tumi andhar nishiithe dhruvatara, tomare dekhile smarane rakhile keu nahi hay dishahara. Dishahara means "one who has lost their way." But a traveler, wherever they may be, whether in the desert, in the jungle, or sailing in the ocean, when that traveler sees the pole star they know what direction they are headed in. The pole star points the way north. *Andhara nishiithe* means "in the dark night." *Tumi dhruvatara*—you are the pole star. *Tomare dekhile*—one who sees you. *Smarane rakhile*—and one who remembers you. One who sees you and one who remembers you, such a person never loses their way. *Tomare dekhile, smarane rakhile, keu na hay dishahara.*

So you see, these songs are meant for sadhakas, for spiritual practitioners. They are not simply songs. They are a part of spiritual practice.

It was quite late, well after nine, when I finished my evening meditation and Dada came to fetch me for dinner. This is not unusual in India, especially at Gadopur where Dada and Didi rarely finish their spiritual practices before

6 A book delineating basic practices and observances for practitioners of Ananda Marga sadhana, including various social codes.

eight-thirty.[7] *Afterward Dada came to my room to make sure I had everything I needed to be comfortable for the night. He was sorry, he said, that he didn't get the opportunity to answer any of my questions that day, but that we would begin our work tomorrow for sure. Then he told me this story:*

C: In 1956 Baba told me to go to my village home and hold a *tattvasabha*."[8] I said, "Baba, what is a *tattvasabha*? We don't know what this is." The Marga had just been founded the previous year. So Baba explained to us what he meant by *tattvasabha* and told myself, my wife, another lady acharya, Ajinadevi, and Acharyas Harisadhan, Shiva Shankar and Ram Tanuk to go to Gadopur. Before we left Baba told us what questions the pundits would ask and dictated the answers to us. We did as Baba directed. The six of us went to Gadopur, held a gathering in the village square and had a debate on spirituality and Ananda Marga with the priests. They were satisfied. Pundits are never satisfied, but the people attending the conference, they were satisfied, and many people took initiation. We remained busy till noon the next day. That evening a few people from the village came to me and asked me if I would explain to them the following morning about the significance of *astapash* and *satripu*.[9]

I agreed, and I was glad that I had time to think it over. You see, in those days we had no philosophy, nothing of the kind. Today you have a vast literature, you can educate yourself. But in those days our only treasure was whatever Baba had told to us. Now I had heard about *astapash*, the eight fetters, and *satripu*, the six enemies, from Baba, but they were not fully set in my mind. So when I went to bed that night I started thinking about them, one by one, and explaining them to myself. It was a sort of mental rehearsal for the next morning. And while I was rehearsing I fell asleep. During the night I had a dream, and in the dream Baba explained to me the meaning of *astapash* and *satripu*. When I woke up I was very happy because I had gotten the answer, the complete answer.

This is how knowledge comes. It may come through thinking, through

7 Didi means "elder sister" and here refers to Dada's wife, Acharya Ram Pari Devi, who was the first female initiate and first female acharya in Ananda Marga. It is used for women in the same way as "Dada" is used for men.

8 *Tattvasabha* means a public conference on spirituality and spiritual philosophy.

9 *Astapash* means "the eight fetters"; they are: fear, shame, hatred, doubt, bondage of lineage, complex of culture, vanity and backbiting. *Satripu* means "the six enemies"; they are: longing for earthly objects, anger, avarice, attraction, pride and envy.

dreams, through realization. Nobody knows in what form it will appear, but it will come. In those early days I didn't have the capacity to think so deeply, or to realize so much, so it came to me through a dream. Of course, Baba had already told us what questions the pundits would ask. "They will have no other questions, apart from these questions," he had said. And then he dictated the answers to those questions. When we arrived in Gadopur, the questions the pundits asked were the exact same questions that Baba had coached us for. So it was a successful *tattvasabha* and my visitors the following morning were quite satisfied with my explanation of *astapasha* and *satripu*. Baba did it but I got the credit. Actually, I got the credit for doing nothing. I was just a medium. It was he who was explaining through me, answering through me.

So, this can happen and will happen in everybody's life. You will also get the answer one day to all the questions that arise in your mind. You will get the answer from within yourself.

Do you know the history of Newton? Newton was known as a great scientist. But how did he know that the earth had gravitational force? Where did this knowledge come from? Not from any book, not by hearing it from somebody. It came from within himself. He started concentrating on a particular point; when his mind was fully concentrated on that point, the flow of knowledge came from his unconscious mind to his conscious mind, and he gave the world the theory of gravitational force. So it is with everyone. Everybody has all the knowledge of the universe hidden within themself. You need only know how to access it. Yogis learn how to do this through meditation. So go on meditating, go on meditating. One day you will develop the ability to know the answers to the questions that arise in your mind.

D: But in the meantime we can take the easy course and ask you.

C: Yes, yes, that's true. To save time, it's just saving time. To save time you ask those who are capable of giving you a reply. Or you consult such books and treatises that give you the answer.

What might otherwise take you ten years to learn, you can learn in one year by asking the right questions or through study. So it's not bad; it's quite good, in fact. Asking questions in order to know the reply, or looking into books, authoritative books, is quite good because it saves you time. Otherwise you might have to go on concentrating, or thinking, or meditating for years together before you get that same answer. But if you ask the right question you can know it immediately. However, there are times or circumstances when you don't have the opportunity to ask that question. In that case you have no alternative but to think and think and meditate.

You are tired now. I will not disturb you any more.

June 4

THE NEXT DAY WAS a fasting day. Dada came to my room after morning meditation and sat down beside me. I had my typewritten list of questions laid out in front of me on the bed. He picked up the first page, squinted a bit and started reading it to himself. After a minute or so he looked up and said, "How long will it take, do you think, to answer the questions? Not very long, I should think."

But I thought it would take quite some time. Then he read the first one out loud and said, "You see, the answer is very simple. It will take hardly one or two minutes." And so it did. But the spiritual discussion had begun. The questions were only a springboard and by the time we took a break, two hours had passed and still the bulk of the questions remained. Afterward I told Dada that I wasn't sure that there would ever be an end to these spiritual questions. For every one that gets answered, two more arise, and this way the devotees are never at a loss for entertainment.

D: Dada, why is morality necessary for spiritual progress?

C: Morality elevates the mind. If a person doesn't follow morality, if they act against morality, then the mind comes down to a lower level. When the mind is elevated one gets success in one's spiritual practice. When the mind comes down then naturally the spiritual practice, the concentration of mind, the meditation, cannot be good. It's a simple answer. The elevation of mind required for spiritual practice can be acquired through morality. So it is not only necessary; it is compulsory.

D: What is the difference between savikalpa and nirvikalpa samadhi?

C: In the words of Baba, only one sentence: complete or full concentration of mind is savikalpa samadhi and complete destruction of mind is nirvikalpa samadhi. The fully concentrated mind is concentrated in the inner Self. A sound is produced but you don't hear it because the mind is not connected to the gateway of the ear. So the wave carried through the ear doesn't reach the mind. We hear through our ears, true enough, but who hears? The mind. We smell through our nose but who perceives the smell, the different fragrances? The mind. You put a flower in front of the nose of a man who has been made unconscious through drugs and when he gets up, can he tell you what kind of fragrance it was? Why not? His nose is in working condition. It is because the mind is not functioning. So when the mind is fully concentrated it is closed in the inner Self and remains completely detached from the different senses. That state is called savikalpa samadhi.

D: But what is the difference between that and simple unconsciousness? When a person is unconscious their mind is also not connected to the senses. How would you describe the difference between simply being unconscious or stunned, and being in samadhi?

C: Unconsciousness is beyond your control. You have become unconscious due to the effect of something. But in samadhi you are in complete control. You close your mind yourself; it is not due to any drug or injury or a blow with a blunt instrument. Such things make you unconscious but in savikalpa samadhi you are not actually unconscious. In savikalpa samadhi you retain the thinking capacity within your inner Self. There you feel: "I am, he is; I am, he is." But when you become unconscious, you don't feel anything.

So in savikalpa samadhi, although the mind is not at the doors of the senses, it is still functioning inside. It is connected to the Cosmic Mind. When you get up from samadhi you can describe where you were, what condition you were in, what you felt. You can explain it. But when someone who was unconscious or in deep sleep gets up, they cannot tell you what they have seen or what they have heard. Were they thinking at all? No. The thinking capacity is completely lost in the unconscious mind. But when the mind is conscious, and when it is closed within through our own efforts, it is still functioning. But since I have withdrawn my mind from the doors of the senses, I am no longer connected with the external objects. I am only connected with the internal object, that is, the Cosmic Mind. That is the difference between unconsciousness and savikalpa samadhi.

And in nirvikalpa samadhi you have no mind. The mind is completely merged into consciousness and consciousness is so subtle that it cannot be two. As soon as the mind enters into consciousness it becomes one with that Universal Consciousness. Not Cosmic Mind — Universal Consciousness, Cosmic Consciousness.

When a person gets up from nirvikalpa samadhi they cannot explain what they had been feeling. The power of understanding and the power of explaining belong to the mind, but once the mind merges into consciousness it ceases to exist. That is why it is said that complete destruction of mind is nirvikalpa samadhi.

Consciousness is so subtle that there can be no difference between unit consciousness and Cosmic Consciousness. I will give you an example. Take a large expanse of water. Though water is limited, it will do as an example. Now there are millions of points in that body of water. You go to a pond and stand at the bank. You will see that the pond is full of innumerable drops of water. Now touch the water at one place and pull out your finger. You have touched a particular drop of water. But that drop of water is not separate from the main body of water. It is part of it. While you were touching the water with your finger you were touching a particular drop, but that drop is inside the pond. Only when it comes out of the pond can we say that it is different. If it is once again put in the pond it becomes one with that pond.

Swami Ramakrishna Paramahansa once gave an example. Somebody asked him a question about the difference between the Cosmic Consciousness and unit consciousness. He gave that person a bottle and told him to go and fetch some water from the tank. He went to the tank and brought the water. Then Ramakrishna told him to seal the bottle. He sealed it. Then he told him to go ahead and put it back in the tank, then take it out again and bring it back. He put it in the tank and then brought it back. "What happened?" Ramakrishna asked. "You put this water inside the tank, yet the water is still inside?"

"Yes, because the bottle is there."

"Oh, I see. Then take it back to the tank again and this time, when you put it in the tank, break the bottle and then bring it back." So he broke the bottle and the water mixed with the water in the tank. When he brought the bottle back Ramakrishna said, "Why, this bottle is empty!"

"Of course," he said, "you told me to break it. The water mixed with the water in the tank."

"Yes." Ramakrishna replied, "That is the covering that doesn't allow us to feel the Cosmic Consciousness. Break that cover and you will be one with the Cosmic Consciousness."

Ramakrishna was not a learned man. It was only with great difficulty that he was able to write his own name. He was illiterate, but he had that inner knowledge, the knowledge that he gained through meditation, and he used to use such examples to teach the people.

He used to tell this story. Once someone was going somewhere and he saw a crowd of people standing on the bank of a reservoir. He went over there to see what was happening and saw a man walking back and forth on the water of the reservoir. "Oh, you are doing wonders," he said. "How long has it taken you to earn this power."

"Twelve years," replied the man.

Then he said, "Oh, so sorry, after twelve years you have only been able to earn one anna." One anna is four paise. Then he went away.

It was very cheap in those early days. You could take a boat across a river for one anna. But suppose today you have to pay five rupees to cross the river in a boat. So after laboring hard for twelve years he was able to earn five rupees. What is implied is that the show of power is not good, rather it is bad because one's power is gradually spent, and one day the person loses their power and becomes a pauper. Generally, people who go astray and start giving such demonstrations for show, or for name and fame sake, or for money's sake, lose their mental strength and power after some years; they may even become lunatics.

Is it clear then? Savikalpa samadhi means complete concentration of mind. Normally the subtle waves emanating from external objects reach us through the doors of our senses. The wave of the red color from a rose touches the retina and then the mind recognizes the flower. The fragrance reaches the nose and the mind feels, "Oh this is the fragrance of that flower." But when the mind is not at the door of the senses, when it is closed in the inner Self and completely detached from the external objects, it is called savikalpa samadhi. The mind is there in concentrated form, feeling the Cosmic Consciousness, so afterward you can say, "Yes, it was very pleasant, I liked it very much, I was very happy, even now I feel so satisfied." This much you can explain, but in nirvikalpa samadhi you cannot explain even this much because the mind has completely disappeared.

D: What about the different stages of savikalpa? Could you explain them?

C: You see, actually there aren't any different stages of savikalpa samadhi. Savikalpa is one, when the mind is fully concentrated and closed in the inner self, but before you reach that stage you go through different experiences. You don't simply dash there in a moment. You proceed gradually, like a man walking to the market. Let us say it takes him twenty minutes to reach the market. The closer he gets, the more his experience of the market changes. Suppose you are five hundred yards away. Some music is playing on the loudspeakers, somebody is shouting. The closer you get to the market, the more those sounds change. You may say that these are the different stages of the market but actually they are not. This is the path that takes you to the market and as you walk you get different sorts of experience.

Savikalpa samadhi is savikalpa samadhi. But the closer you get, the stronger your feeling. First a weak feeling, then a little stronger, then even stronger, then much stronger, and finally you reach the goal. You know you are getting close to your goal because of the feelings you experience. Take the example of the market again. You can judge how close you have gotten by your experience of the waves emanating from the market. First you hear the music playing. Then you can hear somebody shouting out the prices: "Mangos, mangos, ten rupees per kilo." Perhaps at some point you begin to see the tops of the tents in the distance. So you can judge your progress in this way, but I wouldn't say that these are different stages. They are the points you pass, step by step, as you move closer to savikalpa samadhi.

In nirvikalpa samadhi your mind merges into your unit consciousness. Unit consciousness means that particular point from which your mind has emerged. That point is your unit consciousness. But that point is not separate from Cosmic Consciousness. We say unit consciousness only because that is the particular point from which my mind has emerged. But when my mind merges into that particular point it doesn't become one with that particular point only; it becomes one with the whole Cosmic Consciousness, because unit consciousness is already one with Cosmic Consciousness. That state is nirvikalpa samadhi or *gunatiita* or *nistraegunya*.

It is said that there are three different forces acting in the universe, *sattva*, *rajas*, and *tamah*. They are the binding forces, the *gunanmritta*. *Gunanmritta* means "bound." *Gunatiita* means "that which is beyond bindings." Arjuna was instructed by Lord Krishna, *traegunyavishaya veda nistraegunyo bhavarjuna*. *Veda* means knowledge, *jinana*. *Traegunyavishaya veda*. *Veda*, or knowledge, is bound by these three *gunas*, by these binding forces of nature, or *prakriti*, but you have to be *nistraegunyo*. You must rise above these binding forces.

Traegunya vishaya veda. It means that however far knowledge takes you, it remains bound by these three forces, but you have to go beyond those binding forces. You have to become *gunatiita, nistraegunya* while in your physical body. And what is that state? Nirvikalpa samadhi.

So it is very difficult to say anything about nirvikalpa samadhi because there is no mind. About savikalpa samadhi you can say—"Oh, very pleasant, very happy, very calm and quiet"—but even this you can't say about nirvikalpa. You don't know what happened to you. Of course, when you get up you feel fresh, you feel happy, the mind feels elevated. And knowledge comes. Knowledge will definitely come because when your mind, my mind, or anybody's mind becomes one with Cosmic Consciousness, it gains access to all the knowledge that is there in the Cosmic Mind. You will have certain power, you will know things, but you can't explain the state that you were in for five minutes or five hours or five days. Nirvikalpa samadhi cannot be explained.

This also happened in Ramakrishna's life. His disciples asked him to explain to them about nirvikalpa samadhi. He told them to wait and then went into nirvikalpa samadhi. When he became normal again he said, "No, no, it is not possible to explain. How can I explain it? He who can explain is not there."

Do you remember the song I sang last evening? *Nirava rate tomari sathe, na bala katha anek rayegecche. Nirava rat, tomari sath*—that means nirvikalpa samadhi. *Nirava rate, tomari sathe, na bala katha anek rayegecche.* Many things remained unspoken with you in that *nirava rat*. How can I talk? The mind is not there. The mind is completely merged in him. So that is nirvikalpa samadhi.

D: But when you come out of nirvikalpa samadhi, then you know that you have been in nirvikalpa samadhi.

C: Yes, you know it, but you can't explain it. You know it because you feel a certain sort of calmness, satisfaction and mental strength. And you get knowledge. Then you realize where you have been.

D: Dada, when the mind merges into nirvikalpa, why is it that one comes out? Who is there to bring you out? How do you come out if there is no mind?

C: Here the theory of action and reaction comes into play. Whatever action we do has its reaction and that reaction becomes an object of action in the next stage. Let us say, for example, that I have just eaten. Now I feel satisfied, I don't feel hungry, because I have eaten. So eating was the action, and the reaction, the result, is that I no longer feel hungry. I am fully satisfied. Then the next stage comes. That food which I have eaten will not remain in my stomach forever. It will be digested and again I will feel hungry.

Suppose I have taken chilis, red chilis. Afterward I feel very uncomfortable because they are so hot. But if I take something sweet then I feel better. This is also action and reaction. I ate the chilis and they gave me some trouble. I ate something sweet and I felt better. I ate a mango and felt better. So every action has its reaction.

Now we are bound to face the reactions of whatever actions we perform in the world. They are held in store for us until we exhaust them, and as long as they are not exhausted the binding force of nature affects us. A person is born, grows into a child, then a youth, and eventually becomes old and dies, but the mind doesn't die. Only the body dies. The mind leaves the body when the body is no longer fit to dwell in and remains in the Cosmic Mind, but because it is bound by its reactions it doesn't become one with the Cosmic Mind. It takes another physical frame in order to face those reactions, regardless of whether they are good or bad. That is the cause behind rebirth, the philosophy of rebirth. Whatever reactions we didn't face in this life become our binding force. We have to come back again in another form to face those problems. Likewise, when you go into nirvikalpa samadhi those reactions still remain, and you have to come back to face those problems, to face those reactions.

Of course, in some cases it so happens that the sadhaka, year by year, is exhausting the old reactions without creating any new ones. Now a day may come when my old reactions are finished. On that day, if I go into nirvikalpa samadhi I will not return. So what does a sadhaka do who wants to stay and sit in nirvikalpa samadhi every day, but who has no reactions to act as a binding force? Before sitting in nirvikalpa samadhi he takes a mental resolve. He resolves, for example, that I will remain in nirvikalpa samadhi for one hour and then again I will come back in this physical frame to work in this world. And that becomes the binding force, that becomes the reaction. That mental thinking, that mental resolution, becomes the binding force. Then, when you enter into nirvikalpa samadhi, that force brings you back after the designated time. If you took a resolution for one hour then after one hour you will come back to your body and take up your work.

Often, a saint will decide to stay on for a few years to do some work, because those who come and get nirvikalpa samadhi don't go away leaving many problems for others to face. They try to help others. So they resolve in their minds: I will stay here for five years more and do such and such work. That resolution also becomes a binding force and enables them to stay for five more years.

D: What happens to a person when they die if they have been going into nirvikalpa samadhi every day but still have not exhausted all their reactions? Will they have to come back again and take another body?

C: Yes. Unless you exhaust your reactions the binding force will act upon you. What generally happens is that when a person sees that they have a certain amount of reactions left that would force them to take another body then they stay on to finish them. For example, that gentleman who told me, "You will get it when the time comes."

D: What was it he said in Bhojpuri?

C: *Samay aya ta mili*. You will get it when the time comes. Now that gentleman used to live in a hut inside a garden.

D: I visited that place yesterday. Hrishikesh took me there.

C: Yes, he used to live there in that small cottage. One day he was walking in the garden and he fell down and broke his hip. After that he could only move around with the help of crutches. Some people advised him to get it operated on and set, but he said, "No, no, it is not necessary. Let it be. I am able to get around on crutches and that's good enough." Then, some months later, he fell down again and broke his wrist. When he saw that it was broken he said, "Oh this bone is also broken." As if nothing serious had happened. Then again he went about his business. Again some visitors requested him to get a cast put on or get some treatment, and again he said, "Oh no, leave it as it is." Then somebody asked him, "Why are you facing these problems? There are so many methods nowadays to correct it. Why don't you take help from modern medical science?" "No, no, Babu," he replied, "leave me alone. I don't want to come back again."

Only this simple answer. Many people would not have understood what he was talking about. But now I understand what he meant when he said, "Leave me alone, I don't want to come back." I doubt that the people who advised him to take the help of modern medical science understood what he was talking about. They might have thought, "Oh this man has become *pagal*, mad."

So you see, many saints who do not want to come back will exhaust their reactions in similar fashion, in concentrated form within a short period. Suppose I have ten reactions to exhaust. I can finish those reactions in ten years or in ten months. If I take ten years to finish the reactions, then it will feel very easy. But if I want to finish them in ten months or one year or two years, then they will come in concentrated form. The reactions will be stronger, the trouble will be greater. But at that stage, if you have the power to get the reactions exhausted, then your mind also has the strength to tolerate them. Whatever trouble arises, the mind doesn't feel it. It tolerates it. It's like the difference between a strong man and a weak man. The strong man can easily carry a weight of fifty kilos on his shoulders but a weak man has trouble carrying a weight of only thirty kilos. So it is with mental strength. If a person is mentally strong they can exhaust in two years the reactions that someone else might need to spread out over twelve years.

So many people, saintly people, who have the capacity to know how many reactions are pending, know that if they leave their body with unserved reactions they will have to come back again in another frame to face them. Rather than do this they invite those reactions to come. They become mentally prepared to face them; then they face them and go away. Such was the case with that gentleman who said, "No, no, leave it as it is," when people advised him to take advantage of modern medical science. "I don't want to come back again."

D: Dada, you said that saints or elevated people no longer create reactions; they can then work to finish their reactions. What is the process or method of working without creating reactions?

C: No one can live on this earth without working, without action. Breathing is an action, eating is an action, even thinking is also an action. And when actions are there, the reactions are also bound to be there. We can't stop acting, so how then can we stop the reactions? What is the solution?

The solution is sadhana, and in sadhana the second lesson is especially meant for this.[1] If you can surrender all your actions to him you will not be responsible for the reactions. Do whatever you do, act in whatever manner you act, but surrender those actions completely to him. This is what second lesson teaches. If you are firm in your second lesson your reactions will gradually go on diminishing, and a day will come when your mind will be so well-established in that process that your actions will not bring any reaction.

Lord Krishna instructed Arjuna: *Sarva karman paritya ja manekam sarvyam*—forget everything, surrender completely to me, and I will rescue you from all your reactions. That is the essence of second lesson. If a spiritual practitioner is fully established in this process, if they are able to surrender completely to him, they will not have to face the reactions. The reactions will dissolve of and by themselves. That is why morality is also essential. You asked me earlier why morality is essential for a spiritual practitioner. Morality is essential because it helps a person to elevate their mind. When the mind is elevated it becomes very easy to surrender. And when you surrender to him completely you are freed from all reactions.

So you see, everything is connected—morality, surrender to God, always remembering him through Guru Mantra, the mantra of second lesson. If you think about it you will see how closely interconnected they all are.

D: Dada, I have a couple of more questions about samadhi. First of all, some people say that one can be in savikalpa samadhi and still move about and do their work. Is that really possible?

C: No, it is not possible. You cannot be in complete savikalpa samadhi, but you can be in a half-samadhi state. In the half-samadhi state the mind works, but only in a limited manner. You can do the essential things—moving, sitting, replying to somebody's questions, eating—but this is not possible in complete savikalpa samadhi because in complete savikalpa samadhi the mind doesn't function. It becomes completely closed in the inner Self. Every action, you see, has its root in the mind. First you get the idea that you have to go to Patna; then you get ready and start. But in savikalpa samadhi the mind is not functioning. How can you move about? Unless the mind thinks, "I have to go to Patna", you

1 Here he refers to the second lesson of Ananda Marga sadhana where the sadhaka or spiritual practitioner learns to ascribe Godhood to the actor, the action and the object of the action through the use of Guru Mantra.

will not get ready and go. So it is not possible. If you are in full savikalpa samadhi it is not possible to act.

However, you can raise your mind to a higher level, close to savikalpa samadhi but not in savikalpa samadhi. In that state you can act, and when you act in that state you will not do anything wrong because your mind is already elevated. It is very close to savikalpa. Whatever you think, whatever you do, whatever you speak, will be of a higher level. No wrong can be done by a person who is able to keep themself close to savikalpa samadhi.

D: Can one keep one's mind in half-samadhi and still be active enough to, say, give a lecture?

C: Yes, yes. That is possible, because your mind is not completely enclosed in the inner Self. It maintains some connection with the external objects through the senses. The doors to the senses are open, but in a very limited manner. In that state the mind will only grasp those things which are essential. If somebody abuses me I will go on working and moving. I will not feel it. I will not mind it. Otherwise, if I am in normal condition and someone abuses me, I may get excited. I may get agitated or angry. But when you are very close to savikalpa samadhi, when you are moving about, talking, acting in that state, then you don't feel the effect of good or bad. Somebody abuses me—well and good. Somebody praises me—well and good. All are equal for me. Let them abuse. Let them praise. Both are equal for me.

So one should always try to remain in a state that is close to savikalpa samadhi. In other words, one should always try to keep one's mind elevated, and with an elevated mind no one can do any wrong. Every action will be the right action—according to the principles, according to the ideology. It is said that one should follow *yama* and *niyama* and the Sixteen Points,[2] but

2 *Yama* and *niyama* are the ten basic moral principles of yogic sadhana, and the first two limbs of the eightfold astaunga yoga given by Patanjali. The five principles of yama are: non-injury, truthfulness, non-stealing, avoiding over-consumption, and seeing everything as an expression of God. The five principles of niyama are: physical and mental cleanliness, contentment, service, spiritual study, and meditation on the Supreme.

The various yogic practices taught by Shrii Shrii Anandamurti have been compiled and given the name "Sixteen Points." Yama and niyama, for example, are included under one of those points.

it is very difficult to follow yama and niyama and the Sixteen Points. That only becomes possible when the mind is elevated, and to elevate the mind, practice is essential. So do as much practice as you can. This will elevate your mind, and with an elevated mind it will be very easy to follow yama and niyama, Sixteen Points, and all these things. Remember, no wrong can be done by a person who always keeps their mind in an elevated state.

D: Dada, you are easily able to remain articulate and fulfill all your worldly duties. But in Anandanagar there is an old man, Makhanjii, who was your cook for many years. When I see him walking around or attending functions he doesn't seem to be maintaining much connection with the world. Perhaps he just doesn't make any effort to come back into normal consciousness?

C: Why should he try to come into normal consciousness when he doesn't have any responsibilities? It's better to live in that state. A person is very happy in their inner Self. A person feels very satisfied in that state; they don't feel the need of anything. If you give them food, they will eat whatever you give them. You will also feel that way if you practice for some time.

You know, people like to have food that is according to their taste. Add some more chili, add some more oil, fry it. Then they are happy. But once your mind is elevated you will take whatever food you get, as long as it is not harmful for the mind or body, and eat it with full satisfaction. You see, today is *amavashya* [new moon]. You are fasting, but you are talking, sitting with me, moving about. You don't feel any trouble. Rather, you don't even remember that you haven't eaten unless someone reminds you of it. So long as we were talking you didn't remember that you were fasting, but now that I have pointed it out you remember: "Oh yes, I am fasting." Why? Because your mind was in that spiritual flow.

D: Dada, some people believe that Baba withholds samadhi from some of his disciples, especially his workers,[3] so that they will work properly. A worker once told me that once you get samadhi you won't have much desire to work, and because of that Baba often withholds that experience until a person is very old.

C: Do you remember Baba's story about Dhruva and the sage Narada? One

3 The *sannyasis*, or renunciate monks, of Ananda Marga are commonly called workers since they have dedicated their lives to service.

must work in accordance with the stage of life one is in, but in all stages of life a person should never forget their spiritual practice.

Now, it is true that after you attain samadhi you feel like living in that state forever, but since you are living in a family, in a society, in a country, in this world, you have certain responsibilities. I am living in this house. I have a responsibility to repair this house. If I don't do it, I fail in my duty. This house gives protection against the sun, rain, strong wind, and so on, so it is my responsibility to keep it repaired. Likewise, if I am married I have my wife, I have my children, and I have a certain duty toward them as well. It is my responsibility to provide them with food, clothes, medical facilities, education, etc. But suppose after achieving samadhi I don't feel like doing all these things. I think, "Let me sit in meditation all day long and remain in samadhi." In that case I will be doing them an injustice. After enjoying some samadhi I will get up and ask my wife for food, then eat and again go and sit in meditation? I will leave my clothes for someone to clean? I will leave my room for someone to clean? So then everybody else has some duty toward me but I have no duty toward others? That is not right. Therefore, once a person achieves samadhi they must take a resolution to do service to others. And when you make this resolution, when you resolve in your mind, "Yes, I will do service to others", that will make you act. It will give you a sort of goading; it will create a force that propels you to act, to do good to others.

So, while it is true that a person who gets samadhi feels like remaining in that state all the time, we have a human body, we live in a society, in a family, in some area, and because of this we have some duty and we should not fail in our duty. If we fail in our duty, then that also will be an action, and that action will come back to us in the form of a reaction, and that reaction will become our binding force.

Suppose my neighbor's house catches fire. Now there is no such thing as accident in this world. Everything is incident. Everything has its cause, so there must be some cause behind this also. Then why should I go and help him? He is suffering the reactions of his own actions. Why should I go and help him? Well all right, that's true. He is suffering because of his own actions. But if I don't help him then I am also acting, and that action will have a reaction, and that reaction will be a negative reaction for me because I have failed in my duty to extend help to others. *Jagat hitayaca.* My duty is to extend help to others. He might be facing his own problems, but my duty is to help others to overcome their problems.

If I don't fulfill my duty because I'm following this philosophy that he is facing his own reactions, then that action of mine will bring me an adverse reaction.

D: We have many sadhakas who have been doing sadhana for many years, for example, some avadhutas,[4] but who have not yet achieved samadhi. Can it be that in some cases Baba is holding back samadhi so that they will do more work.

C: In some cases, perhaps, but not in all cases. Why? Being an avadhuta doesn't automatically make one a very good spiritual practitioner, and being a *grihi* [householder] doesn't mean that one is an ordinary spiritual practitioner. Baba created the avadhuta cadre for work, for social service, for doing relief, education and welfare work. The reason behind this is that family people get less time to do this sort of work. They should also do it, but Baba wanted some whole-time workers who could devote all their time, twenty-four hours a day, for such work.

You see, what is spirituality? In a simple sentence I can say: Be good, do good. "Be good" means to do spiritual practice strictly. If you carry on your spiritual practices strictly then your mind will become elevated. You will become good. You will have a pure heart and a pure mind, and your thinking will always move in the proper direction. So spiritual practice—"be good."

"Do good." When your mind is elevated you will not be happy if you see others suffering. So you extend your help to them. So "do good." Be good and do good. *Atma moksartham, jagat hitayaca.* Spiritual practice for oneself and *jagat hitayaca*—do good to others. So avadhutas or avadhutikas and family people are all alike in the sense that both have to do spiritual practice and both have to do good to others. The difference is that a family person gets less time for doing good to others while an avadhuta can utilize all their time apart from sadhana. The entire day is at their disposal for doing good to others. This is why Baba created this cadre in 1962. Up until then family acharyas did the work. The Marga was founded in January 1955, and between then and 1962 all the work, whether relief work or dharma pracar—teaching spiritual practice to others, talking about the spiritual philosophy—everything was done by family people. But when the organization continued to expand, Baba

4 Sannyasis or renunciates who practice a special type of meditation called *kapalika* are known as avadhuta or avadhutika in Ananda Marga.

needed some whole-time workers, some volunteers who could dedicate their entire time to this work.

Now a family person may be a very good spiritualist. An avadhuta may be a very good worker but the family person may be superior in practice. The avadhuta may be inferior to them in sadhana and vice versa. An avadhuta may be very good in sadhana, and a family person may not be so good in sadhana. Being a family person or an avadhuta doesn't confer any sort of priority for spiritual practice. It depends on the individual, how much time they devote, how sincere they are. So avadhuta or family person, it makes no difference. The only thing is that one should be sincere in practice.

Now, with the avadhuta, since a cadre has been created for this purpose alone, to do service, if they fail in this respect they are more responsible than the family person. If I fail to extend help today to somebody and an avadhuta fails to extend help to somebody, he will be considered more responsible than me. The action is the same, but in his case the offense will be greater.

D: So the reaction will also be greater.

C: Greater. So such a person will have to be very serious. If they don't understand this and neglect their duty then they will have to face the reactions.

So there is no question of becoming avadhuta only for spiritual practice. If you want to spend all your time doing social service, doing good to others, extending help to suffering people, then in that case you can become an avadhuta, but don't do so only for spiritual practice. Spiritual practice can be done at home. When Baba initiated me he told me that there was no need to go to the hills or to the forest. Live in your house. Close your room and that will be your cave. You are all alone there. Suppose you practice sadhana for two hours. Your room is closed for those two hours. You are all alone. That is your forest, your jungle, your cave.

So one should not become an avadhuta for spiritual practice alone. Yes, if you want to serve the suffering humanity or the suffering creatures—not only humanity: plant life, animal, bird life also—then become an avadhuta. But if circumstances don't permit you to become an avadhuta or avadhutika then you should not feel any inferiority complex. "How can I be a great spiritualist? I am a family person." No one should feel like that. All one requires to do spiritual practice is a human body. Once a person has that, they have all they need to reach their spiritual goal.

D: Dada, we practice Ishvara Pranidhana to attain savikalpa samadhi.[5] I have heard that in some cases certain musicians, especially in north Indian classical music, are able to enter into samadhi while playing music, simply through their concentration in the aesthetic realm.

C: That depends on one's level of mind. Not everyone has the same level of mind. Your level of mind, my level of mind and someone else's level of mind are all different. Nobody knows who is at what level. Somebody may already be very close to that achievement. Suppose I am here, you are there, somebody else is there, and the point we are trying to reach is here. From that place the point is far away, from there it is closer, and from here it is very close. So it depends on the different levels of mind. Achieving samadhi depends not only on one's efforts but also on the level of mind one had reached prior to this life. One person may be able to reach that point with very little effort while another person, despite more strenuous efforts, may not reach it by the time that person does because of the different levels of mind.

Swami Ramakrishna Paramahansa attained savikalpa samadhi without a teacher. The urge to do practice came from within himself, that is, it was a reaction carried over from his past life. In his past life he must have been a practitioner, and his mind had reached a certain level. When he came again in a human body he brought that level, that mental level, with him. As a result, he was able to attain savikalpa samadhi with just a little practice and without a teacher. Only afterward did he meet Totapurijii, his teacher, who helped him to attain nirvikalpa samadhi. Not everybody, however, can think of reaching savikalpa samadhi without a teacher because everybody's mind is not at that level. So one can get samadhi very quickly or one can get it with great delay. It all depends on the level of mind and, at the same time, the effort one puts in. That is also important.

D: Then by concentrating on music one can actually go into samadhi.

C: Yes, yes, but the music should have a spiritual vibration. Prabhat Samgita is one such music that has a spiritual vibration. It is just possible that while singing *ami base achi nadi tiire tahari ashay, he karnadhar kathay*, or listening to the cassette, you may go into samadhi. But the spiritual vibration should be there. Without the spiritual vibration the music may drag

5 Ishvara Pranidhana is the first lesson of Ananda Marga sadhana.

you away from your spiritual ideation. Such music will not help you to go into samadhi. So there must be a cause, and if the cause has a spiritual vibration, that is, if the music is such that it emanates spiritual waves, then it can become the cause of that effect—samadhi. So certainly one can get samadhi—savikalpa samadhi, not nirvikalpa samadhi—through the vibration emanating from a certain kind of music.

D: And through kirtan also.[6]

C: In kirtan what happens? When you concentrate your mind you are thinking about the Supreme. You are calling him, you are remembering him, and as a result the mind gradually becomes more and more concentrated in him. It forgets the external world. I am shouting for him, I am calling him, I am looking at him, I am remembering him. The mind is fully concentrated in him. Gradually it becomes so concentrated that you get savikalpa samadhi. So one should always sing or listen to good music. Good music means music with a spiritual vibration. And kirtan. These things can help you to achieve savikalpa samadhi.

Yesterday I quoted the example of Newton. Many people had seen apples falling to the ground prior to him. But nobody came forward to say that the earth has gravitational force. Why was Newton able to discover this when others hadn't? It was because his mind had reached a very high level of scientific thinking, and so, when he concentrated his mind—"Why, why, why? Why is this happening?"—he got a flow of knowledge from his unconscious mind. "Ah," he said, "it is because the earth has gravitational force." So concentration of mind, through any channel, will bring you the desired result. Newton didn't think about God. He thought about the attraction of the apple. Why are objects always attracted toward the earth? He concentrated on that point and he got the result. He got the knowledge. Likewise, if somebody concentrates their mind on the Cosmic Existence, they will achieve that Cosmic Existence. They will get the proper knowledge, the correct knowledge about that Cosmic Existence.

D: What is the proper ideation when we are singing kirtan?

C: While doing kirtan it is better, whenever possible, to close your eyes. If you are moving about and singing kirtan then this may not be possible.

6 The chanting of mantras, usually accompanied by the Lalita Marmika dance. Kirtan was popularized in India by Chaetanya Mahaprabhu.

But if you are sitting and doing kirtan, or standing in one place, or moving in a circle inside a room, then it is possible to close the eyes. Now this is the practical side. This is not theory or philosophy. Close your eyes and take your mind gradually up through the chakras as you do in Bhuta Shuddhi and Asana Shuddhi.[7] Take it to the final point, the *sahasrara* chakra.[8] Then try to keep the mind concentrated on that point while you recite the kirtan mantra.

D: Should one then do the same visualization that one does in Dhyana?

C: No, the visualization that is done in Dhyana should be done only in Dhyana and in no other practice. Concentrate on a point as you do in Ishvara Pranidhana, but that point should not be at your Ista Chakra, which is different for different people. It should be the same for everybody, at a point in the sahasrara chakra. Go on reciting or singing the mantra. When the mind gets fully concentrated it becomes elevated and helps in spiritual practice. If you sit in Ishvara Pranidhana after kirtan you will have more success with your meditation.

D: Dada, previously you emphasized the importance of getting proper satsaunga.[9] But if one is not getting proper satsaunga can one also get satsaunga from books?

C: Yes, definitely. Satsaunga doesn't only mean spending time with good people. Reading good books is also satsaunga. So we have two kinds of company, good people and good books. Both are our companions. One can have satsaunga either with books or with people or with both.

D: So the satsaunga I am getting through our conversations qualifies as both since these conversations will also become a book and other people will have a chance to enjoy them through that medium.

7 Bhuta Shuddhi and Asana Shuddhi are part of the withdrawal process that is taught in the first lesson of Ananda Marga sadhana in order to prepare the mind for the recitation of mantra.

8 The seventh or crown chakra, or psychic center, located at the top of the cranium.

9 Literally, "keeping company with the truth." Generally it refers to having the company of other spiritualists.

C: That's good. I don't know how far it will help others but at least your idea is very good.

D: As long as we are on the subject of satsaunga, what advice would you give to someone who lives in a place where there are no other spiritualists? How can they maintain as elevated a state of mind as possible while going about their daily activities?

C: I would advise them to carry good books with themselves. One. There are also cassettes available with good talks. When they are alone in their room and taking rest, or when they are eating, or whenever and wherever they are alone, they can read those books or listen to those cassettes. Nowadays, with the improvement in science, you have such apparatuses that you can listen to spiritual talks and the person sitting next to you won't be disturbed. So even in the train or on the plane you can have your spiritual talks with you. And if nothing is available your mind is there. Close your eyes and think about the Cosmic Existence. Carry on your half Ishvara Pranidhana.[10] If you have neither a book, nor a cassette, nor a spiritualist to talk to, then in that case close your eyes and think of him. That is satsaunga.

D: Many people find it difficult to do mantra japa. They are not able to successfully recite their mantra during their daily activities. What techniques or advice can you give them?

C: The human mind is such that it needs practice to become successful at doing something. If you want to become a good musician you have to practice. If you want to become a good football player you have to practice every day for at least an hour or two. So is the case with spiritual practices also. Everyone forgets their mantra in the beginning. So you need to make a habit of it and the habit should be such that even if you don't think about your mantra it comes automatically.

From our childhood we have been eating in the morning, then again at noon and again in the evening. We were taught this in childhood and gradually it has become our habit, a well-established habit. Now, even if nobody tells you that it is time for lunch, you remember. "Oh, it's time to eat lunch." This is a habit.Likewise, you develop the habit of saying your

10 The repetition of one's mantra when one is not sitting in formal meditation. Also known as *japa*.

mantra through practice. In the beginning you have to work at it. You forget your mantra. As soon as you remember, you start doing it again. Again you forget it, and again, as soon as you remember, you start doing it. There is no other way to learn except through practice.

I will quote again from the *Gita*. Arjuna told Krishna that what he was instructing him to do was very difficult to achieve, and then asked him how to achieve it. Krishna said: *Abhyasesu Kanteya*. Kanteya means Arjuna. "O Arjuna, it will come through practice." So there is no easy solution except practice, practice and more practice. *Abhyasesu Kanteya*. And that practice needs the backing of a strong desire to achieve the desired result. So one needs to devote some time every day for this practice. In the beginning you will forget. Everybody forgets. There may be a few exceptions, but by and large everybody forgets in the beginning. But once you are able to form the habit through practice it will become automatic.

You see, when we walk we never think about what we are doing. Now I am lifting my right foot and placing it in front of me. And after the right foot is placed, I raise my left foot and put it forward. Nobody thinks about this. You start moving and automatically your feet take you where you want to go. It is a habit. One doesn't need to think about it. Let us suppose I am going to the market in Mahua. While I am walking I think about some problem. The mango orchard needs to be sprayed for insects. The place has to be cleaned. I will ask so-and-so to clean it and I will pay him such-and-such amount for doing the work. I am thinking about all these things but the movement of my feet is not disturbed. Why? Because of habit. So you should make the mind so habituated that it remembers automatically.

D: When one is trying to develop this habit does one need to practice the ideation of the mantra as well? Will the ideation come automatically just by repeating the sound or is it possible to go on repeating your mantra but never remember your Ista.[11]

C: You know the meaning of the mantra, and when you know the meaning of your mantra you will definitely remember your Ista. The meaning reminds you of your Ista because the meaning is connected with the Supreme. So everyone should know the meaning of their mantra and

11 The word *ista* refers to one's individual spiritual goal or spiritual ideal.

they should recite it with full awareness of the meaning. Then they will not forget their Ista.

D: Dada, could you say something more about the benefits of japa?

C: Every thought, every action, everything we do, either mentally or physically, creates a sort of vibration. Japa is also a mental action and it creates a spiritual vibration. That vibration spreads throughout the nerves and the nervous system with the result that the body becomes physically able to experience, in a pleasant rather than an unpleasant way, the movement of kundalini.[12] And that vibration also helps to awaken the kundalini. Through the constant touch of that vibrational force the kundalini awakens and moves upward. That is the benefit of doing japa.

D: You once said that nirvikalpa is also a practice and that a yogi should sit in nirvikalpa for some time every day. Is the same true for savikalpa, or does one sit only in nirvikalpa once one has attained the ability to enter into it?

C: No, because savikalpa is a stage on the path and the path must be clear. You must rise upward gradually. The kundalini, or serpentine power, resides in the body. It is a sort of energy. It is not seen but it is there. When it rises upward it rises through a path or passageway, so that passageway should be clear and unobstructed. To reach nirvikalpa means that the kundalini awakens, rises up through the *sushumna nadi*,[13] which is in the spinal cord, until it reaches the top chakra. That is nirvikalpa samadhi. But on the way the kundalini automatically passes through the other chakras, and the moment it passes through the sixth chakra you get savikalpa samadhi. You are not thinking about attaining savikalpa samadhi but it comes of its own on the way to nirvikalpa samadhi. You are not going into savikalpa samadhi, you are going into nirvikalpa samadhi, but you must pass through it. The moment that the serpentine power passes through your

12 Kundalini refers to the psycho-spiritual energy of the individual. It is said to reside in the lowermost chakra in a form that resembles a coiled snake. In most individuals this energy is dormant, but through meditation it can be aroused and when it reaches the two uppermost chakras the spiritual aspirant experiences savikalpa and nirvikalpa samadhi respectively.

13 The psychic canal located within the spinal cord through which the kundalini passes.

Ista Chakra you get savikalpa. But it continues to rise, and from savikalpa you pass into nirvikalpa.

D: Dada, is it possible to see the kundalini or to have some awareness of it?

C: No, the kundalini cannot be seen. Electricity is moving in this wire. You can't see it, but just touch that wire and the shock will let you know that there is electricity in it. So it is with kundalini. I am sitting in front of you. I can't see your kundalini and neither can you, but you can feel it.

Well, there are so many different kinds of experiences. It is said that the kundalini is lying dormant at the bottom of the spine in the muladhara chakra. Through the incantation of mantra, through the waves created by meditation, it is awakened. Suppose a man is sleeping and you go and touch him. "Please get up, please get up." He is receiving the sound wave and also the touch wave, and due to these he gets up. He may be sound asleep, but if you do this three or four times — "please get up, please get up" — he will get up. His sound sleep is broken. It is like that. The kundalini is dormant, it is sleeping, but the waves created by meditation, by the incantation or recitation of mantra, repeatedly dash against the kundalini and wake it up. Once awakened, the kundalini has a tendency to rise upward. When it starts rising, a certain kind of physical experience is felt. Now what will happen if my body is not physically able to tolerate it? I will feel a very great heat. I may feel so much heat that I will start perspiring. This is because my nerves are not yet fit to tolerate the movement of kundalini, or, I should say, the vibration created by the movement of kundalini. You may sweat. You may even feel like vomiting. When the body becomes fit enough to tolerate the movement of the kundalini then you will not feel that kind of heat or nausea or perspiration. After the kundalini has risen up once, twice, ten times, a hundred times, you become used to it. Then, instead of feeling great heat or perspiring or feeling nauseous, you start feeling just the opposite. You start feeling a pleasant shivering. You feel a very cool, quiet, calm mental wave. Your nerves also become very calm and quiet. You feel a very pleasant sort of physical sensation. What began as a troublesome or uncomfortable experience has changed into a pleasant one. That is why one must make one's body ready to welcome the rising of kundalini.

Now, how do we make the body fit for the rising of the kundalini? Through constant practice. Daily you practice and daily a sort of vibration is created that spreads throughout the nerves. That is the first thing. Then food habit. Your food should be such that it keeps the body cool, calm and quiet. The mind should also be quiet, not agitated. So your food should be *sattvic.*[14] Then, through practice the nerves will gradually get used to that vibration. If you are not used to running and you run a mile, the next day you will feel pain in your knee joints, your ankles, your thigh muscles, and so on, but if you keep on practicing then after one month or two months or six months it will become normal for you. A man who walks ten miles every day doesn't feel any difficulty at that distance, but send a man ten miles who is not used to walking even one mile and he will become exhausted. So you see, it's all a matter of practice. If one keeps on practicing, then gradually one's nerves become capable of absorbing the vibration created by the rising of kundalini. Proper food will also help in making those nerves fit for absorbing that vibration. Asanas [yoga postures] are also important. They have an effect on the different glands and on the nervous system. Pranayama, the breathing exercise, also helps. In fact, each part of the eightfold practice is equally important.[15] Nothing should be neglected.

Ishvara Pranidhana is the practice that enables you to achieve savikalpa samadhi, but if you are doing only Ishvara Pranidhana without making your body sufficiently fit to allow the kundalini to rise, then you won't achieve it. To have success one must make the body physically able to absorb the vibration created through the rising of kundalini. And the physical body can be made fit through asana, pranayama, regular Ishvara Pranidhana, proper food habit, and so on.

D: As the kundalini rises do you actually feel any physical sensation in your *sushumna nadi*?

C: Yes, yes. You will feel a sensation in your backbone area, a shivering feeling. You will feel something moving in your backbone. Suppose you

14 According to yogic philosophy there are three coexistent forces, or binding principles, in nature: *sattvaguna*, or sentient; *rajaguna*, or mutative; and *tamaguna*, or static. Every manifest object is dominated by one of these forces. The principle foods that fall into the category of *sattvic* are most vegetables, fruits, grains, and dairy products.

15 The fundamental practices of yoga were organized into an eightfold system, called astaunga yoga, by the great sage Patanjali more than two thousand years ago. The eight parts are yama, niyama, asanas, pranayama, pratyahara [withdrawal], dharana [concentration], dhyana [meditation], and samadhi.

tickle a person and they start laughing. They feel a kind of shivering which makes them laugh. Likewise, when the kundalini starts rising the person gets a sort of vibration or tickling sensation that makes them shiver. In some cases, people start crying.

D: So then the occult symptoms we hear about are all caused by the movement of the kundalini. In certain scriptures one can find a list of the different occult symptoms, like shivering or the hair standing on end or involuntary shouting.

C: Exactly. A sadhaka gets different kinds of experiences when the kundalini starts rising up. What kind of vibration they experience, and whether it feels pleasant or unpleasant, depends on the particular body—to what extent that body is fit to absorb the vibration. There are some people who get a ticklish feeling from a gesture alone. You haven't even touched them but they feel like laughing. They start twisting and trying to keep away from you. And then there are other people who can resist the sensation for a few seconds before they start laughing. So it all depends on the physical fitness of the particular sadhaka. The fitter the body, the less vibrational shock one experiences, and eventually there is no vibrational shock at all. But as long as the body is not fit, this experience is painful to some extent, at least in the beginning. Suppose you feel like vomiting. It's painful. You can't go and eat. You will have to get up and take rest for some time. So a sadhaka has to make their body fit through food habit, asana, pranayama, regular practice of Ishvara Pranidhana, regular bath and other practices. Only then will their body be able to absorb the vibration that emanates from the upward movement of kundalini. These things are important and every sadhaka should follow them.

D: What is the difference between *mukti* [liberation] and *moksha* [salvation]?

C: Mukti means going and coming, going and coming, with the guarantee that you will not go down to lower levels. That person has achieved such a high spiritual level that even when they leave this world it is guaranteed that they will return in a human body.

D: By high level you mean savikalpa samadhi?

C: Yes, a person who has achieved savikalpa samadhi and leaves their body, but who has not completed the sadhana, who has not achieved nirvikalpa samadhi and exhausted their reactions, they will come back, but their human body is guaranteed. They will get sadhana in the next life. That is also guaranteed. They will return and start progressing from the point that they had reached in their previous life. With a minimal amount of effort they will start rising up like Ramakrishna Paramahansa did. So that is mukti.

But moksha means that you have achieved nirvikalpa samadhi, you have exhausted your reactions, and you don't want to come back also. You have resolved that this is the end; I will not return. I have done my duty and I will not do anything more. Then, when one merges finally into the Cosmic Existence, it is moksha. And when a sadhaka merges into the Cosmic Existence but comes back again to face the unserved reactions then that is mukti, not moksha. So the final stage is moksha. Of course, mukti is a very high achievement, but it is not the final stage. The final stage is moksha.

D: Then, in *Caram Nirdesh*, when Baba says *mukti pabei pabe* [their liberation is a sure guarantee], he guarantees mukti not moksha.

C: For moksha you will have to make some effort.

D: So let us say that a person has achieved nirvikalpa samadhi, but has not yet exhausted their reactions. Then, at the time of death their mind merges into nirguna.[16] Will they still have to come back and take another body?

C: Yes.

D: That will be mukti?

C: Yes, but with mukti your physical body is guaranteed. You will not go down to a level lower than the human level. And your spiritual pursuit is also guaranteed.

D: From where you had left off before. I see. Is it possible that a sadhaka can fall from the path after they have achieved savikalpa samadhi through their practice? Is there still the possibility of degradation or downfall?

16 The unmanifest Cosmic Consciousness. *Nir* means "without" and *guna* means "qualities."

C: Yes, yes, yes. There is always the fear of downfall. That is why Patanjali has said that there are eight practices, not seven, and the eighth one is samadhi. So samadhi is also counted as a practice. Samadhi has to be practiced, otherwise there is every possibility of coming down.

Suppose I have achieved samadhi and then I say, "I have achieved everything. What is the need now of wasting time and sitting in samadhi. Let me do some work; let me talk to the people." Gradually I will start coming down instead of elevating even higher. My mind will become progressively weaker and, as a result, one day I will come down to the level from where I began. So even after achieving samadhi one must practice samadhi every day, otherwise there is the possibility of downfall.

At this point some people came to visit Dada and he switched over to the local language, except for a few brief moments after reprising Shankaracharya's song Bhaja Govindam.

Bhaja Govindam, bhaja Govindam, bhaja Govindam, mor hamate; andam galitam palitam munda...

It is good advice. Shankaracharya's advice is: O people, O fools—*mor* means those who have no knowledge—O fools, remember him, remember him, remember him. You have become very old. You have lost all your teeth. Your limbs have become very weak. You are moving with the help of a staff. Still you are aspiring for worldly pleasure. O fools, remember him, remember him, remember him.

Then it is time for some rest and noon meditation. Dada's visitors take their leave and I go to my room to enjoy the afterglow of the morning's conversation.

In the late afternoon, once the sun starts to dip behind the house, Dada again asks Ram Pirit to set up some chairs in the courtyard. I realize now that this is a daily ritual, that the chairs are there because Dada invariably has visitors at this time of day. Within a few minutes I notice an old man strolling leisurely up the walkway and Dada turns to me to say that Punditjii has come, an old class-friend of his. He is the same age as Dada, a venerable old village patriarch with a walking stick, thick glasses, and an old faded t-shirt and dhoti made of homespun that has been washed so many times that the original colors cannot even be guessed at. They may have once been white but they could just as well have been blue. As he approaches, Dada smiles and says, "You see, here in the village many people have nothing to do, so they look for some way to idle away the time. We will talk for some time and then he will continue on his way."

Punditjii greets Dada and then sits down. An animated conversation ensues in what, as near as I can gather, is a mixture of Hindi and Maethili. Both of the old men are quoting Sanskrit verses, and at one point Punditjii laughs and throws up his hands. I cannot understand everything they are saying but I can understand enough to know that Punditjii is saying "Oh, I cannot remember all these old verses. How can you!"

It is just before six. Twilight is coming on. Dada is fresh and energetic, and the world is melting into magic. The Maethili they are speaking is not classical Maethili, but Vajika Maethili, which is influenced by Magahi to the south (Patna, on the other side of the Ganges) and Bhojpuri to the west (across another river that marks the border of Bhojpur). The three colloquial forms of Maethili had been the subject of one of Baba's discourses during that Gadopur DMC, and Dada had been explaining all this to me earlier during an impromptu language lesson. I find myself musing over this and trying to follow them as they shift from Hindi to Maethili and back again. Maethili is closely related to Bengali and I find myself able to understand bits and pieces of it, although my comprehension increases dramatically when they switch to Hindi.

The discussion continues. Now they are talking about different geographic areas. Dada is leaning back in his recliner and Punditjii has his feet drawn up on the seat of his chair. He is counting on his fingers, reciting a long list, then explaining something and using his finger to emphasize his various points. Now another pundit arrives. His dhoti and t-shirt are relatively white and decidedly newer. He is younger, about sixty and when he sits down he removes his t-shirt, a young man in this gathering of old men. He wears the sacred thread worn by Brahmins and some Ksattriyas,[17] and around his upper arm is a tied thread with a single large rudraksha bead. The thongs are ubiquitous.

Now the conversation turns to language. Chandranathjii tells a story illustrating a particular point about grammar. It reminds me of how Baba would make grammar not only interesting but fascinating, with stories, anecdotes and colorful illustrations and insights into the hidden psychology and history of language. From language they move on to Malda mangos and how they have been available in the market for the past ten

17 The second of the four main Hindu castes.

days, but how these mangos have no taste because they have been ripened with carbide. They are from Bhagalpur, Punditjii says. They are talking Hindi now and my comprehension is pretty good but I decide to go back to my editing, lifting my head from time to time when something in the conversation catches my interest.

As the light fails Sitaramjii, Dada's farm manager for the past fifty years, shows up from his post in the mango orchard. It takes him some minutes to make it up the walkway, with his slow but regal gait befitting his eighty-three years. He has a brass pot in one hand and a stout bamboo staff in the other. When he finally reaches our circle he flicks his staff against the base of Punditjii's chair who turns and greets him with a short laugh. Then he ambles over to the veranda to deposit his pot and staff. He returns with his shirt off and sits in a free chair, drawing his feet up and casting his solemn glance around from side to side. Now the old men are silently staring off into space, into the coming darkness that is making it difficult for me to see this page as I write. These people move slowly but they are healthy and alert, a perfect symbol of the virtues of village life. The bats are flying now. Their time of day has begun. I go off to take a halfbath and when I return the pundits are gone. I sit down with Dada and ask him if I could trouble him with a few questions before sadhana. In answer, he tells me this story.

C: One day Baba came to my place unexpectedly. In those days he used to pay people surprise visits from time to time. During this visit he was walking up and down on the veranda—it was a long veranda—and at one point he stopped and said, "Look here, Chandranath. Human life is limited; one's power is also limited. So within a limited time and with limited power what can one do? How much can one do? So go on doing sadhana and whatever time is left over from doing sadhana try to spend that time doing service to others."

I said, "Baba I don't get enough time for sadhana. I am always being disturbed.

"Why?" he said. "How are you being disturbed?"

I said, "Baba, many people come to me to learn about the philosophy, about spirituality and spiritual practice, how to do spiritual practice. So I talk to them, I teach them the lessons, and then they come again for further lessons. Often they bring a friend or a relative with them to meet me. It's a continuous chain. Moreover, I have to go to the office as well. I have my job and whenever I come home from work there are people waiting to talk to me. So I have to take time out from my sadhana to talk to them, convince them, teach them the lessons."

Then Baba replied, "When you talk to them you are talking about spirituality, is it not? You are teaching spiritual practices? So count it as part of your practice."

So no, it is no trouble to answer your questions. It is a part of my spiritual practice. And this can be called satsaunga.

The light is failing so Dada suggests that we go on the porch and sit in front of a lamp so that I can read my questions. But I like it here in the courtyard, even more so, perhaps, now that the sun has gone down. It is cool and the twilight has an atmosphere all its own that I want to enjoy without any artificial lights for competition.

D: Dada, I have many questions concerning devotion. Perhaps we can talk about one or two now and then continue with this subject tomorrow. First of all, what is devotion? People have so many different ideas about this.

C: In short, the human mind is always attracted toward some object or some subject. It never remains idle. This attraction is a must. And there are two kinds of attraction. The attraction by the Great, or the Cosmic Existence, or Infinite Existence; and the attraction by the external objects of the created universe. When the mind is attracted by the external objects it is called common attraction, but when the attraction is toward the Great, when the mind runs after that Infinite Existence, it is called devotion.

As far as attraction toward external objects goes, we may call it by different names but we can't call it devotion. If we say devotion toward the family, devotion toward the society, and so on, it is not the correct use of the word "devotion." Attraction toward the Great is devotion and attraction toward worldly objects is attraction.

Now what happens in the case of attraction by the Great? When one's mind is attracted by the Cosmic Existence, for whatever reason—it may be due to study, to the company of saintly people, to sadhana, to the grace of the guru—whatever may be the reason, whenever there is attraction by the Great, the mind always feels happy if it is able to follow the path through which it is attracted. What I mean to say is, a person's mind is attracted by that Cosmic Existence, and when that person starts moving toward him they feel very happy. If they don't get an opportunity to move in that direction they feel unhappy. Or suppose they are deliberately not moving in that direction. Then they feel repentance. So a person feels happy and satisfied when they are able to move on the path of spirituality.

Not only that. When one is attracted by him, one's mind is always engaged, always engrossed in his ideation, his ideas. And when the mind is always engrossed in his ideation then that person will never think of base or mean matters. When one never thinks about mean matters then one's mind is always rising up, always being elevated. It doesn't come down to the lower levels. So through devotion a spiritual practitioner moves upward. Their mind is elevated and when the mind is elevated anything can be achieved. One's concentration will be better, one's spiritual practice will be successful, and samadhi will be easy to achieve.

Now the question crops up: How can one develop devotion? I have just alluded to the fact that devotion can be gained in a variety of ways: the grace of the guru; the company of saintly people; reading good books; doing spiritual practice rigorously; always thinking about him, about the Cosmic Existence, with the help of your second lesson. All of these are part of your practice. Of course, guru's grace is not a practice, but all the rest are practices, and these practices help a person to elevate their mind. When the mind is elevated, the attraction of the Great becomes greater. And when the attraction is greater, the devotion is also greater. So they are interconnected—elevation of mind and attraction of the Great. When there is attraction of the Great, the mind will be elevated. When there is elevation of mind, the attraction becomes greater.

So these are the methods through which a person can develop devotion, and devotion is a must because without devotion the final attainment becomes very difficult. So a spiritual practitioner should follow all these things. Then there is the grace of the guru. That is not within our control.

D: How does one get the grace of the guru?

C: This is an important question. The other things are within the scope of my capacity. I am capable of doing them. But how can I get the grace of guru? Once, long ago, in one of the DMCs at Bhagalpur, Baba said that without the Lord's grace no one can achieve the final goal, and no one can get his grace by begging. Baba used the words: *Bhik mamanese* grace *nahim milta hai*—you can't get grace by begging. Then how can you get it? You have to snatch it from him. But how can we snatch it from him? He is all powerful. I am just a very weak unit being. Is it possible to snatch it from him? No, it is not possible to snatch it through our own strength. So then, what can we do?

The answer is to do something that will force him to bestow his grace on you. Something that will make him feel helpless in that regard. This is the meaning of snatching. You force him into such circumstances where he has to bestow his grace upon you. And what can we do that will make him want to bestow his grace? Do what he wants you to do. If you do what he wants, then he will be so attracted to you that he will bestow his grace. And what does he want us to do? He wants us to do *atma moksartham jagat hitayaca*. So you see, ultimately we come to that same point. Do your sadhana regularly, sincerely, seriously, and do service to others. The key is sadhana and seva, spiritual practice and service.

So we started talking about devotion and we end up at sadhana and seva.

D: Dada, at one place Baba mentions the five *bhavas*,[18] like *dasya bhava, madhur bhava, sakya bhava*, and so on. Can you say something about the practice of the *bhava*s. Should we practice certain *bhava*s? Is one higher than another?

C: These are the mental inclinations or attitudes of mind. What is *sakya bhava*? Feeling that he is my friend. *Sakya* means "friend" and *sakya bhava* means "attitude of friendship." But you see, all these *bhava*s are just in the beginning stages. If you go on practicing seriously, sincerely and rigorously they all are left behind. So there is no need of going into all the details and descriptions of *sakya bhava*, and so on.

Some people say *piya ki doli*. *Piya* means "husband." *Piya ka desh*—to the land of my husband. Many poet-saints have used this word. *Putra bhava*. *Putra* means "son." You must have heard the story of Lord Krishna's childhood? Nandana and Yashoda had this *putra bhava*. Arjuna had *sakya bhava*. But a regular sadhaka need not think about all these matters. Leave them aside. They have some place, no doubt, but only at the lower stages. People follow these different methods in order to awaken devotion. But in my opinion they are not necessary for a strict, sincere and regular sadhaka. Let us keep ourselves confined to practicing the eight parts of yoga combined with social service and this will give us devotion.

18 The traditional attitudes that the spiritual aspirant adopts in order to relate to God, such as looking upon the Lord as one's friend or as one's lover or as one's father or mother.

D: And kirtan.

C: Yes, kirtan comes under sadhana. Kirtan, bhajan [devotional songs], meditation. These are all parts of sadhana. And doing good to others is service. If we can keep ourselves engaged in sadhana and seva all the time, either physically or mentally, it will awaken devotion within us. Even when we are not acting physically, we can think about it—how to do, what to do, where to do, under what circumstances. This will not only awaken devotion, it will elevate our mind, and with this elevation of mind our devotion will go on increasing. As the mind elevates, the stronger the devotion becomes. So let us forget those different attitudes toward God or the Cosmic Existence. That is for those who have not gotten the real path, who have not gotten a sadguru [true guru], who have not gotten a scientific method of practice. It will do them good, no doubt. But when the higher stages are open to us we should take advantage of them. Just because we have to pass through grade school doesn't mean that we should remain in grade school forever. We have a chance to go to the university, so let us go to the university. Let us keep on moving onward, higher and higher.

Even before I was initiated I was doing something, what I learned through reading books or listening to saintly people. But I only did those things until I came in contact with my spiritual teacher. The day I came into contact with him I felt satisfied and I never cared again for the practices that I had been doing before meeting him. Nevertheless, what I had been doing was good and it may very well be due to those practices that I got such a guru.

Suppose you are climbing a staircase and you have reached the fiftieth step. Along the way you have passed the tenth step, the twelfth step, the twentieth step. All these steps have helped you to reach the fiftieth step, but once you have passed them what is the value of going back? So once devotion is awakened, the lower stages should be forgotten. Do not waste time with them. Let us move onward, let us move forward. What can be achieved through the practice of those mental inclinations is already yours. Use this now for your further progress.

D: So it is enough to remember Baba and move ahead?

C: Baba's ideation is different from those different *bhavas*. Don't think of Baba as your friend. If I am an old man I shouldn't think that Baba is my son. If I am a young man I shouldn't think that Baba is my father.

Not like that. By now I have realized that he is a great teacher. He is the divine personality who has one foot in the Cosmic Existence and another in the created universe. So when I have a guru like that there is no need of thinking that he is my son or he is my father or he is my friend or he is my brother. There is no need of that. Take him as your guru, the real guru, the form in which we have received him. Baba has said in *Ananda Sutram*: *Bhava bahavatitayoh setu taraka brahma*. Taraka Brahma is the bridge between manifested and unmanifested. *Bhava bhavatitayoh. Bhava* means "manifested" and *bhavatiita* means "that which is beyond the manifest", that is, "unmanifested." *Bhava bhavatiitayoh setu. Setu* means "bridge." *Bhava bhavatiitayoh setu taraka brahma.* Taraka Brahma is the bridge between the manifest and the unmanifest. So when we know that we have gotten a teacher like that then there is no need of taking any other attitude toward him. Let us all adopt the same attitude and through that attitude we will develop devotion toward him and we will receive his grace. Once devotion is aroused, grace will come of its own. That is what Baba meant to say. Snatch his grace.

D: This feeling of devotion, how does it differ from emotion or sentiment?

C: Emotion is temporary and not as strong as devotion. Devotion is a well-thought, well-planned, well-established subject. Emotion comes suddenly and goes suddenly, and its duration is short, while devotion is permanent. So devotion is superior to emotion. Emotion can go both ways: it can be good; it can also be bad. Sentiment can be good; it can also be bad.

Suppose I am following a particular religion. Certain religious rites are prescribed in that religion and I have become very orthodox about them. Even if you suffer because of this, it doesn't matter to me. Let the other person suffer. Not only them but hundreds or millions of people like them. I will observe my religious rites without compromise. Well, that is the bad side of sentiment. What are these different sentiments: linguistic sentiment, regional sentiment, caste sentiment, religious sentiment? They are all narrow sentiments.

So sentiment or emotion can be either good or bad, but devotion is always good. There is only one direction for devotion and that direction is toward the Great. So it is always good. It is the sure road to success, the path that leads to the goal, so there is a great difference between emotion or sentiment, and devotion.

D: So one can feel both emotion and devotion for God?

C: Of course. When you are a devotee the good side of emotion will come of itself. When one has become a devotee, when one has developed devotion within oneself, then emotion will always rise up inside. You see, when you sing Prabhat Samgita or when you sing kirtan, you feel very happy or very attracted. That attraction or happiness is the rising of emotion; it is due to the rising of emotion in the proper direction. So once you have devotion the right sort of emotion will come of its own. But it cannot be vice versa. Emotion may arise but it will not lead to devotion if that emotion is not in the right direction. That emotion or sentiment may be misleading.

Nowadays, in Pakistan, the Shias and the Sunnis are killing each other. Why? Because of religious fanaticism. They are following the same religion, Islam, but they have some differences in certain religious rites, and because of that they are inimical to each other, they are killing each other. Well that is emotion, that is sentiment. How can I say that it is good? It is bad. But if a person has real devotion toward God, toward Allah, they will never indulge in killing others because of that sentiment or emotion. That sentiment or emotion will be controlled by their devotion and their devotion will not allow them to go down the wrong path. So devotion is always superior to emotion or sentiment. It will always control emotion or sentiment. No one should care for emotion and sentiment. One should care only for devotion, and if one has devotion then the good emotion or good sentiment will come of its own.

D: Dada, in the beginning sadhana takes a great deal of effort. As one gets closer to the nucleus and achieves some elevation, does it require less effort, that is, does it becomes more natural?

C: Yes. In the morning I talked about habit. It will become automatic. In the beginning you have to put in a lot of effort, but gradually the mind becomes so habituated, so imbedded, so engrossed in its ideation that it comes of its own, without any effort. It becomes very easy. Even while working, even while eating, even while taking bath, you will remember him. You will always remember him, always see him, mentally. With progress in sadhana and devotion it becomes easy—very, very easy.

June 5

THE NEXT MORNING I had one of the deepest meditations I had ever experienced. I sat there on the edge of an internal expanse and felt the desire well up within me to disappear. What a joy it would be to simply let this individuality go, to dive in and lose myself in that endless flow. I had a taste of the joy of being hollow, like a reed for the Lord to blow through. There is nothing to fear, I thought, in giving up this individuality to him, and everything to gain. But, of course, it was only a taste, a passing whiff of the divine fragrance, and I knew I owed much of that experience to the charged atmosphere that I was meditating in. Here I was living for these few days with not one saint but three, for there was no mistaking the attainments of Dada's wife and Sitaramjii. And in a house where Baba had once stayed, and about which he had once said that in the future many people would come there to enjoy the spiritual vibration.

During breakfast we talked about fasting—the benefits, how to prepare for a fast and how to break it. I was surprised to learn that Dada had fasted four times a month without water until his early seventies because Baba had said that four times was better than two.[1] Nowadays he feels too weak to talk or get out of bed if he fasts, so he takes some fruit and milk on fasting days.

Dada had to go to town to collect his pension so I spent the rest of the morning with his two grandsons, Devavrata and Hrishikesh. Devavrata explained to me some of the prevalent superstitions and prejudices that many Indians have about foreigners, and Hrishikesh got me into a long discussion about the endemic corruption in India and what needs to be done about it.

1 Regular fasting is a traditional part of yogic practice. In Ananda Marga it is recommended to fast at least two times a month. Monks fast four times.

After lunch Devavrata brought me some ripe mangos from the orchard, the first of the season, and Dada and I sat out on the veranda for a few questions.

D: There is a certain M. who claims that in the early part of Baba's life most of his time was devoted to sadhana, or at least to being alone in his room and apart from the organization; he says that only in the last twelve years of Baba's life did he give so much emphasis to organizational work and service activities. According to him, Baba was setting an example that first a person should devote most of their time to sadhana, and only when they become very successful in sadhana, very elevated, should they then work for the society. Can you address this? What is the proper balance between sadhana and seva, and how can one achieve that balance?

C: First of all, it is not possible for anyone to sit in sadhana all the time. At the very least, one has to get up from sadhana to take care of one's personal duties or responsibilities—food, toilet, bathing, and so on. Now if a person does nothing more than this, does it not amount to selfishness? Yes, do your sadhana, but there should be a balance between work and sadhana. Just as you spend some time taking care of your own personal necessities, you should also spend some time doing work for others. There should always be a time marked for sadhana and a time for duty—I call it duty. Doing work for others is a duty.

Now, we read in the *Gita* that Lord Krishna advised Arjuna to lead a balanced life. *Yuktaharaviharasya yuktacestasya karmasu yuktasvapnavabodhasya yogo bhavati duhkhaha. Duhkhaha* means "remover of *dukha*," "killer of *dukha*." *Dukha* means "misery." When does yoga become the remover of misery? When you lead a normal life, a balanced life. *Yuktaharavihara* means "balanced"—in your food, in your relationships with people, in sleep, in work. Krishna advised Arjuna to maintain this balance in every sphere of life, not only in sadhana. If a person leads this sort of balanced life, then for them yoga becomes the remover of misery—*yogo bhavati dukhaha.*

Essentially, what this boils down to is that not sadhana alone but sadhana combined with duty, worldly duty, makes a person successful in their yogic practices. So this duty is also compulsory. In one of his discourses, Baba has said that no matter how much sadhana you do, you will not get salvation unless you do service to the suffering.

So it is not correct to say that we should only do sadhana and once we have achieved something then we should do service to others. Rather, it is misleading. You will not achieve anything if you do not do service to others. Combine your sadhana with service to others. This is what Baba had been preaching since the very beginning of the organization. What to speak of the organization! Baba initiated me two years before the organization was founded. It was founded in 1955; I was initiated in 1953. At the time of initiation Baba told me, "Your duty is not only to look after your own self. You have to do service to others also. *Atma moksarthamjagat hitayaca*. Sadhana for self and service to others.

As soon as he founded the organization in January 1955, he started introducing different departments for social welfare. In 1956 he introduced the idea of cooperatives and asked us to open up a cooperative for the local people who were being exploited by the merchants and traders. In the long run we couldn't compete with the merchants of the town, but he supplied the inspiration and we followed through on it. We were not successful, true enough, but he planted the idea in our minds that cooperatives can save the people from exploitation, and even though we failed we knew that someday someone else would come forward and do it successfully. In 1956 he also introduced departments for education, relief and welfare, and had us establish social service projects. So how can one say that he started in this line very late in his life? He had been working along these lines from the very beginning. All the social service aspects of Ananda Marga were introduced long ago, at the beginning stages. So I must strongly disagree with what M. has said.

D: Dada, I wonder if you could offer some advice to help people find the proper balance between the amount of time devoted to social service and the time devoted to sadhana. I meet some people who feel an intense pressure to work or do service, and consequently they do less sadhana. They say that forty-five minutes or a half hour is all the time they can afford to devote.

C: No, that also I do not accept. Why only forty-five minutes? If the scheduled time is one and one half hours, then do it one and one half hours. You can't claim that you don't get enough time. You get time for everything else but you don't get time for sadhana? I don't find any logic behind it. You see, last night, just to give an example, I went to sleep at 12:30. Why did I go to sleep at 12:30? Because in the evening I was not satisfied with my sadhana. So at eleven o'clock I sat on my bed and began doing my sadhana. I took about one and one half hours and went to sleep at 12:30. And in the morning, when I got up, I was very happy. So nobody can advance the reasoning that they don't get enough time. You have to make time for it. Sadhana should be taken very seriously. Otherwise one's life will not be balanced.

Somebody says only sadhana; another says only duty. Neither approach is indicative of a balanced life. A balanced life means both. Lord Krishna has said as much—not only a balance between sadhana and service, but a balance between sleeping, eating, and everything else as well. *Yuktahara. Ahara* means "food." *Vihara. Vihara* means "mixing", or taking pleasure or seeking pleasure from external objects. *Yuktahara viharasya, yuktacestasya karmasu.* Your efforts or work should also be balanced. *Yukta swapnava bodhasya.* Sleeping and waking should also be in balance. Some hours should be set aside for sleeping and some for working. At every step of the way we should try to lead a balanced life. So if someone says that forty-five minutes for sadhana is enough, I will not agree. If someone else says that we should spend the whole day doing duty, I will not agree with them either, just as I do not agree with M.'s contention.

If I am to continue working in this world then I need some rest. So I have to sleep. Since I use this body to do service, I must keep this body fit. For that I have to eat. So eating, rest, clothing, all these are necessary for the body. All these should be provided for the body. The body should be kept fit. And why should I keep the body fit? For two reasons—sadhana and service. So keep the body fit and do sadhana and service. Do everything in a balanced way and earmark a satisfactory amount of time for sadhana.

I have often expressed that we should, as far as possible, fix a particular time for doing sadhana. Suppose someone is dying and I say, "No, this is my time for sadhana. I will not help him." This is not correct. I must help. But, of course, such things don't happen every day. This is an emergency. In an emergency we may break our rules for a greater cause, but otherwise we must fix a time for sadhana in the morning and in the evening. Suppose we sit at six o'clock in the morning. Let it be six o'clock every day. Suppose we sit at seven o'clock in the evening. Let it be seven o'clock every day. If eight o'clock, then let it be eight o'clock, but we should try to sit in sadhana at a fixed time. And we should make a daily effort to stick to that time, just as an office-goer sticks to their time. If you have to be in the office at nine o'clock then nine o'clock means nine o'clock. So it should be for a sadhaka. Six o'clock should mean six o'clock.

So a fixed hour should be set for sadhana, both in the morning and in the evening, and the place should be fixed as well, at least as far as possible.

Suppose you are staying in this house for four days. Then for each of these four days you sit in sadhana at a particular place, the same place. Not today here and tomorrow over there. You did it yesterday on your bed, you have done it today on your bed—do it tomorrow also on your bed. So the time and place should be fixed.

And the third thing is food. People do not consider diet to be an important part of spiritual practice, but it is. Food affects the body and the body is the seat of the mind. The brain is a part of body, and the mind functions with the help of the brain. So the brain should be healthy. For a healthy brain, the body should be healthy. For a healthy body, the food should be healthy. Now, by healthy food I do not mean food that will help you to become a wrestler, but rather food that makes the nerve fibers and glands calm, cool and quiet. Nothing should be eaten or drunk that agitates the mind or agitates the body or nerves. So equal importance should be given to food, sitting place, and the time for sitting. These are essential for a sadhaka.

D: Then to continue in this vein, I have heard some people claim that it is not essential to be vegetarian to make good progress in sadhana.

C: No, it is essential to become a vegetarian for doing sadhana. First of all, let us scrutinize this claim. Generally we find that the principle diet of those who became great saints in the past was fruits and green vegetables. Why? Well, food definitely casts some effect on the nerves, and the brain is composed of nerves and nerve fibers. The brain, in turn, is the carrier of mind, the seat of mind, so whatever affects the brain also affects the mind. Suppose somebody drinks a bottle of wine. That person will become agitated, rather their thinking becomes agitated, and they can no longer keep themselves under control. Somebody quarrels, someone else weeps, a third person laughs, and in each case their behavior is completely different than their normal behavior when they are sober. This shows that the liquid they have ingested has definitely affected their mind.

In India people take a drink called *bhanga*, which is made from a type of green plant. The leaves are plucked and dried in the sun and kept in bags. They take a few spoonfuls of those leaves, mix it with sugar or juice or even with water, and they drink it. Within a short time you will see them with their eyes half-closed and their speech slurred. When they try to walk they stumble. Their nervous system has become intoxicated and as a result they lose control over themselves, over their speech, their behavior, their movements. That is the effect of a few leaves mixed with water and sugar. There are some foods and drinks that cast their effect immediately. There are others that do not have any immediate outward effect. The effect is slow and gradual, like slow poisoning, and in the long run they damage the nerves and nervous system. Once a person becomes used to such things it becomes difficult for them to give up the habit because if they don't use them they feel uneasiness or tiredness or pain.Likewise, whatever we eat or drink has some effect. Some things have a greater effect and some things have a lesser effect, but everything has some effect on the body, nerves, brain, and, most importantly, on the thinking, on the mind. This needs to be carefully considered before one decides what to eat. For a sadhaka the main thing is concentration and meditation, and for concentration and meditation you need a cool mind, and for a cool mind those foods that make the mind agitated should be avoided by the spiritual practitioner. There are certain kinds of foods that keep the nerves cool: fruits, green vegetables, milk and milk products. They don't agitate the nerves.

Now this is a matter of experiment. Anyone can perform this experiment by first doing sadhana for a period of time, say six months or one year, while following a strict vegetarian diet with an emphasis on fruits and milk products, and then changing their diet to include onions, garlic, red chilis, and generous amounts of tea or coffee—leave aside liquor, or meat and fish. Only those things that are also vegetables. Practice this for six months or one year and see how much it affects your sadhana. Of course, if the person finds it to be bad after only one month then they should give it up. This is an experiment. There is no use continuing it once you have gotten the results.

A sadhaka should avoid foods that produce heat in the glands and agitate the nervous system, and such a diet has been the subject of experiments by yogis since very ancient times. All along they have been saying that a sadhaka should not take meat, fish, eggs, onion, or garlic, and that fruits, milk products, green vegetables and grains are good for meditation. They make the body strong without agitating the nerves.

The sum and substance comes to a strict vegetarian diet. With an agitated mind it becomes very difficult to concentrate, and if the concentration is not good, one's progress will be slowed. It cannot be said that one won't progress at all, but one's progress will be slow. But then, if we want to do something or achieve something, why go slow? Let us progress quickly, and for that let us eat the food prescribed by yogis since ancient times.

So I must say, a strict vegetarian diet is very helpful, in fact, essential for a sadhaka.

D: What is the appropriate amount of time to spend in meditation per day, and does it differ from person to person?

C: I can tell you what Baba told me. He took a promise from me in July 1955 to sit for one and one half hours per session. I started sadhana in 1953, but Baba started teaching me vishesh yoga in 1955.[2] Before initiating me into vishesh, he first asked me if I was prepared to sit for a minimum of one and one half hours per sitting. It is a minimum, not a maximum. So I would prescribe one and a half hours.

D: Also for a sahaj yogi?

C: Yes, yes. Definitely. Before I took up vishesh, I was doing sahaj yoga and I was devoting that much time. Sometimes even more. Sometimes two hours, sometimes two and a half hours. So, combining my experience and the teachings of Baba, I would say that one must devote one and a half hours per sitting. Twice daily, once in the morning and once in the evening. It's not asking too much.

The other times you sit for sadhana you can sit anywhere from fifteen minutes to half an hour, depending on the time available. Before you eat lunch, before going to bed, and when you get up. You have to do something at these times, so that something can be fifteen minutes, twenty minutes, half an hour—as the time permits. Say I wake up and sit in Guru Shakash,[3] but I feel the urge to go to the bathroom. So I will get up and go, as the circumstances dictate. But that too should not be less than fifteen minutes.

D: Then for a normal person you recommend two main sadhanas and in addition to this a short sadhana before leaving the bed in the morning, again before lunch and again before going to sleep at night.

2 *Vishesh* means "difficult" in Sanskrit. There are several different systems of meditative practice in Ananda Marga. The general system is called sahaj yoga (*sahaj* means "easy") and consists of six different lessons, including Ishvara Pranidhana and Dhyana, which have already been mentioned. Vishesh yoga is the advanced practice.

3 A type of meditation that is practiced as soon as one wakes up and before leaving the bed.

C: For a sahaj yogi I would advise fifteen minutes Ishvara Pranidhana and fifteen minutes Dhyana before going to bed and before eating lunch. And in the morning, when one wakes up, then Guru Shakash instead of Ishvara Pranidhana and Dhyana.

D: You advise this also for family people?

C: Yes, yes. It makes no difference for sadhana whether one is a whole-time worker or a family person. Whatever I advise regarding sadhana is meant both for family people and renunciates.

D: Dada, a short while ago you listed three main points that are very important for sadhana. What other advice would you give to someone who wants to make good progress in sadhana?

C: We talked about some of the other points yesterday. Second lesson, mantra japa, and service to the suffering creatures—not only human beings but everything in this creation. The plants should also be protected. Birds and insects should not be killed unnecessarily. At every step of our life we should try to do service to others. Leaving aside the three points that we already discussed, these are the other essentialities for quick progress—second lesson, japa, and service to others. I have already pointed out that Baba has made it clear that you will not achieve progress unless you do service to the suffering, no matter how many hours of sadhana you do. So all these combined together will allow a person to achieve progress in their sadhana and ultimately achieve the final goal.

D: How important is satsaunga to one's spiritual progress?

C: It is very important. Why? As you think so you become, and you think according to the company you keep. You and I are sitting here together, talking together, dining together. Now whatever subjects we talk about keep our mind engaged in thoughts revolving around those subjects. So our choice of subject will certainly have some effect on our mind. And the subjects we discuss are according to the company we keep. So satsaunga is equally important for a sadhaka. When we are in the company of good people, spiritual people, then we remain engaged in good talks, and these good talks supply our mind with good ideas; they help us develop good thinking. This helps a sadhaka to concentrate their mind on that Cosmic Existence. So in my opinion satsaunga is very important.

Each and every action has its origin in mind. Whatever we may do — be it physical labor, talking, shouting at somebody, abusing somebody, praising somebody or showing affection to somebody — it begins in the mind. The words we speak have their origin in the mind and likewise our physical actions. You came to this place only after you first thought of coming here. So the action of your coming to this place originated in your mind. If we think thoughts of doing harm to others, then our actions will follow suit. And then there are some people who are so blind that they think of doing things that are harmful to themselves. But by keeping good company a person develops good thinking, and this good thinking makes one act in the right way. So — good company, good thinking, good actions.

D: Dada, in western societies there is a lot of misunderstanding about the concept of guru, or the necessity of guru. There are some teachers who teach that a guru is not necessary at all and can, in fact, be dangerous because when a person surrenders to a teacher they are liable to get misled. Thus many people advise others not to accept a guru, but just to be sincere with their sadhana. In your opinion, what role does the guru play in the life of a sadhaka and what is the necessity of having a guru? Can liberation be attained without having a guru?

C: Can liberation be attained without guru? Well, I would have to say no. It is not possible to attain salvation without a guru. The reasoning behind this we can address later. First let us look at the history.

Lord Krishna, Lord Shiva, Christ — they were great people, great human beings. Did they have a guru or not? Well, there is no historical record about their having had a spiritual teacher, as far as I know. But even then they practiced something. They went into seclusion to practice. Where did they learn their practices? They must have learned them somewhere.

Now we can't say for sure about Christ, Shiva or Krishna, but it is well known that Buddha visited a guru and lived with him for some time. After that he went into seclusion to practice, and he practiced very rigorously, something which is not possible for everyone to do. The exception should not be made the example. How many disciples of Buddha became real Buddhas after him? So the exception should not be made the example. It is said that such persons are carriers of light from the Cosmic Ray. He was created by the Cosmic Existence itself.

But if we are to talk about the normal person, then I must say that a guru is necessary and without a guru it is not possible to attain salvation. If it were possible then why did Buddha go and preach after achieving salvation? Why should he have expended so much energy moving about the country and teaching people to do this and that practice. He himself acted as guru after he achieved enlightenment. Why should he do that if a guru were not essential?

Let us come to the life of Sri Ramakrishna. He could not achieve nirvikalpa samadhi until he met Totapuri and accepted him as guru. Totapurijii asked him if he would like to do *adwaita* sadhana. *Adwaita* means "singular entity." That Cosmic Existence is infinite. He is the singular entity, the only existence. So he asked Ramakrishna, "Do you want to do *adwaita* sadhana?" Ramakrishna said yes and with Totapuri's help he was able to achieve nirvikalpa. Ramakrishna was already close to reaching the goal but he needed somebody's help to bridge the final gap and he got that help from Totapuri. Later, Totapuri left and went away, but out of respect for his guru, Ramakrishna himself taught his disciples *adwaita* sadhana. Nowadays you will find so many ashrams named Adwaita Ashram; they were named by Ramakrishna's disciple Vivekananda. Adwaita Ashram—Almora; Adwaita Ashram—Dantoli. Because his guru taught him *adwaita* sadhana, *adwaita* became a respected word.

So guru has its importance in the life of a spiritual sadhaka. And not only in a sadhaka's life, but in everyone's life. You go to a college; you go to a school. You want to learn mathematics; you want to learn literature. You need the help of a guru, even for the most ordinary things. You need somebody to teach you literature, to show you how to become a good literary person. If you want to learn Bengali you need the help of a person who knows Bengali. You need a Bengali dictionary; you need some books in Bengali. So even for ordinary education in schools and colleges you need a teacher.

Likewise, in the field of spirituality everybody needs a teacher, but here it is even more essential. The vibrational force, the vibrational strength that we get from the guru helps us to move forward in our sadhana. The mantra he gives us carries with it a special vibration. If I simply pick up any mantra from anywhere and recite it internally and concentrate on it, it will not help so much. Let me explain why.

The mantra that the teacher has given us carries the vibrational force created by him. You go and stand on the bank of a river. Keep on shouting all day long, "There should be a bridge here, there should be a bridge here." There will be no bridge and everyone will say that a madman has come to the bank of the river and he is shouting, "there should be a bridge here, there should be a bridge here." But suppose the chief minister of the state comes, stands on the bank and says, "There should be a bridge here." What will happen? Immediately his staff will start working and after some time there will be a bridge there. Why the difference? You were shouting the very same words but nobody was listening. Everybody was laughing. Today a certain person comes, orders that a bridge be built and, lo and behold, a bridge is built. Why? Because his words have the strength of the chair of the chief minister of the state behind them. Likewise, if we just pick up any word from anywhere as our mantra and start reciting it, it will not help. It must have the vibrational force of a spiritual teacher.

Now let us come to our teacher. He has said in *Caryacarya Part II: Varabhaya aur janusparsha mudra ke pravarttana dwara Shrii Shrii Anandamurti ne jis shaktispandan ki srsti ki hai, tumlog usika sahara lekar apne ko aur jagat ko sarvatmaka kalyan ake path path par lekar age barho.* What is the meaning of these words? He says: "Anandamurti has created a vibrational force through the two *mudras*,[4] *varabhaya* mudra and *janusparsha* mudra"—those mudras are for meditation. "Take help from that vibrational force and go ahead. Do not go ahead alone, but take others with you also on the path of *sarvatmaka kalyan*, the path of all around welfare."

And continue down through the history. Every great saint had some sort of vibrational force behind him, in other words, some spiritual teacher, some spiritual guide. So, in my opinion, it is not correct to say that we can manage without a teacher. We can't even learn the alphabet without a teacher, what to speak of spiritual practices.

Now let us move to the philosophy. The philosophy says that God is infinite. And the Infinite has no hands or feet or eyes or tongue or throat. So how can he act in our presence and how can we grasp him? No human mind can grasp the Infinite Existence. It is beyond the limited capacity of our minds. So there needs to be a link between the Infinite Existence and the finite existence. And who will serve as the link? No one but he. The Infinite Existence alone can become the link. He creates a body out of the five fundamental factors that he has created, and this body becomes his medium. He projects his ideas, his theories, his works through this body. The Infinite acts through that body and this is what is called guru.[5]

4 *Mudra* refers to a ritual gesture, usually of the hands or fingers. Realized gurus will use mudras to transmit certain spiritual vibrations.

5 In *Ananda Sutram*, Anandamurti says: *Brahmaeka guru na para.* Brahma (Supreme Consciousness, God) alone is the guru, none other.

Lord Krishna told Arjuna: *Paritranaya sadhunam vinasaya ca duskritam dharmasamsthapanathaya sambhavami yuge yuge.* "To protect the virtuous and destroy the evil-doers, I come often and establish the realm of Dharma." Here Krishna is connecting his mind with the Infinite Mind. *Sambhavami yuge yuge.* "I come from time to time."

The guru is God. The Infinite himself is guru, but he has to act through some medium. It is just like a bridge. We are in saguna.[6] The creation is in saguna. It is in the mind of the Cosmic Entity, but beyond that there is the Cosmic Consciousness. So the guru acts as a bridge between this created universe where we exist and the Infinite Consciousness. If you want to cross this river you need a bridge, and with the help of that bridge you can cross with great ease and comfort. So guru is necessary. In the realm of spirituality the final attainment cannot be achieved without his grace.

Now if somebody says that by surrendering to a teacher you may be led down the wrong path, well, that depends upon our own scrutiny, it depends on us. Let us scrutinize carefully whether or not the personality whom I am accepting as my teacher has the capacity to guide me. True, not everybody is capable of judging this. A child or a half-developed person may not be able to think deeply about such matters. But an intelligent person, whether they are educated or not, has the ability to understand such things; they can judge whether or not this teacher has the capacity to lead me toward my goal. If a person feels that such and such teacher has the capacity to lead them, then let them lead. If one feels that the teacher doesn't have the capacity to lead them, then go in search of another.

When I was young I read a book by Paul Brunton called *A Search in Secret India*. He travelled first to Egypt but he didn't feel satisfied there, so he came to India and after visiting India he wrote the book. In it he describes how he went in search of a teacher. He travelled all over India and visited many people who were reputed to be saintly people. But he didn't feel satisfied with any of them. Finally he went to Arunachalam, to the ashram of Ramana Maharshi. Now he didn't talk to Ramana, he didn't question him, he didn't get any answers from him. He simply sat in front of him for *darshan* as so many others had.[7] Now, as far as I remember, he wrote that while he was sitting there Ramana opened his eyes and looked

---

6 The manifest Cosmic Consciousness, or manifest creation. *Sa* means "with" and *guna* means "qualities."

7 *Darshan* means "sight." It refers to seeing the guru physically or listening to them speak.

at him and when he did he felt a sensation pass through his body and he went into trance and remained in trance for some time. When he came out of his trance he was very happy, very satisfied, fulfilled. Mr. Paul Brunton then accepted him internally as his guru due to this experience, due to his first-hand knowledge. It's like that.

I began searching for a teacher in 1951 but I didn't find one to my satisfaction until March 1953, after a search of nearly two years. It was the help or gift of Providence that wherever I went I didn't feel satisfied. But when I first heard about the man who would become my teacher I felt something, a sort of satisfaction and a strong urge to meet him and talk to him. And once I met him, saw him, talked to him, I felt even more satisfied. And when he initiated me I cannot even begin to describe how satisfied I felt, how happy I was.

So it's like that. A person should scrutinize carefully and decide for themselves where and when they should surrender. If they don't feel like surrendering, they should not surrender. There is no compulsion in it. To simply go anywhere without discriminating first and surrender—that is not the teaching. You surrender where you feel satisfied, but in any case a teacher is essential, a must.

D: If a person is searching for a teacher, is there anything they should look for that can help them know whether or not such and such a teacher has the ability to lead them to their spiritual goal?

C: There is no formula for finding a teacher. The one essential thing is that if you feel satisfied when you look at them, talk to them, listen to them, then accept them as your teacher. If you don't feel satisfied, don't accept them.

Well, this too differs from person to person. Different people have different mental vibrations and if my mental vibration and your mental vibration don't tally then we will not like each other. The contrasting forces will clash. A bad man may visit a highly elevated saint and not wish to accept him as his teacher because the vibration emanating from that saint, the waves coming out of the mind of the saint, do not feel pleasing to a man who is evil by nature. The force of the saint is contradictory to his own, so he feels uneasy around him and leaves as soon as he gets a chance. This depends both on my vibration and on that of the guru. So there is no hard and fast rule or formula for how we can test a guru. What happens is that when we hear about a particular teacher or meet them, a sort of attraction arises within, an urge I should say, and that urge goads a person to accept someone as their guru.

Muktya kancha sadguru prapti. If you have the sincere urge for salvation then you are sure to get a true guru. Perhaps you remember that in my case I went to visit a certain teacher and asked him for initiation. He refused me and told me that I would get it when the time came.

D: Yes, the mahatama that lived on the other side of the rice paddies.

C: Yes, and when I finally met my teacher for the first time, his first words to me were, "Has the time come?" Now add my experience to the aphorism in *Ananda Sutram,* which says, *muktya kancha sadguru prapti.* "When the sincere urge for salvation arises, a person gets the sadguru." *Sadguru* means "correct teacher", "right teacher." This is as much as I can say about guru. The rest people have to figure out for themselves; they should have their own experience.

Kabir has said—Kabir was a saint in the thirteenth century in India—he said that he didn't consider himself to be either Hindu or Muslim. He said, "I am a man fashioned out of the five fundamental elements; I am neither Muslim nor Hindu." At the time the Muslims and Hindus were fighting each other for power.

Kabir composed many verses, and in many of them he has talked about guru. In one verse he says:

> *Guru Govind dono kare kaho lago pay*
> *Bali hari guru apano Govind diyo dikhai.*

Guru means "teacher"; *Govind* means "God." God and teacher, both are standing before me. Whom should I salute first? First I must salute the teacher who has shown me God. Kabir said this in the thirteenth century, seven hundred years ago. In another poem he has said:

> *Jura jao re ham jani*
> *Sadguru kajeri caran pakale kahai kahane jane*
> *Guru kijiye samajh bhujike*
> *Guru wa gun galtane ankush gahi baethiye*

Whatever is created will come to an end one day. Nothing in this universe is permanent; everything is bound to come to an end, even the yogis who are practicing in the jungles. Both yogi and jungle will disappear; nothing will remain. And there is a circle, a chain, of coming and going, but *sadguru kajeri caran pakale kahai kahane jane*. If you surrender to a guru, if you take shelter in a sadguru, a real teacher, then *kahai kahane jane*, where is the coming and going? That means, you will get salvation.

But he goes on to say *guru kijiye samajh bhujike*. When you accept somebody as your guru you must be very careful. When selecting a teacher you must be very careful. *Guru kijiye samajh bhujike*.

And what will happen to your faults, to your mistakes? The qualities of guru, or the vibrational force of guru, will act on you like an *ankush*. *Guruwa gun galtane ankush gahi baethiye*. You might have seen someone riding an elephant in India sometime. Someone sits on the neck of the elephant with a pointed iron rod and whenever the elephant doesn't listen he just pokes it and directs the elephant to move in a particular direction. That pointed iron rod is called an *ankush*. So he explains in this poem that the vibrational force of the guru sits on you like an *ankush* on the head of the elephant. The vibrational force of the teacher sits on your faults like that *ankush*. So that is the value of a teacher.

D: Is it necessary that one's guru be in physical form?

C: So long as the guru is physically present it is better to have contact with them as frequently as possible, but when they are not physically present, then in that case we should not feel disappointed or wonder how we can get help from them. In that case, Dhyana is very essential. Dhyana is always essential because it is a part of sadhana, but through Dhyana we get the guidance we need, the proper guidance. The vibrational force that Baba has spoken about in *Caryacarya part II* regarding *janusparsha* and *varabhaya* mudras is received through Dhyana. So even when the teacher is not physically present one can have contact with their vibrational force.

D: So those sadhakas who come into a path after the guru has departed, such as that of Ananda Marga, can—

C: They will have to be taught the process and shown the mudra. The guru has taken what we call *samkalpa* in Sanskrit, or resolve. It is his *samkalpa* that people will get help through this mudra, even when he is not physically present, so that the sadhakas can progress in sadhana and attain nirvikalpa samadhi in their Dhyana. So no one should feel discouraged, or feel that it is not possible. It is possible. Of course, this is not something to be written about; it is a matter to be discussed among spiritual practitioners. We find that since Baba has left his physical body we are getting more vibrational force than we used to get when he was present. This suggests that when he was present he was controlling it to a certain extent, just to see that we put in more time and more effort in sadhana. But since he left his physical body he is giving more help through his vibrational force.

So no sadhaka should feel disappointed that the teacher is no longer physically present. In 1956 Baba said that through *janusparsha* and *varabhaya* mudras a vibrational force has been created and that force will help everybody in their progress. He left his physical body in 1990, but he said this in 1956. Let us have confidence in what he said and avail ourselves of that vibrational force.

Now you feel happy in my company. Later on somebody will feel happy in your company. Again somebody will feel happy in their company. So there will be a chain like this. Maybe for a thousand years, maybe for two thousand years. Nobody knows for how long it will go on, but it will go on in this way.

Once Dhyaneshananda was sitting with Baba, taking notes; he was so interested in what Baba was saying that he forgot to keep writing. Baba looked at him and said, "Dhyaneshananda, is it not necessary to write down what I am saying?" Then he realized that he had stopped writing and apologized. Then Baba said, "Look here, I am telling you things that nobody else will be able to tell you. Others will come and say other things, but nobody will say these things. I will also come again after three thousand years and say something more, but in a different language."

These are the intricacies that can never be solved. Because in this infinite universe everything is infinite. But we are concerned with our own existence and our existence is confined to sadhana and seva. So let us be very sincere and serious in our sadhana and seva. That is the ultimate.

Tonight at the dinner table Dada told me something about the history of Gadopur. There are just over fifty margis here in a village with a total population of only six hundred. It has been the seat of saints for as long as people can remember. In the sixteenth century a famous saint lived here who showed many miracles to the villagers. They built a shrine to him and a temple that are still standing. Then there was the mahatma that Dada visited. Saints and sannyasis from all over India used to come to visit him. He died in nineteen fifty-six but people still visit his cottage. Then there was another sannyasi-saint who lived here not so long ago. He was still alive when Baba came. After Baba left Gadopur, this sannyasi told the local people that Baba hadn't come for Chandranath. He had come for him. He knew there was one person rotting here and he came to lift him up and rescue him. Shortly after Baba's visit this sannyasi left his body.

And today it is not only the seat of one saint but several.

June 6

MORNING SADHANA WAS WONDERFUL again. Every day in Gadopur gets better and better. As usual I was up with the sun around a quarter to five. I could hear the wooden sandals of Sitaramjii clomping around in the next room along with his soft "Jaya Baba's", and reverberating underneath the tiles. It is cool in the morning but once the sun gains a little bit of altitude it starts heating things up fast. I have been bathing at the well rather than in the bathroom, both because I want to leave the bathroom free for Dada and Didi and also because I love taking bath under the open sky. The water from the well is quite cool, enough to give me a shiver or two in the cool morning air but so invigorating.

Last night Dada sat down with myself and Ram Bachanjii in the courtyard to enjoy the late night tranquility. It must have been close to 10:30. They talked over some farm matters and I told Dada that I had been out there in the dark typing up the things he had been saying about Gadopur over dinner. He added a couple of more things, including the story of the village's first revolutionary marriage.[1] In 1964 he arranged the intercaste marriage of his niece here in Gadopur. The boy was intelligent, well-educated, and handsome—all in all a good match. The couple now have five children and have had a happy life. But the entire village opposed the marriage and they especially opposed Dada for having arranged it. They couldn't stop it from going through but for some years afterward they remained inimical to Dada. They tried to prevent any of the local people from working for him so that he would have no one to plow the fields, to fetch water, to work in the house. But as the years went by they changed

1 Intercaste, interfaith or interracial marriages are called "revolutionary marriages" in Ananda Marga and were strongly encouraged by Baba to help break down social barriers.

their opinion and grew to respect him very much. They saw over time that these Margis were good people, principled people, honest and just people. Now whenever there is some dispute in the village they bring the matter to Dada to settle and they accept his decision.

Dada is not feeling well today. The heat has been excessive. There is no electricity to run the fan and he is feeling the effects. It requires some effort for him to sit down and talk, but he does so anyway. Before we begin talking he does some Dhyana. I can see the whites of his eyes behind the half-closed lids, the pupils involuntarily rolling up toward the crown chakra. His face shines. His lips curve into an intoxicating half-smile. I can feel the vibration wash over me as clearly as if I were seated by the seashore, being sprayed by the crashing of the breakers. It dawns on me once again that I am with a man of God, and for a few moments I realize what a rare opportunity this is. I think back to what Dada had been saying a couple of days before about half-samadhi and this time I find myself far more aware and curious about the state of mind he is in while we talk, trying to catch a glimpse of the place from where he is talking.

When Dada comes down into normal consciousness to deal with his daily duties (like taking perfect care of his guest, making sure I have the best room when I come, his room which catches the breeze from three sides and stays cooler than the rest), it is easy to miss who he is. You may mistake him for a nice old man, gracious and dutiful, but catch him in these moments when he allows his mind to rise into higher states and there is no mistaking that you are in the presence of a rare being. He is the ideal sadhaka, a living example of what I would like to become, and in many ways the barometer of what progress I have made.

D: Dada, if we are only puppets in the hands of God, if everything happens according to God's will, then to what extent are we responsible for right and wrong? To what extent does the human being really have free will?

C: We are responsible only for our actions, not for the results. The results come as reactions to our actions, so we have our free hand, our free will, our independence, only in action.

Every action brings with it a reaction, and when the reaction comes then we become helpless because the reaction comes according to a certain law of nature, and that law cannot be changed. So we have to be careful while acting, and if we are not careful while acting then we have no choice but to reap the consequences of those actions in the form of reactions. So we should not say that we are simply tools in the hands of Providence, but rather that we ourselves offer to become tools due to our actions.

In the *Gita* it is said: *Na kartrtwam na karmani lokasya srjati prabhuh, na karmaphala samyogam svabhavastu pravartate.* The Lord says, "I do not do anything and I do not make anybody do anything; nor do I give the collective fruits of anybody's actions to them in order to make them suffer. Everything happens according to the law of nature." And what is the law of nature? That every action has its reaction. *Svabhavastu pravartate.* Everything happens according to the law, and that law is action and reaction. So one must be very careful while acting, because one has control over one's actions only. No one has any control over the reactions, the results. Again in the *Gita* Lord Krishna has said: *Karmanyeva dhikaraste ma phalesu kadacana.* "You have authority over the actions alone, not over the results."

So we are tools no doubt, but we are tools because of our own wrongdoing, because of our own folly. If we are careful while acting, and if our actions are such that the reactions are not of a painful or binding nature, then we become free. If we are careful then we are not tools, rather he becomes our tool. He becomes so pleased with us that he bestows on us everything we need or require. Generally speaking, he has already supplied us with everything we need. Look at this created universe. It has everything we need, but due to our own folly and mismanagement we suffer. In society there are certain rules. If we follow them then everything is peaceful. But when antisocial elements rise up they disturb the entire society. Whose creation is this? It is the human beings' own creation. We do wrong and we suffer for it. So I should not blame him, or claim that we are tools and that he is making us dance as he wishes. No. Lord Krishna has said, "Neither do I do anything, nor do I make anybody do anything; it is the law of nature that is taking its course." And what is that law? Action and reaction. If somebody puts their hand in the fire their hand will burn because this is the law of nature. You cannot blame the fire or blame God for having burnt your hand. It is your own action that is the cause of your hand being burnt. So a person should be careful while acting. Then and then alone can that person be considered a wise person.

D: Many sadhakas have questions about the occult powers, the *siddhis*.[2]

2 The *siddhis*, or occult powers or supernatural powers, manifest themselves in a sadhaka when that sadhaka gains complete mastery over the different chakras. Mastery over a certain chakra gives the practitioner control over the corresponding

What exactly is meant by occult power, when and how does a sadhaka get occult powers, and are there certain times when it is okay to use them for the welfare of other people?

C: Occult power is of little value, nor is it difficult to achieve. It is easy to achieve, and it is of little value because if one uses one's occult power it becomes the beginning of one's downfall.

I say it is not very difficult to achieve. I don't know whether or not you have had a chance to see any mesmerizers. I have seen several during my school days, young men who could do peculiar tricks with cards and could put a man to sleep. Later I realized that this level of occult power can be achieved within only six to twelve months. You practice *tratak*, a kind of process where one does nothing but concentrate ones eyes on a particular point, or a particular light, or a particular star, for a certain number of hours per day. Within six months, or maximum one year, you will get the power to exercise a kind of control over someone else's mind. Of course, that person should have a weaker mind than you. If you come across a mesmerizer you will find that they generally select some youngster of twelve or fourteen or sixteen years of age, not a mature adult of forty. They need a mind that they are easily able to influence.

Occult power means to throw the strength of your mind out through your eyes or your words. The easiest method is to throw out your power through your eyes. Through words it is a bit more difficult, and through thinking alone it is far more difficult. Ordinary mesmerizers cannot do this. It can only be done by great Tantrics, great sadhakas, great yogis. They can influence the external world through their thought alone.

In this respect Baba once told a story about Lord Buddha. Once, while Lord Buddha was moving around from place to place and preaching, he visited Vaeshali. Vaeshali was then the capital of the republican government of the Licchavis, the Licchavi dynasty. When he reached Vaeshali he stayed in a mango orchard. Buddha never stayed inside a village. He always stayed on the outskirts, in some garden or orchard. When the people heard that Lord Buddha had come to Vaeshali they came from all parts of the capital and assembled at the mango orchard. There they requested him, "O Lord, we are suffering very much. Our town is suffering from a

---

element associated with that chakra. For example, mastery of the first chakra brings control over the solid factor, or earth, and thus the ability to materialize objects at will.

cholera epidemic. People are dying every day. We don't know what to do. The physicians have failed to stem the epidemic."

Then Lord Buddha replied, "All right, it will be okay." The villagers returned home satisfied and from the very next day the cholera epidemic was over. Whatever cases of infection had already happened, had happened, but no one else fell sick.

Baba asked us to explain what Buddha had done but we couldn't. Then he said, "There is a nucleus for each and every happening in this universe, a central point from which that ray of light emerges. In this case, negative *microvita* were flowing from a particular nucleus and spreading into the city of Vaeshali,[3] and due to this people were contracting cholera. What Lord Buddha did was to apply his mental pressure, his mental force, to that nucleus. He knew where that nucleus was and how to apply that force. An ordinary person cannot know this but Buddha knew, and by applying pressure on that nucleus with his mental force he was able to stop the flow. Something may be coming out in lakhs and crores,[4] but once it is corked the flow stops. When Lord Buddha put his mental pressure on that nucleus, the flow stopped and there were no new cases of cholera.

What Buddha did is very difficult to do. But these ordinary things—to change a card from one to another at will, to put a man to sleep, to make someone talk as I want them to talk—such things are very easy to do. Both types of powers can be called occult powers, but this show, this sort of game for money's sake, or if not for money then for name and fame, this is bad. It doesn't do anyone any good. The person who is being hypnotized suffers. Repeated hypnotism weakens the heart. At the same time, the person who is doing the hypnotizing will gradually lose their power and become mentally weak, so much so that one day they may become a madman, a lunatic.

So occult power is not a good thing. It should never be used and nobody should aspire to attain it. If it comes, then let it come like a milestone on your path. This is our journey of spirituality. Many kinds of milestones will come along the way. Let them come and let them pass; we should not stop at any milestone. We should go ahead. So occult power is not good.

Now let us return to what Buddha did. What he did, he did for the good of society, for the good of humanity. This should be done, yes, but

3 According to Anandamurti, *microvita* are the smallest entities in existence, far subtler than subatomic particles. They fall within the realm of both physical and psychic expression.

4 One lakh equals one hundred thousand. One crore equals ten million.

it should only be done by such persons who have the authority to do so. Buddha had the authority to do so and he used that authority. But suppose you have some power, and somebody you know is suffering from a headache. You go and touch them and their headache disappears. Why should you do this? Have you got the authority to do so? No, you do not. You are not a guru. You are not a spiritual guide or teacher. An ordinary sadhaka should not use their occult powers, even for the good of others. Try to help them to the limit of your human capacity, not through your supernatural or supermental capacity. Leave that for the great teachers, the great guides, like Buddha or Ramakrishna.

We, as sadhakas, do not have the authority to use our occult powers, even for the good of society. We should act like human beings and do good to the society with our human efforts. It is foolish to go and sit in seclusion and think, "Oh, let me do some good to the society with my occult powers. I will achieve occult power and then I will use it for the good of society." No, you must be authorized to do so. A district magistrate is authorized under the law to do certain actions. His father, who lives in the same house, is his elder, his superior. The district magistrate shows respect to his father, but does the father have the authority to wield the power that his son is wielding in office. No, because he is not authorized. The same goes for the son of the district magistrate. Neither of them are authorized, only the magistrate himself is.

So the general principle is that nobody should care for occult power, nobody should aspire for it, and nobody should use it. This is the general rule. If you use it, you not only harm yourself, you also harm the person on whom you are using your power.

Now I will explain the philosophy behind the rule. Every action has its reaction and one who acts has to suffer the reaction of that action. Now suppose some person has done something wrong and someone else has done something good. Good results are coming to the latter person and troublesome or vexatious results are on the way for the first person. These results, whether good or bad, can come in concentrated form or they can be spread out. Suppose you are due to be happy, and suppose your reactions dictate that you should enjoy a certain level of happiness spread out over ten years, but you want to enjoy a greater happiness than you are enjoying. Then your happiness will be concentrated into one year or ten months. You will enjoy those ten months or one year and then for the next nine years you will be in continuous trouble. You have exhausted what was in store for you; your pocket is empty.

Likewise, let us suppose someone is due to suffer grief over a period of ten years. That grief is spread out; it is not in concentrated form. But if that person wishes to finish those reactions quickly then they will have to make themselves strong enough to suffer ten years of grief in a single year, in concentrated form. Now I have no authority to interfere or effect any changes in that schedule. Neither should I make anybody suffer for twelve years in place of one year, nor for one year in place of twelve. I should neither do anything to make it concentrated nor to spread it out. Suppose I start suffering from a headache and you relieve me of that headache. My suffering is not over. That reaction remains, waiting to be expressed. It will come out again some day in some form. Again you relieve me and again I will have to undergo that unexpressed reaction. All you are doing by relieving me is creating a constant chain of suffering. Had you left me alone in the first place I would have suffered that one night, but after that I would have been okay. My reaction would have been exhausted. Now, instead of suffering for one night I may have to suffer for ten nights due to you. You are under the impression that you are helping me, but rather than being helped I am worse off than I was. I would have only had to suffer for one night, but now this problem keeps returning at intervals over a longer period of time, and I am all the more unhappy for it.

So these changes in the law of nature should not be effected by anybody. Nobody should try to use occult power. Whatever was possible for me to explain, I have explained. Now you think it over and go on practicing. These powers will come by themselves, as I have just said. They are the milestones in your journey. They are bound to come. But ignore them when they do and move ahead. There is nothing valuable to be gained in them and everything to lose.

D: Dada, there are certain types of psychic healers who effect cures through their mental powers rather than through medicine—laying on hands and such things. This is prevalent in some countries.

C: Here also. In fact, the mahatma who told me "you will get it when the time comes" used to do this in the beginning, after he resigned from his job and returned to Gadopur to live in his garden. People would go to him and say, "Oh, my son has a very high temperature, please help me. He is very restless." The mahatma would then tell that person to go and pluck a certain flower and bring it to him. He would take the flower and then give it back to him and tell him to place it by the side of the boy's pillow.

The man would take the flower, go and put it next to his son's pillow, and the next day the boy would be cured. This went on for some time. Then one day his teacher came to see him. His teacher was an old man, about a hundred years old. He came and stayed with him for a few days. And while he was there he told him, "Look here, my boy; what are you doing? You are spending the little treasure you have earned. You will be a pauper again after some time. Don't do it." That was all he said, but after that the mahatma, his disciple, completely stopped doing such things.

Well, such things are not good. People think they are doing good to the sufferer but they are not. Rather, as I have just explained, they are extending that person's suffering. This kind of psychic healing will not bring the suffering to an end. *Avasya evam bhuktavyam.* This means, unless you spend it, unless you consume it, unless you exhaust it, it will remain in store for you. So such things are certainly possible but by stopping the reaction at a certain point, all you are really doing is extending the period of the person's suffering and that is not good. I have given you one example. People were coming to this mahatma for petty matters and he was helping them, thinking that he was doing them good, but when his teacher warned him then he stopped and never did it again.

D: Dada, the occult powers such as *mahima*, *laghima*,[5] and so on—do they come to all sadhakas at some point, and at what point do they come? For example, if you achieve savikalpa samadhi, do you automatically get occult powers?

C: This concerns sadhana. You know that the serpentine power, the *kulakundalini*,[6] lies dormant in the lowest chakra, the muladhara chakra. There is one English writer whose book I read sometime in 1956 or 1957. His name, if I remember correctly, was John Woodroffe. The book was called *The Serpent Power*. In this book you can find descriptions about the kulakundalini. Now in the philosophy of yoga or rather the science of yoga sadhana, the serpentine power, which is called kundalini in Hindi or Sanskrit, lies dormant in the muladhara chakra. Through the

5 The eight major occult powers referred to here, such as *laghima*, the ability to enter the intermolecular spaces of any entity and direct it according to one's wishes, are obtained when the sadhaka gains complete mastery over the fifth chakra.

6 *Kundalini* literally means, "coiled serpentine"; *kula* refers to the lowermost vertebrae of the spine where the kundalini is said to reside. The kundalini is the spiritual force of the individual.

vibration of mantra, or the incantation of mantra, and through the waves created by meditation, the kundalini awakens, and once it awakens, its natural tendency is to rise up through the *sushumna nadi*, through the canal in the center of the spinal chord. The *sushumna* starts at the muladhara chakra and goes to the sahasrara chakra; it is the passageway through which the kundalini travels. Now when the kundalini rises up it penetrates through each chakra in succession. The first chakra that it penetrates is the muladhara chakra, which is the controller of *ksititattva*, or solid factor. If a yogi, a practitioner, has the capacity to raise their kundalini up to the muladhara chakra then they get a certain power. And what power is that? The power that is connected with the solid factor. So that person will be able to materialize a flower. You and I are sitting with that person and they say, "Oh, would you like a flower? Then have it." And the flower materializes. "Do you want a biscuit?" And the biscuit materializes. Anyone can do this who has the capacity to raise their kundalini to the muladhara chakra.

Now the next chakra that the kundalini passes through is the svadisthana chakra, which is the controlling point of *jalatattva*, liquid factor. I told you the story that Ramakrishna used to tell about the man who had the ability to walk on water. That meant that that man had the capacity to raise his kundalini up to svadisthana, and therefore he had control over water. Likewise, if a person raises their kundalini up to the manipura chakra then they can spread fire and can walk on or through fire without being burnt. They have control over fire.

So it's like that. Power comes gradually as the kundalini rises upward. Once it rises above the vishuddha chakra the person gains control over all five fundamental factors, over all matters relating to the five elements. For this reason it is said that a person becomes powerful when they achieve savikalpa samadhi. Savikalpa samadhi means that the kundalini has become established in the ajina chakra, the sixth chakra, and that in turn means control over all five fundamental factors.

In practice what happens is that we see the powers coming gradually. But if a person, once they reach muladhara, gets in the habit of playing with their power over solid matter—materializing sweets, biscuits, flowers, and the like—then they remain at the muladhara chakra. They take a seat there and go no further. Suppose you have started for Patna. On the way you pass through Hajipur and you become charmed or fascinated by Hajipur. You start moving here and there in Hajipur and forget all about Patna. You will never get to Patna if you remain there. So a sadhaka has a goal. They must not stop at any milestone along the way. Forget the milestones and go ahead.

With occult powers there is always the danger of being attracted, fascinated, or charmed by them and forgetting the main goal. You remain lying by the roadside, somewhere on the path. So I advise a sadhaka to forget occult powers completely. If they have occult powers, then they should forget that they have them. Because if they don't they will use them someday and they will suffer for it. This is the mandate of the guru, the order of guru. You should never use your occult power. Baba has expressed this clearly and directly in many of his discourses—no sadhaka should ever use their occult power. They should neither be desirous to acquire them, nor should they use them if they have them. Anyone who violates this, violates the mandate of guru. So occult power is not a good thing. Rather than leading a person to their final goal, it will stand in their way and drag them down.

We should help society and other living creatures, no doubt, but for that we should use our human capacity, not our supernatural or supermental capacity. Keep your supermental power in reserve for your own progress.

And it so happens that a person who enjoys certain supermental or supernatural powers, when they do some human effort they are helped by God and are generally successful in their endeavors. When a good person makes an effort to do good to others, you will generally see that the people get some benefit from what they do because nature helps. The good that a good man does for others definitely reaches the other person, the society, the entire world. So let us work for the good of society with our own human efforts, according to our individual capacity. Whatever occult power we may have will remain with us and help us in our mental progress on the path of spirituality. And if I am good, if I am sincere, God will help.

D: Dada can you say something about the value for a spiritual practitioner of following a particular routine.

C: Everyone, according to time, place and circumstance, should frame a routine. What is the normal routine? Get up at four-thirty, do Guru Shakash. Take a break for bath and morning duties. Then sit for your regular sadhana. After that, get up from your sadhana, give some food to your physical body so it can act, and go out to do some work, some social service.

Now social service is of many kinds. Social service doesn't mean walking around asking people what they want. First you should visualize what is going on around you, think about what is happening, and then think about how to improve it, what you can do. At the moment you are trying to write a book. That is also a kind of social service because you are gathering knowledge, you are gathering experience, and out of your knowledge and experience you are going to write something. Others will read it and it will help them. They will not have to go through the same strain that you have had to go through. It will be easy for them to gain access to this kind of knowledge. So that is also a kind of social service. There are so many kinds of social service.

Baba divided social service into four kinds. He used the words *viprocit*, *ksattriyacit*, *vaeshyacit* and *shudracit*. *Viprocit* means help through knowledge or intellectuality. *Ksattriyacit* means helping through one's physical strength, or providing shelter or protection to somebody. A nurse bandages a fractured leg or gives an injection, a compounder dispenses medicines—these are *ksattriyacit*. *Vaeshyacit* refers to economic aid, giving food or clothes, and *shudrocit* refers to purely physical service. In some hospitals there are dressers. The doctor gives instructions as to how the bandage or splinter should be applied, and the dresser does accordingly. So the doctor gives his intellectual knowledge, *viprocit* seva, and the dresser does the physical work, *shudracit* seva.

So there are so many methods, so many different ways or systems for doing good to others. All have equal importance. Suppose a hungry man comes to me and I start preaching to him about spirituality. That is of no good to him at that moment. It is not the proper way of doing him service. This is *viprocit* seva, no doubt, telling people about spirituality, but here the man doesn't need *viprocit* seva. He is hungry. He needs food. So here *vaeshyacit* seva has more value than *viprocit* seva. Another man is suffering from a migraine. He needs a pill. Is this the time to pull up a chair, sit by his side, and start telling him that God is infinite, that you must concentrate on him, that you are a human being and the object of a human being's life should be to attain salvation? No. He is in no condition to listen to you because he is in so much pain. There is no way that he can concentrate on what you are saying. Rather he will feel annoyed. So first give him some medicine, give him some medical treatment.

So one is to select what is to be done according to the circumstance, the time and the place. Whatever is necessary at that particular place, with that particular person, under those particular circumstances.

Now back to the individual routine. Get up at a certain time, do this, do that—food is necessary, bath is necessary, rest is necessary, and for our own education some satsaunga is also necessary. We should make some time to read some good books or talk with some good people. So a person needs to form their own routine and decide how to utilize their time properly. Look at me. I am very busy these days. I am getting the house repaired. I am getting the water supply ready so when many people arrive here next week they won't have to suffer for want of water. And then there are other arrangements that need to be made for the people who have sent word to me that they will be coming and staying here for some time. Arrangements so that when they reach here they will not face any trouble. They should have proper sleeping arrangements, a place to sit and talk, food to eat, water to drink, some place to wash and take bath. So I am busy with that. But I am not neglecting my other duties either. If somebody comes to me for advice, I give them advice. I am doing my sadhana, taking bath, sleeping, eating, attending to all of my necessary duties.

So a person has to form their routine according to the circumstances. My guests will come and then they will go away. After that I will be a free man. My routine of today will not remain tomorrow. It will change according to the change in circumstances. The time that I am utilizing now for making certain arrangements will have to be utilized somewhere else. It may be utilized in writing something, or doing something for the good of the village with the help of the other villagers.

So one should frame their routine according to the situation and it should be done with a sincere heart. It should not be a hypocritical routine, rather it should be framed with the idea that one's time should not be wasted. Here I find that when I am not disturbing you, you are using your time in writing, in typing, in thinking. That is quite good. You are utilizing your time properly. Everybody has a similar responsibility to form a routine so that they can make the best use of their time.

And then there are so many instructions and advices as to how to make the best use of one's time—what to do and what not to do. One learns this through satsaunga. There is a saying in Sanskrit: *Nidra tandra bhayam krodha alasya dirghasutra satvasah*. These are the six deficiencies or drawbacks. *Nidra* means "too much sleep." Many people feel very happy while sleeping and they go on sleeping ten, twelve hours a day. *Tandra.* Even though I am not falling asleep, I am sitting here feeling drowsy and getting happiness from this drowsiness. This is also bad. It is a waste of time.

Bhaya. Every time you have to do something you feel afraid. "Oh, writing this book is a very difficult task. It will give me no end of trouble. So much thinking, writing, typing, editing, then I have to go to the press, get the book printed, get it bound, distribute it. Such a troublesome burden. Let me leave it." You are afraid from the very beginning. As soon as you think of doing something you feel afraid. So that *bhaya* is also an impediment. *Krodh*. Over a little matter you erupt, you get angry. As result you can't concentrate and you end up doing something wrong. You are bound to do something wrong because an angry mind, an agitated mind, can never think deeply on any subject. The face becomes red, the blood pressure rises and disturbs the thinking capacity. *Alasya*. Idleness. I am sitting here, knowing that a certain task has to be done. A message has to be delivered. "All right, I will go," I think, but I continue sitting right here. Then at four o'clock I finally go to meet this person and tell them that they were supposed to be somewhere at four o'clock. "Please hurry up." But I have spent the last four or five hours idling my time away, thinking, "Oh, yes, I will go and tell them, I will go and tell them." Out of laziness you inform them at the last moment. This laziness is also an impediment to progress. *Dirghasutra*. This means "procrastination." Something has to be done. "All right, let me do it tomorrow." Your field needs to be cultivated by a certain time, but you procrastinate for three or four days and the field dries up. Now if you sow your seeds it is already too late. So these six things are stumbling blocks in the way of progress. All of these should be kept in mind while making a routine, and not only while making a routine but while acting according to that routine.

Dada has been talking of service and it is precisely at this moment that one of the workers who has been digging the new well out behind the house approaches us with a cut on his foot. The pick slipped, it seems, while he was working and grazed the side of his foot. The moment he sees the cut, Dada is up and attending to the injury, explaining to the man what needs to be done, sending people to bring what he needs, and seeing to it that everything gets done properly. It is a perfect example of what he has been talking about. See what needs to be done for the people according to the circumstances, and do it. Then he goes into the house and returns with the bandage. Someone else has brought some antiseptic and a bucket. Dada cleans and dresses the wound himself, and when he is finished he gives detailed instructions for its care over the next few days. The look on this man's face is priceless. He is grinning from ear to ear, obviously loving the affectionate attention that Dada is giving him. I catch his eye and we exchange winks, as if to let each other know how much we are enjoying this little scenario.

It is late afternoon, and by the time everything settles down again it is time for the workers to call it a day. Once they leave, Dada and I return to our chairs and pick up the conversation more or less where we left off.

D: Is there any advice you can give for raising children so that they develop a liking for sadhana?

C: The first thing I would say is: come visit me, stay with us and watch how I behave with the children. Then think over your experience and write about it. Over these past two or three days you have seen how I behave with my grandson, Devavrata. That is practical knowledge.

But for those who cannot come and stay with me, I would tell them that whether or not they themselves are interested in sadhana, they should talk to their children on a regular basis about sadhana so there is a constant reminder to the child about the necessity of sadhana in a person's life. This doesn't involve any labor or expenditure. Simply talk about it.

Then there are some simple discourses of Baba. Those delivered on the occasion of DMC are a bit difficult for children to understand. Also the Renaissance Universal talks, delivered on the night prior to DMC, are a bit difficult to understand. But there are many short discourses of Baba that are simple and which contain interesting stories. Children who are a little bit older, say ten or twelve or fourteen years of age, may enjoy reading those books. They will help them to become mentally inclined toward sadhana.

Third thing: parents should take their children along with them to different spiritual functions, such as weekly group meditation, seminars, retreats, and so on. These three things combined will help keep their mind engaged in this atmosphere of spirituality, and as they grow they will become more and more inclined toward sadhana.

One thing more: parents must guard against showing certain weaknesses while their children are around. If they don't feel interested to sit in sadhana then they shouldn't let their children discover this. They should carefully conceal this fact from them. They should never express any lack of interest in sadhana while their children are present.

And at every step they should deal psychologically with the children. Never through fear complex but always through love, affection, and reasoning. Never shout at the child: "Why are you doing this? Stop that!"

Instead say: "My good boy, this is not good. Do it this way. This is the right thing to do." They should always deal psychologically with the child.

D: There is some controversy concerning M. He has told a number of family people that if they want to gain real progress in spiritual life, if they want to attain samadhi, then they must be celibate, regardless of whether or not they are a family person. In your opinion, to what extent is celibacy necessary for family people?

C: It is not necessary to be one hundred percent celibate. Tell M. that Lord Shiva is supposed to be the Adiguru, the first teacher of Tantra and yoga on this earth. But he had a wife and children. Lord Krishna is considered to be Yogiraj, the king of the yogis, and he had a wife and children. So ask M. if he means by this to deny their existence—those who propounded yoga and Tantra on this earth. They had families; they had children. So how can anyone say that one-hundred-percent celibacy is necessary? No, it is not necessary. This is the first point.

Second, if everyone preserves hundred-percent celibacy what will happen? Society will cease to exist. Moreover, no creature, what to speak of human beings, should boast that they can maintain one hundred percent celibacy. It may be that one person out of a hundred can maintain perfect celibacy, but in most cases it is just boasting. And where there is a show of celibacy what happens? Society becomes impure.

So to maintain the purity of society it is essential that one get married and have a family. But lead a restricted life. Don't overindulge. If you do, you will fall sick. Your physical body will deteriorate. You will fall prey to different kinds of disease. So while hundred-percent celibacy is not necessary, all of us should lead a restricted life. How much sex is okay depends on the circumstances, physical condition and age. There is a significant difference between a couple of twenty-five and a couple of forty-five. And a vast difference when compared to a couple of sixty. If somebody at fifty years of age has as much sex as a person of twenty-five their health will be broken. So they have to be more restricted than the person of twenty-five. Thus, these things are to be decided according to the circumstances, age, and physical condition.

Furthermore, this person of twenty-five, man or woman, has to take care of his or her partner. The husband has to respect the sentiment of the wife, and the wife must respect the sentiment of the husband. This also has to be taken into consideration before a person can decide how much is proper for them. It is a matter to be decided according to the wisdom of the person, the intelligence of the person, the thinking capacity of the person.

So the general principle is that hundred-percent celibacy is not necessary for progress in sadhana, and incontinence is also bad. One should lead a restricted life, a balanced life. Baba used to call it a balanced life. He gave a series of talks on the theory of *prama*, which means "the theory of balance." Baba always said that one should maintain balance at every step of life. Lord Buddha also advised his followers to avoid extremes. Follow a middle path. The word he used was *mazim nikai. Mazim* means "middle." *Nikai* means "path." Neither hundred-percent celibacy, nor hundred-percent incontinence. Lord Krishna said, *Yukatahara viharasya yuktacestasya karmasu yuktasvapnavabodhasya.* Lead a balanced life in sleeping, awakening, eating, working—*ahara vihara. Vihara* means "mixing" or "taking pleasure from external objects." This also includes the physical relations between husband and wife. It refers to the seeking of pleasure from any worldly object, be it food, flower or anything else. Somebody wants to have a beautiful garland with a nice fragrance every single evening. Well that's too much. It is good to have a garland with sweet-scenting flowers at certain times, but this doesn't mean that one should become mad for it. Everything should be balanced. Likewise when it comes to the matter of the physical relations between husband and wife. It should be balanced and each should respect the sentiment of the other. In intimate relations there are always two people involved, a man and a woman, husband and wife. Both should agree. If one doesn't agree, the other should not pressurize them.

D: Let us say the man wants to maintain celibacy and the wife does not.

C: So let him respect her sentiment. Let his celibacy be postponed until some future date. What is the necessity of doing it immediately? So hundred-percent celibacy is not necessary, and hundred-percent incontinence is to be avoided. Lead a balanced life, the middle path. What Lord Buddha said—*mazim nikai*. What Lord Krishna said—*yuktahara vihara*. What Baba said—*prama* theory. They all advise the same thing.

D: In *Caryacarya*, Baba has said that more than four times per month is not good for health.

C: This is a restriction that has been framed keeping in view both the physical body and the mind, because loss of semen affects both mind and body.

If too much semen is lost then the body becomes weak, and the nerves and nerve fibers become weak. Consequently, the mind also becomes weak because the nerves and nerve fibers of the brain are the vehicle through which the mind functions. If they become weak then the functioning of the mind becomes weak. Thus the restriction. But this doesn't mean that everybody should make it a point to have sex four times a month. If one can limit it to three times or two times, it is even better. But that should be a cooperative effort. It should be with the cooperation of both parties, so that both remain happy. Each should respect the sentiment of the other.

D: I have a question concerning sleep and spiritual practice. First, is it possible to say one's mantra while sleeping, and if so, then how does one go about practicing it?

C: It is possible, but then it is not possible in a day or two, or even in a year or two. This needs a lot of practice. Through constant practice for long years it becomes a habit.

An individual forms many habits over the course of a lifetime, some good and some bad. One has to make some effort to stop the bad habits. Suppose someone has the habit of blinking their eyes while talking. You may have seen some people with this habit. If someone brings it to their attention, or if they become aware of it somehow, then that person may make efforts to check it. They try, but after a few minutes they forget. Later they have to try again. It has become a habit and a habit is difficult to give up.

Likewise, a habit of incantation, or recitation of mantra, has to be formed. And how can that habit be formed? Through constant practice—the practice of Ishvara Pranidhana and the practice of japa. Now when you go to bed at night you don't fall asleep the moment your head touches the pillow. It will take one minute or two minutes. Someone else takes five minutes. So until you fall asleep forget everything else and continue reciting your mantra in coordination with your breathing. If you practice this rigorously, a habit will form and eventually the mantra will continue even while you are sleeping. You may not be aware of it while you are sleeping, but the moment you wake up you will realize that you are reciting your mantra. When you fell asleep you were reciting your mantra and the moment you woke up, whenever you may wake up, you find yourself reciting your mantra. This will convince you that you had been reciting the mantra while you were sleeping also.

There is a story in the *Ramayana*. Once Hanuman snuck into Vibhisan's room in Sri Lanka while Vibhisan was sleeping. And as soon as he entered the room he heard a sound from somewhere, a very feeble sound—Rama, Rama, Rama. That was the mantra of Vibhisan. Hanuman was astonished. Where is this sound coming from, he wondered? It seems to be coming from the atmosphere itself. Then he realized that the sound was coming from Vibhisan who was sleeping on his cot.

It's a story but it demonstrates that even while sleeping the recitation of mantra is possible. But it needs a lot of practice, constant practice, until an unbroken habit is formed. Once this habit is formed, the mantra will continue without any effort on your part; rather, you will have to make an effort if you want to stop it.

D: Sometimes we fall asleep and when we wake up we have no consciousness of the time that has passed. When a person becomes spiritually developed do they eventually become conscious even when they sleep?

C: During sleep the mind's functioning should remain stopped. Unless it remains stopped nobody can get rest. And for rest sleep is necessary. So sleep should be sound sleep. Now what happens is that most people dream. Dreaming is not sound sleep. And if a person keeps on dreaming most of the night, the next morning they will not feel so fresh. They will feel a little tired or a little lazy because they did not get a good sleep. The mind didn't rest properly and when the mind doesn't rest properly then the body also feels tired or exhausted or lazy. When the functioning of the mind stops during sleep it gives complete rest.

Even when the mind is functioning during sleep it should function in a healthy way. What are dreams? They are the functioning of the mind during sleep. Now some people see bad dreams or fearful dreams or even sexual dreams from time to time. Such dreams don't have a good effect, but if a person develops the habit of reciting their mantra during sleep they will be free from these dreams. Generally, bad dreams are not good for health. They prevent a person from getting proper rest. Sometimes semen is also lost which is bad for physical health. So everyone should form the habit of incantation, of recitation of mantra, during sleep.

Now a word or two about the functioning of mind. During deep sleep the mind doesn't function, but it is not unconscious. If I am unconscious then I cannot feel your touch. I won't get up. But if I am sleeping and you touch me, I wake up and look at you because I am not unconscious.

I am sleeping. When I feel your touch, the wave created by your touch strikes my mind and my sleep is broken. But during unconsciousness that wave is not received by the mind. Say a man is made unconscious through anesthesia so he can be operated on. For half an hour the doctor is operating and that touch of the doctor's instruments doesn't awaken him because he is unconscious. But if a man is sleeping and you go and prick him with a pin, he will get up. He is not unconscious. The mind is there, the mind is alert, but it is taking rest. So there is a difference between deep sleep and unconsciousness.

D: Do you find that as sadhana progresses, one spends less time dreaming and more time in deep sleep?

C: Yes. You sleep only for four hours but you get complete rest. If you have spent two hours during the day fully engrossed in meditation then there also the functioning of your mind is stopped. Those two hours, plus four hours sleep—your mind takes rest for six hours. So with only four hours sleep you are quite happy, healthy, alert. There are some people who feel weak and exhausted if they do not sleep for six hours but you feel fresh with only four hours. Why? Because for two hours your mind has already taken rest.

June 7

YESTERDAY MORNING DEVAVRATA TOLD Didi that Dada had been describing one sweet that she used to make for Baba in the old days. Last night that same sweet appeared at the dinner table. She is the ultimate grandmother. After lunch yesterday I was surprised to see this saintly eighty-year-old woman scrubbing the floors with a huge smile on her face. She has an assistant to help her with the cooking and housework but she prefers to do most of the work herself. She decided that the girl wasn't cutting the mangos right for our breakfast so this morning she did it herself. And she was right. Instead of those ragged slices we got these neat little cubes ready to be gobbled up. Heaven is often not so far away. Didi is the essence of hospitality, always alert to see that we have the best of everything.

Today at breakfast the talk turned to mangos. Dada described the best varieties from the different parts of India, and during what part of the season each of them ripened. We have been eating Bombay mangos from one tree in the orchard. They ripen earlier and have the virtue of never being sour, even when they are under-ripe. The best mango from the Bombay area is the Alfonso mango. In this part of Bihar it is the Langra, also known as Malda, especially the white Langra. They are very sour when they are not ripe. Most of the trees in Dada's orchard are Langra and they will be ripe and ready to go starting in ten days. The best in West Bengal is the Hemsagar. Didi told me that she wants to send a basket of mangos with me to the west. They will ripen day by day, she said, so I can go on eating them and still have some to give away when I get there. Today for breakfast we had another sweet, which Dada had described to me yesterday. It is a banana milk pudding, incredibly delicious. This, along with chapatis, fresh mango chutney, homemade butter and, of course, more mangos.

Devavrata found out last night that he has won a scholarship from the Human Welfare Trust for a competitive exam he took part in. The kid is smart, no doubt about it. I mentioned to Dada that it may be due, in part, to his being the son of an intellectual.[1] "Yes, his father is an intellectual," Dada replied, "but he is not so practical." Then I mentioned something Baba had said about the tendency of intellectually or philosophically developed societies to lose adjustment with the physical sphere and that reminded Dada of a story. Once, when Baba arrived at the Jodhpur park office, he went into one of the downstairs rooms instead of going directly upstairs to his room as he usually did. Books and papers were scattered everywhere. Baba asked whose room it was and they told him it was Jagadishwaranandajii's room, a monk with a deserved reputation as an intellectual. "Yes," he said, "intellectuals live like this." Then he turned and walked out.

Dada said that sometimes he finds Amarnathjii just sitting and staring off absently into space. "That means he is thinking something. You walk by and he won't even notice you. That's how it is with intellectuals. They go on thinking."

Then Devavrata walked by and said that half the time, if you ask his father something, he will only laugh.

D: Dada, what is the proper amount of sleep for a normal, healthy individual, and if a person is sleeping eight hours should they make some effort to sleep less?

C: Unless you do meditation, you should not cut back on your sleep because the body needs rest and the mind also needs rest. You may have seen certain madman who hardly ever sleep. Due to this their mind doesn't get proper rest and neither does their body, and this exacerbates their condition. Sleep is necessary and one should not cut down on one's sleep unless one meditates. If the doctor says that you need eight hours sleep, then sleep eight hours. But if the doctor says that I need eight hours sleep, then I won't agree with him. I go to sleep at twelve o'clock and I get up at four o'clock, and I feel fresh. So I would advise those who do not practice meditation to sleep as per medical advice.

Those who practice meditation should judge for themselves how much

1 Devavrata is the son of Dada's eldest son, Amarnath, who at present is the editor of the *Hindi Prout Monthly*, a political and spiritual journal published in Patna.

sleep they need. If you slept for four hours last night and you find that it is not sufficient, that you don't feel fresh, then sleep for five hours the next night. If you find that you feel better, it means that four hours was not sufficient. And if you sleep the next night for six hours and you feel quite fresh then it means that six hours sleep is the proper amount for you. But it may so happen that this amount will continue to decrease. After one or two years you may find that you feel just as fresh with five hours sleep as you felt with six hours the year before. So sleep for five hours only. After another five or ten years you may find that only four hours is necessary, because you feel as fresh with four hours sleep as you felt ten years back with six hours. So everyone should judge for themselves how much they should sleep—what leaves them feeling cheerful and fresh. But it is a fact that the more you meditate, the less sleep you need.

D: There are many different arts that people use to help them lead a proper life, to find out what to do and what not to do. Among these is astrology. How useful is the art of astrology in helping us to know what to do or not to do?

C: Astrology is a science. It should not be discarded. But then nobody should allow their life to drift along with the forecasts of astrology. It is a science and it should be respected, but no one should bow down and surrender to the dictates of astrology. Rather, let me struggle against the flows of astrology, and for a sadhaka Baba has given the second lesson to aid them. "Don't think of going east today. Today is not an auspicious day to travel east."[2] Well, I will travel east with the help of second lesson. Respect it as a science, but don't surrender to it. Take help of your second lesson and do what you want to do.

Second thing. Astrology is a science, no doubt; it tells us that this star or planet is in this position and accordingly you will have this result or that result. And those results are nothing but the reactions of your past actions—it is according to your *samskaras* that these settings,[3] these arrangements of the stars, exist. Nature has arranged it in such a way that you can get the appropriate reaction. But should I then struggle to change

2 The use of astrology for prognostication is quite prevalent in Hindu astrology.

3 *Samskara* literally means "reaction in potentiality." Every action incurs a reaction and the sum total of our unexpressed reactions is our individual samskara. In common western parlance this is often known as *karma*, but this is an incorrect use of the term. Karma means "action", not "reaction."

the reaction? Well certainly you should. Those reactions can be changed or altered by your present actions. So try to do such actions that can change those reactions or lessen their effect. When two opposing forces combat each other an equalization takes place. The meeting point becomes a static point. Suppose there is a tug of war. Ten persons are on this side and ten persons on that side. Both groups are pulling against each other. If the strength of each side is equal then the rope remains where it is. If one side is weaker then the stronger party pulls the weaker party. You have your accumulated reactions seeking expression. Now try to oppose them with actions that will combat their effect. If you can't push back the reactions, at least you can stop them where they are.

In short, it is changeable. Changeable in the sense that the circumstances under which your reactions find expression can be changed due to your present actions; as a result, the reactions themselves are changed. So I will repeat that while this science is true and should be respected, no one should surrender to it. One must do such actions that are able to combat those reactions. And what are these actions? Sadhana and service.

In India you will find many people who believe in palmistry, but the lines on the palm are also changeable. I am not a student of palmistry but I can say from having observed my own palm that there are many lines which were not there previously. New lines have appeared and some old lines have disappeared.

When I was a college student an astrologer came to our town and many people assembled around him and asked him to read their palms. This was in 1941 or '42, long before I got initiated into spirituality. When he read my palm he told me that I would have two marriages. I hated the thought of it, but he was emphatic. "You will get married twice. You have the line on your palm." But something happened and that line disappeared. It may have been due to my feeling, my strong feeling, my mental way of thinking, or simply God's grace. Whatever the case may be, I am now approaching eighty and I have been married my entire adult life to the same woman. What the man foretold proved to be incorrect.

Now look at this line. This line was not in my palm. You see how it branches from here to here. This line started coming out in 1953 after I took initiation, and it's been growing gradually ever since. Therefore I say, don't surrender to astrology or palmistry. Maintain your own thinking and do what is correct. Try to combat your past reactions with your good actions in the present. There is a poem, perhaps it is by Longfellow: "Act in the living present, heart within and God overhead." These two sentences appealed to me very much when I was growing up. "Act in the living present, heart within and God overhead." Have confidence and courage. "Heart within" means confidence and courage. "God overhead." Have faith in him and act in the living present. So we should not surrender to astrology. We must combat the reactions of the past with the good actions of the present.

At this point Dada's grandson, Devavrata, who has been sitting beside us quietly the entire time, chimes in with a poem.

Life is real, life is earnest
And the grave is not thy goal,
Dust thou art, to dust returnest
Was not spoken of the soul.

The poem is also from Longfellow. Dada smiles and makes it clear how much he enjoys Devavrata's contribution.

D: Some people are of the opinion that in order to make good progress in sadhana it is necessary to go into solitude from time to time, but for people who live in the city and are very busy this is difficult to do. They simply don't get the opportunity. What is your opinion?

C: What I have found is that while solitude definitely does one good, one can develop through practice to the point where it ceases to really matter. Even if you are in the busiest part of town you can do your sadhana; it is just a question of practice. For a few days or a few months you may feel some inconvenience, but later on you get so used to it that the sound of the motorcars blowing their horn or the hammering of the mill does not effect you at all. It is just a question of habit.

When Baba initiated me he told me that it wasn't necessary to go to the jungle or to a cave or to some hill to do sadhana. Simply shut the door to your room and that will be your jungle and your cave. You will gradually get used to the circumstances and the place where you do sadhana. And I have found this to be true. So it is not necessary. Just develop the habit through constant practice and you will be able to do your sadhana successfully even in Chowringee. You have been to Calcutta many times so you must be familiar with Chowringee, the busiest part of one of the busiest, most crowded cities on earth. If you have developed this habit of doing sadhana anywhere, anytime, under any condition, then you will even be able to do it while sitting in a hotel room in Chowringee.

While we are talking two people arrive from a nearby town. They have come to Dada to help settle a dispute they have with a third party. They are talking in Maethili, which I can only understand to a limited extent. Afterward, Dada explains to me what they were talking about.

C: … but when we become inimical to one another then all our past actions, which had been ignored until then, are dragged up. This is often the case. When they were united they looked at each other with a friendly attitude and ignored the faults of one another, but now that they are unhappy with each other they are calling attention to their defects. This is the common practice in society. I asked them why they had kept this problem concealed from me until today. They told me they didn't want to vex me with small matters. I told them that small matters become big matters if they're suppressed. Suppose a child gets a thorn in his foot. He conceals it from his elders, from his parents. What happens? The thorn deteriorates, a sepsis is formed and then it has to be operated on. What had been a small problem becomes a big problem later on because the child concealed it from the guardian. It's like that. Had these problems been communicated in the beginning then they could have been mended at the same time, and the situation that they are facing now wouldn't have arisen. So I explained this to them.

Then I said: Anyhow, whatever has happened, has happened. Though the problem has now become a large problem, it has to be solved. Now, before I can consider what can be done, I have to talk to the other party against whom they have allegations. I told them that I would talk to him also, and if a solution could be arrived at in the talk between him and I, then well and good. If not, then I will call all of them together and we will discuss it together. What is important is that the matter should not be allowed to deteriorate further. It must be mended at any cost. So the final decision is this—matters have to be mended—and they have agreed. What the solution will be and how it will be arrived at may take some time, but it is decided that the situation will now be mended. And I promised them that if they are sincere, then my efforts will definitely bear fruit.

D: I have one friend who says that she is now in a very nice devotional flow. Every night Baba comes and takes her away with him. She says she has left the lessons now. She does some sadhana whenever she feels that Baba wishes her to, but she no longer follows any regular routine or discipline. But I notice that you still complete all the lessons of vishesh yoga at least twice a day, yet you've achieved nirvikalpa samadhi. Why do you still do the different lessons? Why not simply spend some time in nirvikalpa samadhi each day and leave the lessons?

C: Well you see, as long as one has a physical body, one should never think that nirvikalpa samadhi alone is necessary and the other practices can now be ignored. You practice a breathing exercise, pranayama. This breathing exercise has a certain effect on your glands, lungs and heart. You do particular asanas. They also have a certain effect on your different limbs, glands and nerve centers. These are necessary in order to keep the body fit, and if you don't keep your body fit it will be very difficult for you to sit in nirvikalpa samadhi. The body must be fit. It is just possible that you are not the master of the nirvikalpa samadhi that you are enjoying today. You have gained something, but it is also possible to lose what you have gained. If you abandon the other practices there will be a gradual deterioration of the nervous system, the nerve fibers, and the glands, or plexuses, with the result that after one year, or two years, or five years your brain will become weak. And if the brain becomes weak, the mind becomes weak. Today you may be able to go into nirvikalpa samadhi at will, but tomorrow you will have to put in extra labor to achieve it; the day after tomorrow even more; the next day much more; and a day will come when you will remain at the lower levels despite your best efforts. You will no longer be able to enter into nirvikalpa samadhi. Again you will have to return to your practices and struggle before you can achieve what you had once achieved. So in my opinion the other practices are also necessary.

Secondly, Baba has said that one who practices only for nirvikalpa samadhi will have difficulty achieving success because unless the lower plexuses are strengthened it will be very difficult to raise the serpentine power to the higher plexuses. Each plexus has to be controlled and strengthened gradually. Now suppose I have achieved this. All my different plexuses, different nerve centers, have been developed, and I have been able to raise my serpentine power from muladhara to sahasrara. Well and good, but samadhi is not the goal; samadhi is a part of practice and it is not the only yogic practice. There are eight parts and samadhi is one of them. Yama, niyama, asana, pranayama, pratyahara, dharana, dhyana, samadhi. So when one attains samadhi one has to practice samadhi every day, and at the same time one should pay equal importance to those lower steps that have helped one to rise to the highest level. Otherwise there is a possibility, rather the probability, of slipping back down again. So nobody should neglect the lower practices.

And thirdly, I should add that at no time has our great teacher ever said that once you achieve samadhi you no longer need to do the other practices. Simply go into samadhi each day and abandon the other practices — never has he said this. Rather he has said quite the opposite. Each and every plexus must be developed and kept strong, and they are strengthened through the different practices that have been prescribed. So nobody should neglect other practices when he or she attains nirvikalpa samadhi. Nor has Patanjali in his *Yoga Sutras* ever said that one can leave aside the other practices after attaining samadhi.

So this is not the correct approach. Such an approach will someday weaken the person, and after a few years they will lose what they have attained due to the growing weakness of the physical body. Here I am not referring to physical strength, but to the physical resistance power of the nerves and nerve fibers. One need not be a great boxer or wrestler, but the nervous system should be strong enough to resist the adverse waves that one is bound to encounter in this world. And for increasing and maintaining that power of resistance, we should continue all the practices. Only then will our mind remain strong, as strong as it has become by achieving nirvikalpa samadhi. Only when we have the support of the physical system. So all the practices should be considered to be of equal importance.

D: In our spiritual practices we are learning to quiet our mind. Does it not create difficulties for one's spiritual practice when one has to do a lot of intellectual work, for example writing, or a lot of thinking during one's daily work routine?

C: You mean to ask if intellectuality may disturb sadhana? No, no. Absolutely not. What is necessary is that when you do a particular job, you should keep your mind confined solely to that job. Suppose you are engaged in some intellectual work. You are writing something. Concentrate your mind wholly and solely on the subject that you are writing about. This is the proper approach. At that moment you should concentrate one hundred percent on the job at hand. Likewise, when you sit in sadhana you should concentrate your mind one hundred percent in sadhana for as long as you are sitting there. If your mind is deeply concentrated in a book, if you are fully engrossed in the ideas of that book, then you do not think of anything else. Similarly, when we sit in sadhana we should not think of anything else. We should think of sadhana alone.

What I mean to say is that a person must concentrate one hundred percent on whatever task they have taken up at any particular time. They should not allow their mind to be diverted. If you are writing and you allow your mind to be diverted to some other matter, what will happen? Your writing will suffer for it. You may make mistakes. When you read a book, concentrate on what you are reading. When you write a letter, concentrate on what you are writing. And when you sit for sadhana, concentrate on sadhana.

So how can intellectuality disturb your sadhana? Our intellectual pursuits don't disturb our eating, do they? They don't prevent us from putting on our clothes in the morning? Then why should they disturb our sadhana? Simply make your spiritual practices a part of your routine and fix the time for your various duties according to that routine. This is my time for getting up, this is my time for going to bed, this is my time for morning duties, this is my time for breakfast or lunch, this is my time for my bath, and so on. Set aside a proper amount of time for sadhana as well. Your intellectual pursuits will not disturb you.

Now in the field of intellectuality there are so many subjects. Someone is thinking about physics, someone else is thinking of a solution to a mathematical problem, a third person is analyzing certain historical facts. Different kinds of intellectual subjects are taken up by different people in their respective fields. The person who thinks of history does not think of physics. The one who is concentrating on physics doesn't think of chemistry. When I think of spirituality, when I think of sadhana, I think of sadhana. If you can develop this ability to concentrate fully on the work at hand then you will not be disturbed by your intellectual pursuits.

But you need willpower. Without willpower it becomes very difficult. Not only for sadhana. To be successful in any sphere of life you must have the strong will to achieve what you wish to achieve. Likewise, you must have the strong will, the strong desire to do sadhana. This strong will is the only requirement.

D: From time to time I have seen people leave the spiritual path who were very rigid in their discipline. Some people feel that if you are too rigid in your discipline it may produce an adverse affect.

C: What is the meaning of discipline? Discipline means following certain rules in certain places and under certain circumstances. Suppose a student is attending class. They have to follow the rules of the class. In other words, the student has to maintain the discipline of the class. They have to bring their books and something to write with. They have to follow a certain dress code, sit in a certain seat, talk with the requisite decorum. These are the rules of the class. If the student follows the rules then we can say that they are a disciplined student. If not, then we call them undisciplined. Is it not so? When I use the word discipline, this is what I understand by it. The following or observation of certain rules under certain circumstances, whether in society, in the family, in the classroom. In my opinion this kind of discipline is not bad; rather, it is quite good because it serves to drive away the chaos and confusion. If no one follows the rules of the classroom then it becomes very difficult for the teacher to teach the students.

In whatever sphere of life you look to, you will find a similar situation. Take the members of a family. Each family member has their own set of rules to follow, a certain way to behave and certain duties to take care of, otherwise the family looses its harmony. The son should observe certain rules when dealing with his mother and others when dealing with his father. The father has a different set of rules for dealing with the son. If the son is not attending to his studies the father may have to scold him or take some disciplinary action. But the son cannot act in the same manner with the father as the father does with the son. So there are rules to be followed under different sets of circumstances and those rules constitute the code of discipline. If they are not followed then the situation in the family, class, office, army, police, or wherever, becomes untenable.

But at the same time one thing must be kept in mind. If certain rules that have been framed are not congenial for the society, or are not to the benefit of the collective, then one should raise one's banner against those rules. This cannot be considered indiscipline. Even though the person has deliberately raised their banner against the rules that are in force, or against the authorities who enforce those rules, those rules are detrimental to the interest of the collective body. So one will have to consider whether the present set of rules are in the best interests of the family or the society or the classroom or the army or the office. Only then should they be followed. Suppose in some office they make a rule that no one will work unless they are paid some extra remuneration for their work. Well that is illegal; it amounts to bribery. This leads to corruption. Such a rule must be opposed and that cannot be called indiscipline.

Thus a healthy discipline should be followed, and rules that go against the collective interest should be opposed. Discipline will never make a person suffer unnecessarily if the rules of discipline are beneficial to the collective body, to the society.

Now as regards spiritual life, a certain discipline also has to be followed. We have learned the rules governing social matters like everyone else and we follow them. That social discipline should not be neglected. If you walk on the road and if you don't follow the traffic rules you will be dashed down by some vehicle, but when we become a sadhaka we become responsible for a special kind of discipline in addition to those social disciplines, a special kind of code or set of rules, and that code is based on yama and niyama.

Now what is yama and niyama? It is a set of rules that guide your moral behavior as well as your ideation about the Lord. Both your dealings with the outside world, with the society, as well as your dealings with yourself. All these are to be guided through the code of yama and niyama, and it should be adhered to strictly. If one doesn't do so, one will be failing in their sadhana because yama and niyama is the foundation of sadhana.

And then there are many things that our teacher has given us along with yama and niyama. We have to practice sadhana. And not just a show of sadhana. It should be a real sadhana, a sincere sadhana. It must be regular. Regularity is included within the discipline. There are so many other practices that I don't need to mention which come within the code of discipline, the spiritual discipline. So a spiritual practitioner is responsible for following the social disciplines of the family, the society, and so on; and in addition to that they have to follow the discipline meant for sadhakas, for spiritual practitioners. But in either case, discipline, as I understand it, is a positive thing.

D: Dada, it is getting late. Perhaps before we stop you could recite a line or two of Prabhat Samgita and explain it like you did the other night. I enjoyed that very much.

C: Ah yes, on that day I explained to those two boys who were sitting here something about Prabhat Samgita.

Nirava rate tomari sathe na bala katha anek rayegecche. *Nirava* means that all is quiet, there is no sound coming from anywhere, from any direction. *Rat* means "night." In the silent night, the peaceful and quiet night, *tomari sathe*, along with you, *na bala katha anek rayegecche*. So much remained unsaid. And what remained unsaid?

Kena go gul bage hazara kanta thake. Why are there so many thorns in this rose garden, thousands of thorns? Go and touch the stalk of a rose. The thorns will prick your finger. So the devotee asks the Lord: Why are there so many thorns in this rose garden? *Kena go nirjhara raksa path vache.* Why is this stream of sweet water flowing along such a rugged bed?

Kamala ghande bhara malina jale phote. Kamala means "lotus flower." The lotus is full of fragrance but it takes root in the mud. Why does such a beautiful flower with such a nice fragrance have its roots in the dirty mud? *Malin* means "dirty." It is so beautiful, so fragrant, but it grows in the dirtiest of places. Why is it so?

Hasite bhara dhara andhara pathe chote. This world is so pleasant. People derive so much pleasure from it, but what is the ultimate result? They come to grief, sorrow, disease, enmity—*andhara pathe chote.* They rush down the dark path, *andhara path.* Why is it so? Why in such a beautiful world do people wander down the dark path?

Sneha mamata bhara raungina khoyabe ghera. This is a poetic description of the pleasures that everyone gets in this created universe—affection, attraction, love. People want to be happy, they aspire for colorful dreams, *raungina khoyabe ghera.*

Kena go srstite kaler chaya nace? Why, in such a beautiful created world or universe does this dark cloud hover? What is that dark cloud? That nobody gets pleasure forever. Pleasure and pain go hand in hand. Nobody can enjoy a particular object forever. A child enjoys life as a child with its mother, playing with its playmates, then they become a student, then a young adult, then a family person, and eventually they become old and infirm, and one day they fall down and never get up. So *kena go srstite kaler chaya nace?* Why is this black cloud of time hovering over this created universe?

Nirava rate tomari sathe na bala katha anek rayegecche. When I was alone with him, when there was no one to disturb us, why did I not ask him these questions? Why did they remain unspoken? Because in samadhi you don't have the capacity to ask questions. You lose your identity. You merge in him. He remains and you disappear. Who then will pose the question? The questioner is no longer there. But as soon as the questioner emerges from that state and becomes a person once again, a created being, they remember that they didn't ask those questions. And they realize that it will never be possible to ask them. The questions only arise once you come out of samadhi. So the questions will always remain unspoken. *Na bala katha anek rayegecche.*

This is the meaning behind the literal meaning, the real meaning, the essence of the thought being expressed through those words.

In the first line of another song the devotee considers themself to be a traveler. Birth and rebirth is the road on which they are traveling, and while traveling the devotee comes to the bank of a river. They have to cross the river, but they can't cross unless somebody helps them to cross. For this a boat is indispensable, and the controller of the boat, the helmsman, is called *karnadhar*. So the devotee sings: "I am sitting on the bank of the river in the hope that you will come and take me across; O my Lord, where are you?" The devotee cannot find him and this makes them uneasy. Where am I? Where is my Lord? He was supposed to come and take me across this river. Then their *akulta*—*akulta* means when one becomes very impatient to achieve something—this feeling of *akulta* goads the devotee to say *base achi nadiir tire tahari ashay, he karnadhar kathay*. I am sitting on the bank of the river in the hope that you will come and take me across; O my Lord, O my *karnadhar*, where are you? These are the songs that the devotees sing to express their spiritual longing.

I had to leave early the next morning so I could be sure to arrive in Patna in time to catch my flight. I finished my practices at 6:30 and came out of my room to find breakfast waiting for me and Didi and Dada as well. It was normally the time when everyone was deep in meditation but they were just as happy to be getting everything ready for my trip. Didi brought a bag of mangos for me, all packed up neatly in plastic and tied securely with a stretch of twine. When I went out to the veranda after breakfast I found the rickshaw waiting for me and a whole party to see me off. Not only the family, but some of the farmhands and a few of the local village margis who I recognized but hadn't actually talked to. It wasn't quite seven yet, a time when everything was normally still quiet in the courtyard, but today there were a good dozen people there, everyone with a bright smile on their face and a greeting for me as Dada put me in the rickshaw and gave the driver some instructions. I found it hard to imagine that they had all come there to see me off at that early hour, but I didn't have any other explanation.

I gave my final namaskar to everyone, Dada last of all, and then headed off down the same country road that had brought me there five days earlier. As the farmhouse disappeared behind the trees, and Dada with it, I felt a sudden determination: I would be back here again to take advantage of Dada's offer, to come not for just a few days but for a few weeks, to enjoy the blissful company, to meditate, and hopefully to leave without any more questions.

PART TWO

PATNA

September 15

THE NEXT CHANCE I had to visit Dada was in September, this time at the house of his eldest son in Patna. The rainy season was officially over but it looked as if someone had forgotten to notify the heavens to turn off the spigots. Patna was full of mud and water from the previous evening's downpour, and nowhere was worse than the residential district where Dada was staying. When my rickshaw driver turned off the main road and started down the street that led into that part of town, he turned to me with a broad smile on his face and said *pani* [water]. And *pani* it was. Within moments the street had emptied into a lake. The water was at least two feet high in most places, and had so completely flooded the surrounding fields and lanes that the landscape had been obliterated. Here and there I could see an occasional tree rising from the surface of the water, looking strangely out of place, and of course, houses. Some houses had enough of an elevated foundation that the water wasn't able to enter the ground floor, but some didn't and you could see the water going right in the front door. I am back in Bihar, I thought. No kind of drainage at all for this entire residential area, nor any government assistance or sign of relief efforts. But people were smiling and trying to make their way to work or to the house or to school as best they could. A school bus passed by and sent waves surging over everyone. The rickshaw drivers were smiling and greeting one another as they passed, joking about the conditions. It was a social event and people were enjoying it despite the hardship. But the going was rough and most of the way my driver had to wade through water nearly up to his waist while pulling the rickshaw.

What should have taken less than half an hour took an hour and a half, but finally we arrived and I was able to take refuge in the safe haven of the second floor apartment where Dada was staying. It was nearing lunchtime by then, and during the meal the topic of conversation turned to *sadvipras* and Mother Teresa,[1] who had just died the week before.

C: A person may have learned many things in their life, but that, by itself, does not qualify a person to be a sadvipra. A person becomes sadvipra by their actions, not by their learning, because they act as a sadvipra acts, and for this reason I would say that Mother Teresa was a sadvipra. She may not have had the training, but she had the internal urge and that was enough. If, by the grace of the Lord, the urge arises within a person to lead a noble life, the life of a sadvipra, then even without any training, without any learning, that person falls within the same category as someone who develops those qualities through training and effort. Some people are born to do good, only good, and I can say that she was a born sadvipra.

The same cannot be said about Nelson Mandela. He may be a good man, a great man, but I do not think that he belongs to the same category as Mother Teresa because he still has some desire in him. He is not without desire; he is not doing completely selfless service. He is a good man and somewhat close to being a sadvipra, but you may not call him a sadvipra. He may falter in some respects, but Mother Teresa lived like a sadvipra throughout her career. She acted like a sadvipra and there is no doubt about her being a sadvipra. Nelson Mandela may be a good man and an honest man, but he doesn't come in the same class as Mother Teresa.

Sadvipra means a person who follows the rules and regulations of complete morality. They must be a moralist, a strong moralist and they must possess the quality of being kind to all creatures, not only human beings or animals, but even to static creatures like plants and trees and so on. Only one who is good to everything, to each and every object on this earth, can be classified as a sadvipra. To become a sadvipra it is not necessary that one become an Ananda Margi. The beauty of Ananda Marga is that it teaches you what to do in order to develop yourself and become a sadvipra. But suppose one becomes an Ananda Margi but doesn't follow the principles Ananda Marga teaches. Then how can they be called a sadvipra? And if somebody who is not an Ananda Margi follows those principles then they are certainly a sadvipra.

A sadvipra is just, honest, kindhearted, and good to everybody. They are making earnest efforts to attain salvation and at the same time they

1 Anandamurti defines *sadvipra* as: Those spiritual revolutionaries who work to achieve progressive changes for human elevation on a well-thought, pre-planned basis, whether in the physical, metaphysical or spiritual sphere, by adhering to the principles of yama and niyama.

are always doing good to others. Wherever they go, a sadvipra feels that it is God who has provided them with the opportunity to do service, and they see him, they see his existence, in every object, every action, every person and every creature. When you do service to humanity you don't feel as if *you* are doing. You don't have this sense of ego. You feel as if he is acting through you, and your service, whatever service it may be, is service to him, to the Lord. Such people are called sadvipra, regardless of what spiritual path they may be following.

D: I remember reading that Mother Teresa used to say that whenever she served people she felt that she was serving God in that form.

C: Then how can anyone claim that she was not a sadvipra? It is the action, the behavior, the manner in which you live that makes you a sadvipra.

D: To be a complete moralist, in the sense that it is understood within the discipline of yoga, one must follow the ten principles of yama and niyama, one of which is Ishvara Pranidhana,[2] which is synonymous with our practice of meditation. Then what about people who do not practice meditation; can they really follow yama and niyama completely?

C: You have just told me that Mother Teresa used to say that she was not serving the person, she was serving God in the form of that person. Now you have your second lesson. What does it teach you? It teaches you to see God in everything, in each and every object that you come in contact with. Mother Teresa used to feel that she was not serving a particular man or a woman but God in the form of that man or woman. So she had within herself the very same idea which you have been taught through your second lesson.

Suppose a person doesn't practice Ishvara Pranidhana in the form that I teach, or in the form that others teach, because they have not learned the process. But if that person follows what Ishvara Pranidhana teaches, if their own inner instincts urge them to follow the principle of Ishvara Pranidhana, then they are following Ishvara Pranidhana. Of course, if such people learn the process of Ishvara Pranidhana they will make rapid progress, faster progress than an ordinary person because they are already endowed with the qualities that come through Ishvara Pranidhana. Now

2 Ishvara Pranidhana literally means "to direct all one's propensities toward God." It is the fifth principle of yama.

other people should not try to copy such types of individuals because not everybody has that internal urge or instinct. Some people are born with that instinct but they are rare. When I mention that so-and-so didn't do Ishvara Pranidhana but was able to accomplish this or that, or develop such qualities, then I must also point out that they had the instinctive guidance from within. So the question arises: where did they get this instinct from? It is because they did spiritual practices or had this type of training in the past. It may have been in the previous life, or in the life previous to that.

This feeling of "I" that you have within yourself, it is a kind of energy, a power, an existence that is separate from the physical body. The body is laid in the grave or burnt on the funeral pyre, but that inner existence that speaks and acts and thinks, this energy, leaves the body when the body dies. It is immortal and thus whatever it learns, whatever it does, it carries the seeds of that experience within itself. In the next birth those seeds sprout and give rise to this kind of internal urge or instinctive guidance that you see in such people. So if everyone says, "I will be Ramakrishna, I will be Mother Teresa," it is simply not possible. You must tread the path shown by those great people. To be like Mother Teresa, or to be like Ramakrishna, you have to follow some discipline and perform spiritual practices, because you do not have that internal urge or instinctive guidance that they had.

What was Ramakrishna? He was a born genius. He attained savikalpa samadhi on his own, without a teacher. Then he met a roving sannyasi, Totapuri. When Totapuri saw him he recognized at once: "Oh, he is a great man." He asked Ramakrishna if he was ready to learn what he had to teach him. Ramakrishna agreed and with his help he was able to attain nirvikalpa samadhi. But Ramakrishna attained savikalpa samadhi on his own because he already carried that seed within himself from previous births, from previous lifetimes. We should not try to copy those born geniuses. They have something that we do not have—that internal urge, that instinctive guidance. But an ordinary person can reach the same level that they reached through Ishvara Pranidhana and yama and niyama and the other practices. For the normal person it is absolutely necessary that they learn and practice all these if they wish to realize such heights. Is it clear?

D: Yes, Dada. Then how would you define the real spirit of Ishvara Pranidhana? What does it mean in essence?

C: Ishvara Pranidhana means to concentrate your mind in a certain direction. Now where do you concentrate? Well, as you think, so you become. If you concentrate on something crude—crude subjects, crude objects—then the mind will become cruder. The principle is: "As you think, so you become." So you have to think of some such existence that can make you subtler rather than cruder. Now the subtlest existence is God. I don't say object here because I can't call God an object. I can only say that he is an existence. So the subtlest existence in this universe is God and you must concentrate on him. There is a process which teaches you to concentrate on him, to fully surrender your mind to him, and that process is called Ishvara Pranidhana. So to become subtle or subtler or subtlest you have to follow that path, the path of Ishvara Pranidhana.

D: So then someone like Mother Teresa, who was born with devotional feeling, is already following …

C: She was already thinking instinctively in this way. You think with the help of second lesson, but she had that internal urge which led her to feel that she was serving God in whatever form he may have appeared before her. She never needed second lesson. It was her instinctive birthright.

So far as yama and niyama is concerned, she followed yama and niyama fully. You never heard a single comment about her that accused her of living lavishly, eating immoderately, or running after material comforts like all these great leaders. She led a very simple life, and she led her life for others, not for her own self. You may say that practice is essential, but that practice was instinctive in her.

Now I took out my list of questions for the first time, the same list I had had with me in Gadopur, and started going through it.

D: Dada, it is easy to see when we sing Prabhat Samgita that it helps in our spiritual practices. But for the majority of people these songs are in a foreign language. Will the effect be the same or similar if we translate them into English, for example, and then sing them, or is it more beneficial to sing them in Bengali, even if the language poses difficulties for us?

C: There are two things to consider here: the words given by a spiritual master, a spiritual teacher; and the idea behind those words. Both are equally important. The idea is important and the words themselves are also important. The words carry a certain vibration because they have been given by a spiritual teacher.

We don't simply pick up a mantra from anywhere; for it to be effective we need to get it from a spiritual teacher, so that the vibrational force of the teacher can be present behind the words. That is the speciality of mantra. Do you remember the example I gave you some time back? Patna is on the bank of the Ganges. Now you go to the bank of the river and start shouting that there should be a bridge here. Will it get done? No, people will think that some madman has come. But if the chief minister of the state or the prime minister of the country goes there and calls for a bridge, then from the very next day someone will start working on it. Why? Because the words you utter and the words he utters carry a different vibrational force. His words have the force of the prime minister, of the post, behind them, and yours do not.

Likewise, in the field of spirituality, a *siddha purush*—*siddha purush* means one who has the capacity to merge their mind into the Cosmic Mind at any time, any place, under any set of circumstances—now if a *siddha purush* gives a mantra then it carries the vibrational force of that teacher. This is why it will not help a person if they take a mantra from some book and start practicing with that mantra. It may help in the long run through that person's own vibrational force. After long practice for ten or twenty years the person may create a vibration of their own and it will gradually have some effect. But if the same person gets a mantra from a *siddha purush* then that word already has the vibrational force of that teacher and they will make good progress in sadhana from the very beginning. Such is the importance of mantra.

Now if we sing Prabhat Samgita in the original language we gain the benefit of the vibrational force that the teacher has infused into those words. Of course, not everybody knows that language and, as I said earlier, the idea or ideation is equally important. So the meaning should be translated into whatever language the person understands. A translation should be available or read out before the song is sung and that will increase its effect. Of course, it is best if the people learn the meaning of the words of the song. People may find the melody attractive even if they do not know the meaning, and the vibration behind it may help their mind to become a bit concentrated toward the Lord, but if they know the meaning then their concentration and the vibration they experience will be much greater. If they know the meaning of the words of the song—"Oh, I am seeing the light; the light is there, but I am not able to reach it. This huge river is in the way. O Lord, where are you? I am waiting on the riverbank for you. Where are you? When will you come to accompany me across, to ferry me toward the light? O Lord, where are you?"—then it will give much more spiritual vibration to the mind than the melody alone can give, no matter how attractive it may be. The mind ideating on the meaning, the inner meaning, and then the melody or the tune—both combine together to create the spiritual vibration. So, it is better to try to learn a few songs thoroughly, to understand the full substance of those songs, instead of learning to sing a hundred songs without fully understanding the meaning. This will have more vibrational effect.

D: One person wishes to know whether or not it is worthwhile to try to get a high post so that one can do more effective service and more good to the society.

C: Nobody should make any effort to get a high post, either in the organization, or anywhere else.

D: He means in society—in politics, or at a university, and so on.

C: If you are invited to assume a certain responsibility, and if you have the time to devote to that work and you think you are capable of doing it, then accept it, but nobody of their own accord should strive to get a higher position or a higher post. You see, this becomes a desire and desire is always damaging. It causes ego to develop. If you have a desire to be the chancellor of a university then your ego is at work. What is the good of such a desire? If people are attracted by your actions, if they think you are a capable person, the right person for the job, they will invite you of their own accord. Why should you strive for it? So in my opinion it is not correct to strive for a high position.

D: Sometimes people believe that if they have a low post or position then they can't do as much good for the society.

C: Then make yourself so popular by your actions, so capable, that people invite you to take up the work. If you are not capable, then keep away. Suppose somebody comes here today and invites me to be the principal of Oxford. Should I accept it? No, because I am not capable of doing justice to that position. Only if you think that you are capable should you accept a post. I could remain as an advisor, but I can't do the spade work. I won't undertake a responsibility that I am not capable of fulfilling properly.

Of course, there may be a good purpose behind your desire. You may want that post in order to do service. But we have just been talking about Mother Teresa. Did she aspire for a high position in society, thinking that in this way she might be able to do more service, that others would be more likely to listen to her and follow her for the good of humanity? Never. She never asked for it; she never strove for it. She simply did service and people recognized her service.

So continue doing good to others and make yourself capable in the process. People will ultimately recognize what you are doing. But if you do service with some desire in mind then it becomes a sort of trading, a business. You become a merchant. I will get this position and then I will do that work. Well that is a kind of trading, and in my opinion it is not the correct approach. Rather, keep on doing good works with no thought at all of any kind of recompense. People will recognize your good works and they will invite you to take up some responsibility. Follow the example of Mother Teresa. She never aspired for any kind of worldly position or influence, thinking that she could do more good to the world if she had greater influence. She went on doing good to others and the world recognized her for it. Be like that.

D: This same person also asks a related question: What advice would you give to help us create more of a spirit of service in our organization, in our mission?

C: In this regard you must follow what the teacher has taught. Human beings have come to this earth for Bhagavada Dharma and Bhagavada Dharma alone.[3] What is this Bhagavada Dharma? Bhagavada Dharma, as Baba defines it, means *artha moksartham jagad hitayaca*. Salvation for oneself and doing good to others. The two go hand and hand, and both are to be adopted by every sadhaka, by every practitioner. *Artha moksartham* means "regular, sincere sadhana." And *jagad hitayaca* means "good to the universe, good to the world, good to others." So a sadhaka's life only becomes complete when they follow both of these. *Artha moksartham jagad hitayaca*. When they do service as well as sadhana. If a sadhaka doesn't do service then they are only doing fifty percent. If they do only service they are only doing fifty percent. Only when they do both, sadhana and service,

3 Dharma means "the essential nature of an entity"; *Bhagavada* means "God." What is implied is that the essential nature of the human being, or the true purpose of human life, is to realize the Divine.

are they doing one hundred percent. That is the teaching of the guru, of our spiritual guide or teacher or master, whatever you may call him. This organization has been established by him with the main objective of this *artha moksartham jagad hitayaca.* One should do sadhana for one's own liberation, and at the same time one must work for the good of others. If one fails to do this, then one fails in one's duty.

Baba has further said that if a person spends the entire twenty-four hours doing sadhana and thinks they will get salvation, they are mistaken because they are doing only fifty percent. Fifty percent is left out. Without service no sadhaka has any guarantee of attaining salvation. This has to be explained to the brothers and sisters. You can never aspire to be a liberated soul unless you complete both. When you do half and leave behind half you should not expect to get liberation.

D: Which is more important, Dada, sadhana or service?

C: Both are equally important. If you are doing only service and not sadhana then at a later stage your ego may develop. You may become selfish. You will be given a hundred blankets to distribute and you will keep the best one for yourself. Instead of adding one of your own, you are taking one from what has been donated. Without sadhana there is every likelihood of a person becoming selfish or egoistic. "I am doing so much good to the people, I am a great man, nobody is equal to me, I am so good." This kind of thinking will develop and become the cause of one's downfall. So sadhana is necessary in order to keep the mind balanced.

The government is engaged in so many kinds of social works. Suppose they have allocated funds to construct roads in a rural area. Some roads get constructed but some do not. In some places the roads are on paper only; they appear on the map, but nowhere else. The government has given a grant to a particular agency, the money has been spent, but only half the work is done—and that with the minimum of cost. What happens to the rest of the money? Well, we all know. It gets distributed among the contractors, government officials, and so on. They were given this money to do good works, but they were not sadhakas, they were not moralists, they were not established in yama and niyama, and in the end they became thieves. They have stolen or misappropriated funds that were meant for the general public. The real spirit of service needs to be awakened in the mind, and for that sadhana is necessary. So both are equally important. They cannot be separated.

D: Dada, what would you say are the qualities of a spiritual person?

C: A real spiritualist is someone who is fully established in Bhagavada Dharma. However, there are many people who have not yet become established in Bhagavada Dharma but who are striving for it, and so long as they are striving they are spiritualists.

I am traversing the path, making efforts to move along the path. How can others judge those efforts? I know that I am striving, I know that I am sincere, I know that I am striving hard to be a real spiritual person. But how will others know? Well, they will know through your actions, not through your sadhana, and that means service. The service you do, and that service alone, will show that you are a spiritualist. Your actions in accordance with the principles of yama and niyama. A person is known by their actions. It is your actions that tell the people around you, your neighbors and friends and acquaintances, that you are a spiritualist, and that action is the fifty percent of Bhagavada Dharma.

So when you do service, that service should be selfless. It should not be a business. It should always be selfless, and if you do selfless service people will recognize you. They will know that you are a real spiritualist, that you are following the path of spirituality. You need not inform anyone of how much you are doing. They will see for themselves.

You see, this path is very difficult. If you start telling people, "I am doing this good work, I am doing that good work, I am doing so much service," then what will happen? Sooner or later your ego is bound to develop, and one day it will be the cause of your downfall. So one should do selfless service, and for that one must bind one's actions to the principles of yama and niyama.

Mother Teresa is on our minds quite a bit these days. Did she waste time propagating the good work that she was doing? No, it was the service itself that she was doing that brought her to the attention of everyone. People could see for themselves that she was doing selfless service. Her actions brought her the recognition of the people. These are the qualities of a spiritualist. A spiritualist is known by their actions, so act as a spiritualist acts, and when the question of action comes into play, follow the principles of Bhagavada Dharma.

D: What are the ways in which one can judge one's own progress? What are the indicators?

C: This is a very good question. In general, it is very difficult for a person to judge their own progress. But there is a change, and after a long gap the person will recognize that they are progressing. You see a child today and again you see them tomorrow. Do you find any change in that child from one day to the next? No. But if you see them again after ten years then you will find a great change. The child of ten has become a young adult of twenty. Every day there was some change, but that day-to-day change is very difficult to perceive. It is only noticed after a long gap. Likewise, in everyday sadhana it is very difficult for a person to notice whether or not they are progressing. But after a long period of continuous, regular and sincere practice one will find a marked change within oneself.

If you think about your past actions and your past feelings, and compare them with your present actions and present feelings, then you begin to recognize how much of a change has taken place. Compare what you were twenty years ago with what you are today and you will find a change. Your way of thinking is completely different. And if you don't find such a change then you will know that there is something wrong in your practice—some drawback in your sadhana or some serious flaw in your practice of yama and niyama. Otherwise, there will certainly be a change. Somebody will feel a complete change, somebody else will feel only fifty percent change, but there will be a change and everybody will feel it.

Now there is one thing more I must explain, which Baba has also explained. A person's progress is pulsative. Say, for example, you are walking. Now when you walk you put one foot forward and then there is a pause before the second foot is raised and put forward. There is a period between these two actions when both feet are on the ground. Likewise, progress in a person's life—in their feelings, their thinking, their sadhana—is pulsative. Until you begin to raise that second foot and put it ahead of the other, you are not progressing. A sadhaka also feels this in their life. Today one feels as if one has done very good sadhana, and then after a month one feels as if all one's efforts are going in vain. They are not getting progress, they are not getting good concentration, they are not able to meditate like they were able to a month ago or six months ago. This is pulsative movement.

Sometimes you feel like you're progressing and sometimes you feel like you're standing still or even going backward. But don't allow yourself to think in this way. Don't allow such thinking to even enter into your mind. Go on doing your work. Our only responsibility is to work, not to think of the results that our efforts may bring. The results will come of their own; we have no control over them. So let us not waste time thinking about the results of our actions. My duty is only to keep on striving, to keep on making efforts to progress, not to bother about the results. Progress will definitely come as long as we keep moving. *Charaiveti, charaiveti*. It means, "keep moving, keep moving." Go on striving, go on doing sadhana and doing service. Someday you will realize how much you have progressed.

Now, of course, those who do very strict sadhana over a long period of time will have certain experiences. They will be able to perceive a certain light, or they will get certain powers. These experiences also make it clear to you that you have gotten somewhere. But then the instruction of the guru is to not allow such things to enter your mind. Disregard them. Suppose you gain the occult power to heat a glass of water. You need not put the water on the stove to boil. Simply look at the glass for some time and the water will start boiling. So why spend money on kerosene or gas or coal when you can simply use your occult power for cooking? Well, don't allow that idea to creep into your mind. Those are milestones in a sadhaka's life. Suppose someone thinks, "Oh, look how much progress I have made. My destination was twenty miles away and already I have covered ten miles. I am halfway there." Then they decide to take a little pause near that ten mile marker and they fall asleep. Of course, they are tired because they have just walked ten miles. And they are happy to have a chance to sit down and enjoy the milestone they've reached. But then they fall asleep, and when they wake up it's evening, it's gotten dark and they can no longer move ahead. They will have to wait until the next morning.

So you see, a sadhaka should never become overly concerned with their progress, otherwise they run the danger of getting stuck at a milestone along the way instead of moving ahead and reaching their destination. If they fall into this trap of being enamored of what they have attained, then one day that sadhaka will become a beggar. All their powers will be lost and it will become practically impossible for them to do sadhana again in that life. That life becomes lost; it becomes wasted.

And then there are other signs and symptoms that a sadhaka feels. If you begin to think of sadhana and service all the time, then you can be sure that you are progressing in the right direction. If the thought starts arising in your mind, "Oh, I have not done sadhana yet. I must do it, I must do it." If this urge is increasing in you day by day. If you begin to feel, "Oh, I have everything I need but the people here are suffering. The water supply is polluted and nobody is doing anything about it, neither the government nor the local landlords. Then let me do something about it." So you go and spend your own money and buy supplies to disinfect the water, so that infection won't spread and people won't fall ill. When feelings like this start developing in you, when the urge for sadhana and service starts increasing spontaneously, then you will know that you are progressing.

D: Let us say a sadhaka is making good progress but then they run into a period where their mind is distracted. Six months ago I was making good progress, but now when I sit for sadhana I don't even seem to be able to make a proper effort.

C: This happens. I have explained why. In a sadhaka's life progress is pulsative.

D: You feel sometimes like you are going backward.

C: No, a sadhaka should never feel that their progress is retarding. It is but natural that a sadhaka sometimes feels dejected, but they should keep this philosophy in mind: "No, I know that my progress is pulsative and that this is the period of pause. That is the cause behind what is happening. I will continue moving, making the best efforts that I can." And then after some time you will find that that period ends.

D: Then it is important not to lessen one's effort. Sometimes you wonder, "What is the good of sitting as long as I do when I am not accomplishing anything?"

C: You should not lose heart. One should think, "No, I know you are pulsative. You are deceiving me; you are cheating me. I will not discontinue my struggle."

Lord Krishna told Arjuna that this maya is very difficult to cross. Maya means "this creation." It is like a game, this constant coming and going, and it is very difficult to overcome. Suppose you compare this maya to a very big river. When the river becomes turbulent it becomes practically impossible to cross it. *Mama maya duratyaya.* My maya is very difficult to cross. But it becomes very easy to cross if you come to me. *Mameva ye prapadyante maya metam taranti te.* Whosoever comes to me will be able to cross it.

So a sadhaka should surrender to him. "O Lord, I feel my progress is being retarded, but this is your game and it is beyond my understanding.

I surrender to you. Do as you please. I will continue my sadhana and my service. Do whatever you see fit to do. I feel I am retarding, but even then I leave it in your hands. I will continue my sadhana and service without pause." That should be the attitude of a sadhaka.

D: A moment ago you mentioned that when one makes good progress on the spiritual path then one attains some occult powers, but if one uses them then it leads to one's downfall. But there are some saints, they say, who display their occult powers all the time. Sai Baba is especially known for this.

C: I have heard many things about him, and at least two of my very intimate friends were with him and practiced whatever was taught to them there. They are no longer living. So I heard from them about his activities, materializing ash for people and other things. Now if you ask me whether or not he is right in doing as he does, I would say that I have no right or authority to interfere in his sphere of activity. But had I been in his place I would never have done so. I do not approve of such things. The great saints never made a display of such things. I have told you about Ramakrishna and the story he told about the man crossing the water by the use of occult power. This story shows what his attitude was toward such things. If you go through the history of other great Indian saints, like Kabir Das, Guru Nanak, Swami Ram Tirth, none of them ever made a display of their occult power. They gave instructions. They taught sadhana. But they refrained from exhibiting their occult power.

Of course, the sadgurus, the true gurus, have the authority to use this power, but that is another matter altogether.

D: On the subject of sadhana, to what extent should we share with others the realizations that come to us in our sadhana?

C: It is not good to share your inner experiences in sadhana with others. "I am getting such and such feelings, I am seeing such and such a light, I am getting this direction or that instruction while in trance." One should not talk of these experiences. Suppose you have learned something in your meditation and you want to share that knowledge with others. Then share it, but don't tell them that you received this in your meditation and that you are passing it on to them. Don't allow them to know that you got this knowledge in meditation. Instead tell them, "this is good to do, this should be done, this should not be done." Whatever instructions or guidance you get in meditation can be shared with others for their guidance, but simply tell them that this is what you feel is the right thing to do. Otherwise ego will develop. It may not happen today. It may come after one year or two years or five years, but ego is bound to develop. People will start appreciating you and praising you. "Oh, he is a very good sadhaka. He has very deep meditation. In meditation he is getting these visions, this knowledge, these experiences." People will flock to you, they will speak very highly of you, and your ego will start increasing. But the guidance you get during your meditation is good. You can share it with others as long as you do it in the right way.

D: What exactly is a *jivanmukta*,[4] a realized soul? Different people have different ideas by what is meant when we say a person is realized.

C: *Jivanmukta purush* means one who has no attachment to his personality or to his personal requirements. They think of the Cosmic Entity all the time, even when they are not in meditation. They never think of themselves or their self-attached objects. That kind of person can be called *jivanmukta*. A realized soul means one who is capable of merging their unit mind into that Cosmic Mind at will. That person has realized him, has realized that Cosmic Existence.

Now "self-realization" is also a commonly used term. Self-realization means you have realized your own soul, and when you have realized your own soul then you have realized him because your soul is a part and parcel of him. The soul is subtle. It is indivisible and immortal. So long as the drop of water is in the ocean, it is ocean. You can't call it a drop. Unless the drop is taken out, you can't call it a drop. It only becomes a drop when it is separated from the ocean. But when the drop is in the ocean, it is ocean. That small drop becomes ocean.

What is mind? Mind is a product of soul. The ideas that come out of soul are mind. Mind is born out of soul. Here "soul" refers to consciousness. There is the Cosmic Consciousness, and within that Cosmic Consciousness there is the Cosmic Mind, and within that Cosmic Mind is the unit mind. That unit mind also has unit consciousness; it is from that unit consciousness that the unit mind has arisen.

Now what is sadhana? Sadhana is the effort to merge the unit mind into unit consciousness, and unit consciousness is already one with Universal

4 *Jivanmukta* means "liberated being." *Mukta* means "liberated" and *jivan* means "life."

Consciousness or Cosmic Consciousness. Here we enter the domain of philosophy. Now consciousness is so subtle that it cannot be separated. The earth, the solid factor, can be separated. Water can also be separated. It is very difficult to separate gas, but it can be done. Ether, you can't separate. We are moving our hands in space, jumping, sitting, making buildings, the earth is spinning in that great void, but that void is inseparable. You can't partition it. And that Cosmic Existence, or Consciousness, is far subtler than ether. How can it be partitioned? If you try to draw a line on the water, you find the line vanishing even as you draw it. But if you draw a line on the ground it remains there unless you rub it out. So the subtler the existence, the more indivisible it is. The subtlest existence is completely indivisible. That is the Cosmic Consciousness.

Now suppose this large circle is Cosmic Consciousness. Of course a circle is finite, but it will serve the purpose as an explanation. And within that circle there are so many dots or points. Now my particular mind comes out from one point within this large circle. It is there that the mind is born. Associated with that mind is a body. The mind is working through this body, that is, the body works according to the dictates of that mind. Now under normal conditions the mind is flowing toward external objects. But what happens in sadhana? In sadhana you withdraw your mind from those external objects. You direct it inside, toward your inner Self, and try to merge your mind into your unit consciousness. The unit mind, when it is withdrawn from external objects and directed inward, merges into the point from which it has emerged, into that unit consciousness. And once it merges into unit consciousness it becomes one with Cosmic Consciousness, because unit consciousness cannot be separated from Cosmic Consciousness. You take a drop of water and put it in the ocean. It becomes one with the ocean. The drop is there but it has become one with the ocean and no one can differentiate it. Likewise, unit consciousness is already one with Cosmic Consciousness but the unit mind feels that it is separate. The moment the mind enters into its original point, that feeling of separation vanishes.

When one achieves that stage through sadhana in this body it is called *jivanmukta*, and that soul is called a "realized soul" because they have realized it. It is a matter of realization. Through the practice of spirituality they have merged their unit mind into unit consciousness, and then again through practice they have merged their unit consciousness into that Cosmic Consciousness. And when they come out they become a normal human being once again. Suppose one sits in nirvikalpa samadhi for one hour or two hours. Thereafter they are a normal person, sitting, eating, laughing, talking to you, moving about, doing everything a normal person does. So such souls are called realized souls. They have become one with the Cosmic Consciousness. And they are called *jivanmukta* in Sanskrit because they are free. They are free from all bondages. Such a person, if they so desire, can leave their body at any moment, anywhere, according to their will. If they need to stay on for some purpose, if something needs to be done, then they will stay on for that period. Suppose they have to do something that can be completed in two years. Then they will stay for those two years, according to their will.

D: Dada, in Sanskrit we use two words for liberation, mukti and moksha.

C: Mukti means that the mind still exists, but in moksha the mind ceases to exist. In mukti one merges into Cosmic Mind. Even when you achieve samadhi, the mind remains. But moksha means the final stage, when one merges into Cosmic Consciousness, not Cosmic Mind. Only that person who has merged their unit consciousness into Cosmic Consciousness, who has achieved moksha, has the authority or the capacity to stay or to go. Such realized souls cannot live in this body, or on this earth, unless they will it. They have to take a determination. "I will stay on for two years so that I can do this work." Otherwise they will leave the body and go away. So in order to remain in the body for some period those realized souls have to take a vow, a sort of promise or resolve, but this cannot be done by someone who has achieved mukti. They can sit in samadhi, they can be one with the Cosmic Mind, they can tell you many things, they can perform many miracles, but they do not have this capacity that the realized soul has.

D: What if the sadhaka has attained nirvikalpa samadhi but they still have some samskara remaining?

C: They have the capacity to exhaust that samskara. They can do it very easily. One who is a realized soul will do it. I told you the story about the mahatma who I went to for initiation but who wouldn't give me initiation. He arranged to exhaust his remaining samskara.

D: Is it possible for a sadhaka to fall once they have reached that state?

C: It is possible, therefore continued practice is necessary.

D: Even after becoming a *jivanmukta*?

C: There is a class of beings who have come for this purpose alone, and it is not possible for them to fall. But they are altogether different. They are said to be a sort of incarnation. God himself is working through their body. He has made them a medium for work, so there is no chance of their falling because he alone is working; there is no one to fall. But for those who are sadhakas, and who have become a realized soul through practice, if they give up their practice, or if they develop ego for whatever reason, then their downfall is bound to follow. Ego leads to self-interest and this will bring them down gradually, step by step, until one day they will become an ordinary person once again. It will not happen in a day, but it will happen one day. That is why astaunga yoga, the eightfold yoga—yama, niyama, asana, pranayama, pratyahara, dharana, dhyana, samadhi—includes samadhi as a practice. Even after you achieve samadhi you must go into it regularly, twice a day regularly at the minimum. If you think—"Oh, I have attained samadhi. I have realized the Cosmic Existence. Why should I continue this practice? Let me now work in the world with my occult powers for the good of the people"—then this kind of attitude or approach will lead to your downfall.

D: And this —

C: The sadhana is called "eightfold" and samadhi is one of these. So after achieving samadhi one should never think that one need not do sadhana anymore. You have to do it, you must do it, and you must do it regularly, every day.

September 16

TODAY THE WATERS BETWEEN my hotel and Dada's place have receded a bit, but not enough to affect the difficulty of the journey. The rickshaw wallah still has his work cut out for him, pulling his vehicle through muddy water that is up to his waist in places. But for me it is a completely different journey than the day before. There is a rightness to everything and a subterranean sense of joy that travels with me as I go, rippling the floodwaters along with the wheels of the rickshaw. It's amazing how a day with Dada can make the mud and the mess of India seem like a divine confusion.

D: Dada, yesterday we were talking about service and how service and sadhana are equally important. Could you explain how service helps to purify the mind? What effect does it have? How does it help us in our spiritual life?

C: You see, while doing service you have to ideate on the Cosmic Entity. The Cosmic Entity is all-pervading. He is present in each and every atom. A sadhaka should remember this whenever they do any action. So while doing service also you have to impose that same ideation. Do not think that you are helping the poor people, that you are feeding the hungry, that you are helping the flood-affected, that you are helping the sick, that you are helping the victims of earthquake or cyclone or epidemic, whatever it may be. God has created this situation. He has put you in this position to give you an opportunity to serve him, and it is he who is accepting your service. Do not think, even for a moment, that you are doing a good deed by offering food to this beggar. Instead, think that the Lord has appeared before me in this shape. He wants my service, so I am offering my service to him.

This is the proper ideation, and to help you with this ideation you are taught the second lesson. If you are successful in this then you will always be thinking about him. What do you do in Ishvara Pranidhana? You think about him. You think of the Cosmic Existence. In this case also you think of that Cosmic Existence, but in an external shape. You are serving the needy people, that is true, but your internal ideation is that you are serving the Lord. Whatever you do, wherever you go, keep him always in your mind. Remember him constantly, and by constantly remembering him you will achieve him, because, as I said yesterday, "As you think, so you become." Since you are thinking about him, one day you will become him.

So service purifies the mind and it also helps to decrease one's ego. If you think that *you* are doing good to such and such person, then ultimately your ego will increase; and ego is always responsible for a person's downfall. Not only in spiritual life, in worldly life as well. Whenever a person becomes overly egoistic it becomes the cause of their downfall.

Take the chief minister of Bihar, for example.[1] He was a great egotist. He considered everybody else a fool and himself a king. His ego was so inflated that everything he said reeked of his egoistic outlook. As a result, nobody has been made unhappy by his downfall. Rather, everybody is quite happy. Only a few goons that were being paid by him are making some trouble.

So ego is the greatest enemy of a human being. Rather, I should better say, ego is a great enemy for anyone, and it is the greatest enemy for a sadhaka. But by imposing this ideation of the Lord, of the Cosmic Entity, the ego will not be able to impede your progress, and one day you will be one with him in accordance with the principle of "As you think, so you become." So service to others with this ideation in mind amounts to sadhana. It is sadhana or Ishvara Pranidhana in the outward world.

D: What about for people whose sadhana is not so advanced? They do service but they often forget that it is God that they are serving. Does their service then have less value?

C: No, no, the value of the service will not be diminished; the value remains. But in the process that person's ego may increase. The one who is being served still benefits from that service, but the ego of the one who serves

1 The former Chief Minister of Bihar, Laloo Prasad Yadav, had recently been sent to prison for his part in a multi-million rupee scam, and was under investigation for other crimes.

may increase and ultimately cause that person harm. It may become the cause of their downfall at a later stage. That is the difficulty.

D: Some people are of the opinion that first they should become more advanced in their sadhana before doing so much service. They may be afraid, perhaps, of developing ego.

C: No, one should practice this from the very beginning. Suppose there is a leper standing on the side of the road. He has trouble walking, which makes it difficult for him to cross the road. Or suppose it is a blind man who wants to cross the road. If you are passing that way you catch the hand of that blind man and take him across to the other side. Then you go on your way. You may feel, "Oh, I have done a good deed for someone," but ultimately that won't cause you much harm. However, if you think that God has come to test you, or to give you an opportunity to do service, and you express your gratitude to the Lord—"O Lord, thank you for having given me this opportunity to do you service"—well, so much the better. But even if you don't take this ideation you have still done a good deed. That will bring you good reactions in the future, and in time, with practice, you will learn not to allow your ego to rise up when you do such good deeds. So service should be practiced from the very beginning along with sadhana. The moment you become a sadhaka, service also becomes mandatory for you.

D: Dada, could you say something about the difference between conventional morality and spiritual morality?

C: There is a story in the *Mahabharata*. The *Mahabharata* is a long historical epic; it is not a fictitious story. During the time of the *Mahabharata*, there was a great moralist by the name of Bhishma, and another by the name of Karna. They were moralists in the sense that they faithfully followed the conventional morality of the time. Arjuna was also a great moralist but he followed the spiritual morality. That was the principle difference between them. Karna and Bhishma were on one side and Arjuna was on the other.

Now Bhishma was said to be such a great warrior that nobody could defeat him in battle. But when he met Arjuna on the battlefield he was vanquished. The same thing also happened to Karna. He was supposed to be invincible but he was defeated by Arjuna. Now Arjuna was not such a great warrior that he could defeat anyone as mighty as Bhishma or

Karna. How then could he defeat two such warriors who were both supposed to be invincible? Bear in mind that in those days no one else would interfere when two people were fighting. Even up until less than fifteen hundred years ago this principle was still observed in India. Nobody would interfere on the battlefield when two people were fighting, and nobody would attack at night. Nowadays we have guerrilla warfare but back then certain principles were adhered to. In the evening the warriors would go to their tents and take rest. Again in the morning they would return to the battlefield and start fighting.

D: They had a sense of honor.

C: That was the inner feeling of the people of that time; they felt it would be immoral to fight secretly. They considered it treachery. When two men are fighting on the battlefield then let them decide who is superior. No one else should interfere. That is how they felt.

So when Arjuna confronted Bhishma, he conquered him. When he confronted Karna, he conquered Karna. When he confronted Dhronacharya, the great commander and military instructor, he also defeated him. Now the spiritual commentators say that Bhishma, Dhrona and Karna were all defeated by Arjuna because he was following spiritual morality and they were following conventional morality. What was the conventional morality of the time? Bhishma knew that the Pandavas, the five brothers, had right on their side and Duryodhana did not, and he said as much. But he believed that he had no moral alternative but to fight for Duryodhana because he was being supported by Duryodhana. Duryodhana provided his food, a house to live in, his clothes, and so on, and this obligated him to Duryodhana. For this reason he felt it was his moral duty to fight for him. He knew he was fighting for the wrong cause, but he felt that he had no alternative. This was the worldly or conventional morality of the time. So here, as depicted in the *Mahabharata*, the worldly morality is defeated and the spiritual morality emerges victorious. So when conventional morality and spiritual morality confront each other we should follow the spiritual morality.

Now some people may decide that under the present circumstances it is okay to steal from the rich and give to the poor. The conventional morality may condone this. However, the real solution in this matter is to construct a society with fixed ceilings on accumulation. Nobody should be allowed to accumulate more than a certain amount of land, a certain bank balance, a certain amount of property. Frame such rules that will prevent people from doing actions which are harmful to the society, such as overaccumulation. Set a legal limit, and if they cross that limit then you can legally confiscate the excess property. This should be the approach, and for that I recommend the Progressive Utilization Theory.[2] Try to control the people who are doing injustice to the society in this way. Not by killing them or robbing them, but by framing a proper set of rules. And so long as the society is not prepared to accept those rules then continue working, continue earning, and do what service you can according to your means.

So spiritual morality is always superior to worldly morality.

D: So by conventional morality you mean the morality that society teaches us. For example, one culture teaches that certain actions are immoral while another culture teaches that those same actions are not.

C: Spiritual morality is given in yama and niyama. To follow yama and niyama strictly is spiritual morality, and everything you do apart from this is worldly morality.

You see, there are certain universal principles. Go to America, go to Africa, go to England, go to New Zealand. Everywhere people will agree that it is good to speak the truth. Everyone will agree that it is bad to steal. No one will condone murder. So these are universal principles. They stand for all ages and all places. Not only in one particular country or society, but everywhere. Certain individuals may not follow these principles, but when confronted with them they will agree that they should be followed. Honesty, good character, non-stealing. These are universal principles which are accepted everywhere, by every society, by every religion. They don't differ from one place to another.

Now there are certain social rules, customs and conventions which can vary according to the time and place. Suppose it is considered immoral in a certain culture to have two wives. Everyone agrees that such a practice is bad. Now let us suppose that somewhere else, in a different culture, there are ten crore women and five crore men. If each man marries one woman then half the women in that country will be forced to remain unmarried. This would create an unfortunate situation for those women, and in that case the rule would have to be changed. A man should be allowed to have more than one wife and it should not be considered immoral. Likewise,

2 The Progressive Utilization Theory, commonly known by the acronym PROUT, is the socio-economic theory of P. R. Sarkar (Shrii Shrii Anandamurti).

if there are ten crore men and only five crore women then the women should be allowed to have two husbands.

These social rules and regulations are meant to be observed according to the time, place and person. They will have to be thought over and reconsidered in each particular place, during each particular time in history. No one can give a set of rules for society that must be followed without allowance for change. They may be followed today. They may be good for the people today. But after one hundred years or two hundred years or five hundred years the same rules may cease to be good for the society. So such rules will continue to change in accordance with the changes in time, place and person. They will have to be thought over carefully by the collective as to what is best in this age and under the present set of circumstances. And what should be the spirit behind them? The spirit behind such rules should be to do good to the mass, to the majority. If they can be beneficial to all, even better. The ideal is: Do good to all. But if you can't do good to all, then do good to the majority, to the mass, though some individuals may be affected.

Suppose you frame the rule that nobody is allowed to accumulate more than a certain amount of wealth. Then the big capitalist may lose something in the process, but their loss is the masses' gain; thousands of people may be benefited by it. So rules should be framed in such a way that the majority is benefited. The comforts of the individual will have to be sacrificed for the comforts of all.

D: What are those key principles that do not change?

C: They are very simple. Do good to all. Whatever action you may take, see that it does good to all. This is meant for all ages. Do not harm anybody, which amounts to the same thing. The methods may vary according to the time and place and person. You have to devise different ways and means as befits the situation. But this principle is unchanging—do good to all, do not harm anybody. We live on this earth, and as long as this earth has been in existence, the fundamental guiding moral principle has always been, at least in theory, to do good to all, to never harm anyone.

Help the needy, serve the needy. This maxim has been propagated since the dawn of recorded history, it is still being propagated today, and it will continue to be for all ages to come. To materialize it, a different set of rules will have to be framed for different places and different ages. But the main principle remains unchanged—do good to all.

D: And the ten principles of yama and niyama?

C: They remain unchanged. They have to be followed, but if I were to sum up yama and niyama in a single sentence it would be: Be good and do good is the unchangeable moral principle.

D: I have a question regarding yama and niyama. Suppose you are in a situation where it isn't prudent to follow the letter of the law. For example, let us say I come to India and they ask if I am an Ananda Margi. If I say yes, they won't let me in the country, so I tell a lie.[3] The situation is such that I feel forced to do so, and I feel that I have done the necessary thing, the right thing, in fact. But then another situation arises where a person thinks, "Okay, we want to do some good work for the people, so let us make some money smuggling some harmless but restricted items so we can support that good work." Now, where do you draw the line? Satya allows you to deviate from the literal truth for the greater good,[4] but in the second case it seems clear that you are violating asteya [non-stealing]. How does one determine where the line is that one cannot cross?

C: If what you are doing doesn't do any harm to anybody. First thing. And second, if the rules that have been framed have been done so out of a spirit of vengeance, or if they are not in the best interests of the country or the society, but rather to cause you harm, then those rules should be violated. If they are not for the good of the society, nor for the good of the people, then they must be violated. You must have heard about or read about the history of the independence movement in India. Mahatma Gandhi defied

3 In 1975 Indira Gandhi declared martial law in India and banned all opposition parties and a number of non-political organizations, including Ananda Marga. Martial law was lifted in 1977, but since that time Ananda Marga has been looked upon with suspicion in some government circles due to its advocacy of Proutist principles and its continuing fight against the corruption endemic to Indian government and administration. Sporadic deportation of visiting Margis continues to this day.

4 One of the five principles of yama. Satya is often translated as "truth" but the actual meaning is "the use of thought, word, and action for the welfare of others." Sometimes this may require deviating from the literal truth. For example, if an innocent person is running from a would-be assassin and takes shelter in your house, then it becomes your moral duty to tell that assassin that they went the other way or that you haven't seen them.

the authorities. He violated the rules. But he was not acting immorally. Instead, I would say that he was following the path of morality, because those rules had not been framed in the best interests of the people. Rather, they were unjust and caused the people unnecessary hardship. You can and should do likewise when you find yourself confronted by injustice, such as the practice of the deportation of Ananda Margis. In that case it will not be an immoral act. But see that you do not do anything that will harm the people or the society. Do not allow that to happen.

So defying the unjust rules of the government is in no way immoral. You have not come to India to do any harm to the people; rather, you have come here for a good purpose. So that restriction should be defied. Wherever there is injustice, it is our duty to defy it. If you can't defy it physically, then do so intellectually.

D: And in the case where a person conducts some illegal business in order to raise money for a good cause?

C: Never do anything which might introduce an unhealthy precedent in the society. Suppose I am a government officer and I accept money—not for my own sake but with the intention of distributing it among the poor. What will happen? When people come to know this they will think: "Oh, he is a moralist, he is a spiritualist, and he is taking bribes. So what can be the harm in taking bribes. Why shouldn't I do it also." This will create a sort of unhealthy precedent in the society. It will lead to the corruption of government officials. Other officers will start taking bribes and they will not have that same good cause in mind. One officer has taken the money in order to donate it, but the others are taking it for themselves and they are causing harm to so many people in the process. In the end your good cause is hampered or damaged because now the very people who don't have the financial capacity to pay are forced to start paying. Their good cause may be lost because they are not capable of paying. And those who are not working for a good cause but have the means to make the payment—they win. An unhealthy precedent has been established and in the end the people suffer for it. Though it began with someone accepting bribes for a good cause, in the end the whole society is vitiated. So there is no justification for doing something wrong to support the right cause.

In other words, both the end and the means should be right and correct. Otherwise it will gradually spoil the society in one way or another. So I do not approve of doing good through illegal means. The illegal method adopted by one spiritualist will be taken up by less scrupulous people and end up doing great damage to the society. It will have an effect of reoccurring nature and that must be avoided.

D: I have heard it said that the years between forty-five and fifty-three are the most fruitful for spiritual practices, given certain changes in the body, mental maturity and other factors. It has also been said that after a certain age the glands start to deteriorate and it becomes more difficult to meditate. What are the best years for sadhana, and is it more difficult to meditate when one becomes old?

C: I am an old man and I don't feel any difficulty. You see, it is simply a question of practice. I read somewhere recently that a young girl, a young teen, successfully crossed the English channel.

D: She swam across.

C: Indeed, a young girl swam across the channel but her muscles didn't give out on her. Why? It is a question of practice. You may be a very strong man, in peak physical condition, but if you have never wrestled and you go up against a man who is an accomplished wrestler then within a short time you will find yourself gasping for breath and unable to keep up. That wrestler can wrestle full-out for half an hour, but you give up after only ten minutes. Why? Because he is used to it and you are not. It is a question of practice.

As I have just said, I am an old man and I don't feel any difficulty, so why should anyone else feel any difficulty? Certainly, it is true that if you are not used to this practice, and then all of a sudden you want to take it up at the age of sixty, then you will feel some difficulty. If you start practicing at the age of fifteen or twenty or twenty-five, then it will be very easy for you when you get older But if you start at the age of fifty or sixty you will feel some difficulty in the beginning. Nevertheless, it is not at all impossible. After some time, when you get used to it, it will be as easy for you as for a youngster.

When I was a young man, in the year 1957, I gave initiation to one gentleman. I was a young man at the time and he was an old man, more than sixty years old. After his initiation he became a very good sadhaka. He followed the rules of sadhana very strictly, he was regular in his practice, and he was so devoted that he could not live without going to see his guru and guide, Baba, whenever he could. Every month, without fail, he would go and meet Baba and spend some time with him. Now he made rapid spiritual progress. He had no difficulty, despite his age. He is dead now, but his whole family is initiated. His eldest son, Aniruddhajii, is a very active Margi who does a lot of social service. He has a very good reputation in his community. So I don't find any basis to support anyone's claim that it is difficult for an older person to do sadhana. I don't agree with them. And I have my own experience to offer you as an example. I don't find any difficulty and I have reached eighty. So it is not difficult. Any person, at any age, can do sadhana and can do it successfully.

D: Dada, are there any differences between female and male in one's approach to spiritual practice or spiritual life? One monk told me that Baba once said that men should do more Dhyana and women should do more japa or Ishvara Pranidhana. Could you comment on this?

C: I differ—differ in the sense that the monk who told you this might not have had understood it fully, or he might have interpreted it according to the ideas in his own mind. In my opinion his interpretation is not correct.

I took initiation and started doing sadhana in the year 1953. My wife saw me doing sadhana and noticed a change in most aspects of my worldly life—changes in my food habits, in my conversations, in my manners and behaviors. Finally, one day she said, "I find a great change in you and I also see that you always do your practices behind closed doors." Baba had told me that there was no need to go to the jungle or the cave to do sadhana. Do it in your own house, in some secluded part of the house. Or lock your room and it will become your cave. So I used to do it inside my room and my wife questioned this. "You do your spiritual practice behind locked doors. What kind of spiritual practice is this that it needs a locked room? And there is a complete change in your talks, manners, behaviors, food habits. What is this?"

I said, "I am following the instructions of my teacher." Then my wife said, " Well, I am a woman. Am I also eligible to do this sadhana?" I told her that I didn't know, that I would have to ask. So she requested me to ask my teacher if he would also teach her or allow her to do the sadhana that I had been taught. Then I went to Baba and I relayed her request. Baba asked me to bring her for initiation on such and such a day. On that day she accompanied me to Jamalpur where Baba was then living. He initiated her and gradually she completed the lessons, one after another.

Nineteen fifty-three passed away, 1954 passed away, then came 1955. The organization was founded in January 1955. Then Baba said, "Now many people are coming and soon many more will be coming. It will be very difficult for me with one physical body to contact all of them, so I have thought of an organization that will have a certain number of acharyas. From now on these acharyas will impart the lessons to the people and the system will continue in this way." First he made Pranayjii an acharya, then myself and four others in a batch, and after only one or two months my wife was made acharya. She was the first lady to be initiated and the first lady to become an acharya. Now in her case, Baba didn't tell her to do more Ishvara Pranidhana and less Dhyana. Rather Baba told her, as well as everybody else, that Dhyana is the ultimate practice. Now let me add something from philosophy. Ishvara Pranidhana is not the ultimate practice. It gives you access to the penultimate step from where you can then enter into the ultimate goal. From Ishvara Pranidhana we get savikalpa samadhi. In savikalpa samadhi a slight sense of duality remains, but in nirvikalpa there is no duality. Only one entity remains. And for nirvikalpa samadhi you will have to do Dhyana. Dhyana alone can give you nirvikalpa samadhi.

Now what do you do when you do Ishvara Pranidhana? You take the ideation "I am he." What does the sadhaka say with the help of their incantation? "I am you." So in Ishvara Pranidhana you have this dual idea: you and he are one. The two entities are one, but duality still remains. In savikalpa samadhi the duality remains. That is not the final goal. But in nirvikalpa samadhi there is only he. Not I; he alone. Thus no one can describe this nirvikalpa samadhi. If you ask me about nirvikalpa samadhi, if you ask me how I felt, well how can I possibly say? But I can describe what I was feeling when I was in savikalpa samadhi.

So when this practice alone can take a person to the final goal, then why should we do less of it? Baba never told this to anybody. Moreover, she is an acharya. If he had wanted the women to practice more Ishvara Pranidhana and less Dhyana then he would have told her to teach this. But such was not the case. As per his instructions, she taught other ladies to perform both practices with the same zeal, the same sincerity, and to allot the same amount of time to both. Because you can't get nirvikalpa samadhi without Dhyana. If you neglect Dhyana, or if you do it halfheartedly, you will never attain nirvikalpa samadhi.

So I don't agree. I have never heard Baba say this, and my wife was never instructed so by Baba. Rather, I have heard Baba point out time and again that for sadhana there is no difference between a man and a woman. And such was the case right from the age of Lord Sadashiva. Lord Sadashiva was supposed to have lived on this earth between seven thousand and seven thousand five hundred years ago, during the Yajurvedic period. The Rigvedic period was over and the Yajurvedic period had begun. He was reputed to be the first teacher of yoga and Tantra. That is not to say that yoga and Tantra didn't exist up until then. They did. Yogic and Tantric practices had been in existence since the beginning of human civilization. The Vedic people were doing these practices, that is, the Aryans who came from the polar regions in the opinion of some people, from central Asia according to others. The indigenous people of India also had their practices. But at that time they had yet to be systematized and they were not popular. Sadashiva was the first teacher on this earth to make them popular and to systematize them. He taught the women as well as the men, and he gave them equal status in sadhana. So I repeat that in sadhana there is no difference between a man and a woman.

In the physical exercises there may be some difference, because the physical frame of a man and a woman differs. There are certain asanas that ladies should not do. Ladies should not do *tandava.*[5] And there are other exercises which are more beneficial for ladies than for men. But in the spiritual sphere or psychic sphere there is no difference. In the Vedic age there were ladies who taught the Vedas and composed portions of them. Madalasa taught this spiritual philosophy. She was supposed to have been the teacher or guru of her own son. So there is no difference regarding spiritual practice between a man and a woman. Both have equal rights. Why should a woman do less Dhyana? It will hamper her progress toward nirvikalpa samadhi.

D: One common remark also attributed to Baba is that women have more sentiment.

C: That is psychology. Psychology has little to do with sadhana. Rather it is sadhana that will determine the psychology. A sadhaka may have one kind of psychology today, but that will change tomorrow due to their meditation. You may be very emotional, very sentimental, very quick tempered, but all of these traits are changeable through meditation. So psychology is not there to guide sadhana; rather, sadhana is there to guide the psychology.

5 A vigorous dance developed by Shiva. The traditional Nataraj pose of Shiva is taken from the steps of this dance.

So whatever the difference on the physical level or the glandular level between men and women—women may be more sentimental or physically weaker—it makes no difference as far as meditation is concerned.

D: This brings up an interesting question for westerners. In western society there is a lot of emphasis on psychology. People go to psychologists when they feel psychological problems, such as fear, low self-esteem, etc., and different psychologists have different methods for working on these problems. People who are unhappy often go to a psychologist hoping that they can improve their mental health and become happier. Spiritual people also make use of these methods. Let us say, for example, that during childhood a person experienced some trauma. They may have been beaten by the parents, just to name one possibility. In the course of time they forget this or block it out, but when they get older it affects them without their being completely aware of it. They may become afraid of other people, distrustful of authority, and so on. One thing that psychologists do is to try to bring these old memories out, and this by itself often helps the person to improve or overcome their difficulties. Some people believe that sadhana alone is not enough, and that these methods are useful to help us do better sadhana in the future. To my knowledge such an approach to psychology has yet to take hold here in India.

C: Psychology is a subject here in India also, but not this approach to psychology.

D: Some people in the west feel that unless you work with your psychology in some similar fashion then you won't be successful in your sadhana.

C: Psychology or knowledge of psychological techniques will not make you a good spiritualist. But if you become a good spiritualist your psychology will become perfect. Meditation will make your psychology healthy, and it will help you to understand your psychology in a far deeper way. If you have dysfunctional ways of doing things you can change that psychology through meditation. So meditation is not to be controlled by psychology; psychology is to be controlled by meditation. It is the meditation that matters, not the psychology. Now, if somebody has some mental difficulties due to the effects of past actions, it may very well be that they will improve through psychological treatment. I have no objection to this. By all means, give them that psychological treatment. But teach them the lessons of meditation as well. That will guarantee their improvement.

Of course, one's approach when dealing with others should always be psychological. If the parents beat the child or threaten them, then that is an unpsychological approach. Such parents could benefit by studying psychology. They are unaware of how their behavior will affect the child. They may want the child to improve, but the child will not improve through beatings or chiding or threats. If you teach someone through threats, they don't learn properly. But if you teach them with affection then they will absorb your lessons more thoroughly. If I teach a child with affection then the child will become so attached to me that they will follow blindly whatever I teach them. But if I threaten or beat them then the child will develop a sort of hatred for me, and they will rebel against whatever I try to tell them or teach them. So an understanding of psychology is a good thing and it should be encouraged in the society, in one's personal life, everywhere. But psychology can never guide meditation; rather, meditation will guide one's psychology.

There is a story about Valmiki. Valmiki was a robber, a highwayman. He used to hide by the roadside, in the nearby shrubs or bushes or jungle. When a traveler would pass by, he would jump out and rob them. Sometimes he would even kill them. Now one time a certain sage was passing through and Valmiki jumped him. The sage kept calm and asked Valmiki, "What do you want, my boy? Do you want money? Do you want food or clothes? What do you want?" Valmiki told him what he wanted, and then the sage asked him what he would do with these things.

"I will eat, I will clothe myself, I will live happily and comfortably."

"And will you utilize these things only for yourself, or for others also?"

"They are for my whole family," Valmiki replied.

"All right, so you will utilize them for your whole family. Now tell me, when you fall sick or when you die, will your family members accompany you in death? Will they also fall sick and share your troubles and your suffering?"

Valmiki was perplexed. "No, of course not. How could that be possible?"

"Then why are you doing all these things that will bring you so much trouble in the future. You know the theory of action and reaction, my boy. You will have to suffer the reactions of such actions one day. Your family won't share them with you. You have told me that yourself. They will enjoy the property you've looted, so they will share your pleasure, but they will never share your pain. So why are you doing all this?"

Afterward Valmiki became a disciple of that sage and today he is famous throughout India as one of its greatest saints. Now look at his past life and imagine how radically his psychology must have changed once he took up spiritual practices. You can claim that the sage used psychology but I would disagree. It is just possible that if I had said this same thing to Valmiki it would not have had the same effect. It was effective because of the vibrational force of that saint, the vibrational force that emanated through his words. That was what impressed Valmiki. It is meditation which gives you that vibrational force. So if a saint or a spiritualist employs some psychological method, that psychological method combined with their vibrational force will be much more effective in creating positive changes in another person than the same method employed by someone else.

You must of heard the story of Kalikananda, Baba's first initiate.[6] Now Baba didn't say or do anything particularly remarkable. Of course, one thing seemed miraculous to Kalikananda, that such a young man could know his name. Baba called him by his name, "Oh, Kalicharan, come here." His name was Kalicharan Bannerjee. But what Baba told him after that was quite ordinary: "Why do you rob to get the money you need. Why don't you do good things? Why don't you earn money in a respectable way?" Finally he asked Baba to teach him how to be a good man and Baba gave him initiation. He became the first disciple of Anandamurtijii, in 1939. Baba was eighteen then and a student at Vidyasagar College in Calcutta.

So what was going on there? Do you think it was the words themselves that impressed Kalikananda? Do you think these words alone were enough for Kalicharan Bannerjee to abandon his evil ways and become Kalikananda? No, it was the vibrational force of Baba's spiritual mind expressed through those words which impressed him and inspired him to become a sannyasi. So psychology is not enough. Psychology is a good thing, no doubt, but only psychology is not enough. Meditation is a must.

And meditation will change the psychology of a person. Everyone has a certain psychological bent right from their very birth. But this can be changed through meditation. The waves created in meditation affect the brain and the central nervous system, and the brain is the carrier of mind. It is the seat of one's mental force. Whatever we do—what we eat, what

6 Kalikananda was the monastic name of Kalicharan Bannerjee, a notorious dacoit in the nineteen-thirties and Baba's first initiate. As the story goes, Baba was walking along a secluded path by the side of a lake on the outskirts of Calcutta when Kalicharan accosted him with the intent of robbing him. Instead, he ended up taking initiation into the spiritual path and later became a renunciate.

we drink, the manner in which we live, the exercises we do—all have an effect on our nervous system. In meditation a vibration is created that pervades the entire nervous system. And because that vibration continues day after day, year after year, it creates an inevitable change in your way of thinking. As you know, the seed of every action is in the mind. First you conceive of the idea of going to the railway station. That action is first born in the mind and only then do you get up and start moving toward the railway station. So since the root of the action is in the mind, if the mind changes then the actions change. Your manner of speaking, your dealings with people, your behaviors, as well as your internal experience will all change through meditation.

I will give you an example. There is one acharya, Akhori Himachal Prasad. He took initiation from me in the year 1955 when I was at Bhagalpur. He was an IPS officer, India Police Service, and he retired as Deputy Inspector General of Police. He lives in Hazaribag now. If you wish, you can go and visit him whenever you like.

Akhori was very fond of eating meat. He had to have some meat with every meal, otherwise he would not feel satisfied. When he took initiation I recommended that he become a vegetarian. After some time he came to me and said, "Acharyajii, it is very difficult for me to give up eating meat. I don't know why. The temptation is so great that I can't do without it."

I said, "All right, I will ask Baba. I can't do anything." Those were early days for me also. In 1955 I had just been an acharya for one year. So I went to Baba, told him what Akhori had said, and asked him what to do?

Baba said, "Go and tell him that he need only remember that he has to give up eating meat one day. Whenever he sits down to eat meat he should think, 'Oh, I shouldn't eat meat. I will have to give it up one day.' But as long as he still has the habit, let him continue. Just tell him to do his practices regularly and not to forget that he has to become a vegetarian one day."

I returned and conveyed this to him. Later, after three or four months had passed, he came to me again and told me that he no longer felt like eating meat. When I asked why, he said, "I don't know why but I don't like it any more. One day I forcibly made myself eat some meat and after the meal I vomited. My tastes have changed."

I will tell you about another person I knew, Mr. Tyagi. He was a contractor. He was a very rich man and he was very fond of drinking costly wine. He used to keep dozens of bottles of different kinds of costly wines in his cupboard. He loved to drink and he loved to entertain friends with his collection. Then he took initiation, but he took initiation directly from Baba. It was before there were any acharyas. Baba never told him to stop drinking. But one day his mind changed due to his spiritual practice and he didn't feel like drinking. A couple of more days passed during which he had a haunting feeling in his mind that he shouldn't drink anymore. Finally he got up one morning, took out his bottles from the cupboard and smashed them, one by one, in the drain of the road outside his house. From then on he remained a strict teetotaler.

So this is what I meant when I said that one's psychology will change through meditation. Utilize psychology wherever and whenever you can, but one should never concentrate on psychology at the cost of meditation. To be perfect, meditation is a must. Learn psychology, read psychology, teach psychology, but always give the priority to meditation. Spiritual practice is guaranteed to change a person's life, and that change will always be for the good.

D: There are some people who have been doing sadhana for a long time and still don't feel satisfied with what they have achieved. I wonder what is happening in such cases. Can it be that these people are not doing sadhana properly? Can you say something for those people who feel they are not making good progress in their sadhana?

C: Some people achieve great things through sadhana in a short time while others do not reach the same level despite many more years of practice. What you have achieved in five years another person may not be able to achieve in ten years. There are a number of reasons for this. Take, for example, a classroom situation. One student tops the class while another is held back and has to repeat the year. The teacher was the same, the classroom was the same, the subjects were the same. Why did one student stand first in the class while his classmate had to remain behind and repeat his studies? Well, first of all what you can grasp, I may not be able to grasp. Second, I may not have the same degree of sincerity that you have. Third, my food may not be of the same standard as your food. I may be eating food that is not good for the nervous system or the brain. Then there is the company one keeps. Your friends may be good people while some of my friends are not such good people, and I spend time with them and get affected by their behavior and their thinking. These different factors all have a profound effect on our sadhana.

Over and above all these factors from the present life are the seeds in the mind that have been carried over from the past life, the reactions in potentiality. The factors I have just mentioned—friends, food, sincerity and effort in sadhana—these are all acquired samskaras. Samskara means the forming of nature. So these are the factors in the present life that affect the formation of one's nature. They are your "earned samskara." And what you have brought over from your previous life is called "inborn samskara." The seed of your individual nature was present in your mind at the time of birth because your mind is essentially the same as it was. The mind doesn't die. Only the body dies. The mind gets a new body and it carries with it the seeds of its reactions from the previous life.

Now I do not have the same inborn samskara as you have, so how can I claim to be on an equal footing with you. My earned samskara in this life may be equal to yours, or even a bit superior to yours, but if your inborn samskara, the seed of that nature which you have carried over from your previous life, is far superior to mine then in that case I can't compare myself with you. You will always be superior to me. However, if I work harder than you do, if I keep on practicing with full sincerity, then my earned samskara will eventually help me to achieve the same success. I may not march along with you, but after you reach the destination I will join you there. Then I will say, "Oh, Devashishjii, I have come too." So it is both the inborn and the earned samskara combined together that make for a person's progress. This is the reason why one student in a class is very intelligent and another is very dull. One becomes a great mathematician while the other does their best to avoid mathematics. If they get the chance they give up mathematics and take up another subject.

So those who have a higher quality of inborn samskara will enjoy very quick progress while others will have to labor harder for a longer period. They will also achieve success, but they will take some more time.

Here we break for lunch. After lunch Dada reclines on his cot in a light conversational mood. After we have talked for some time I remember to turn on the tape recorder.

C: *Pathik ami, pathei basa. Pathik* means "traveler" and *path* means "the way, the path, the road." *Pathik ami pathei basa.* I am a traveler and the road is my home. *Jemani amar jaoya, temani amar asa.* Going and coming—as I go, so I come. I am a traveler and the road is my home.

This is the way of the world, going and coming, coming and going.

I remember once, Baba told me, "You see how people are? Christ was the most innocent creature that this earth has ever seen, but he was crucified."

I asked Baba, "Why was it so?"

He didn't reply. He only said, "If you people will not be careful I will also be tortured very much."

And we saw how he was tortured for more than seven years—seven years and some months.[7] This was in 1956 that he said this, and in December 1971 he was arrested and had to undergo severe tortures before he came out, acquitted by the high Court. This is how people behave. Good people are made to suffer, but good things always come out of their suffering. They sacrifice themselves for others. Such people come for the sake of others.

Again I return to my list of questions.

D: Dada, you were able to lead a long and active professional life. You were a high ranking police official and you had to deal with all kinds of people, with people who were not at all spiritual, yet despite this you were able to achieve success in your spiritual life. What are the secrets of leading a spiritual life under such conditions? What advice would you give people who have to work long hours with people who are not spiritually inclined?

C: After taking initiation I tried my best to follow the principles taught to me by my teacher. Many of my habits changed—food, dress, the way I talked to people, my approach to work. Many people were attracted by those changes while others questioned them and talked against me. One of my subordinates went around saying that there must be some reason behind it. Why is he so good? He must have something to hide. Perhaps he thought that I was trying to cover up some defect or some misdeeds with my good behavior. He didn't say this to me directly but it was brought to my attention by some of my well-wishers. I ignored it. I kept on doing as I was doing. Ultimately people started gaining respect for me, especially my subordinates. They developed the feeling that if they approached me

7 Baba was arrested by Indira Gandhi's government and held as a political prisoner from 1971 until 1978 when he was released by order of the high court following Gandhi's defeat in the elections that followed the ending of two years of martial law. In addition to the harsh conditions of his confinement and various types of mistreatment, he was poisoned in 1973 by the jail doctor acting under governmental order. He fasted for the next five years, four months and one day (until his release) as a protest against that illegal and immoral action.

they would be assured of getting justice. I commanded their respect not out of deference to the rules of discipline but due to my own character. My subordinates gradually became very loyal to me and adhered to whatever I would tell them. So those few people who were talking against me had to keep mum. You see, if ninety percent support you, then the other ten percent have to keep quiet.

If someone needed leave for some important reason then I would grant them leave, even under the most difficult of circumstances. Once there was an election and there was an order canceling all leaves. One young fellow was very disturbed and distressed by this order. A fellow officer of his approached me and informed me that so-and-so was weeping so I called him to my office and asked him what the matter was. He said, "Sir, my marriage has been fixed. I am a poor man and if this marriage is not celebrated I do not know if I will ever get another chance. My mother has called me to come but all leaves are stopped. What can I do? I cannot go home."

So I called the habaldar—the habaldar is the in-charge of a section. I called the habaldar and asked him, "You have ten men in your section. Will it be possible for you to manage with nine? What will happen if you are one man short?"

"Nothing will happen, sir. I am prepared to manage with nine."

"All right then. And nobody is sick in your section?"

"No, sir."

"Then you please manage with nine; leave this one person behind."

So I granted that young man leave and then went to my superior officer, explained what I had done, and told him that I would assume full responsibility for whatever difficulty might arise. He was satisfied with this. If something would have happened with that section, or at the place where that section had been deputed, then the inquiry report would have held me responsible. The young man went home and got married, and the election went smoothly. Now these little things mean a lot. In this particular instance, the news of what I had done spread quickly throughout the force, and that increased my prestige and popularity in the eyes of my subordinates.

Suppose somebody had not received their increment or somebody had not received their traveling allowance. I used to look into it, to make sure that the person in question received what was rightfully theirs, be it money, promotion, transfer, leave, whatever it might be. I always tried to see that justice was done. So I became very popular. In 1975, when a state of emergency was imposed by the Indira Gandhi government, an order was sent to my boss, the commandant, stating that his assistant commandant would be arrested soon and instructing him to be watchful. The arrest order was given by the chief minister at the time. Ananda Marga had been banned as part of the emergency and known Margis were being arrested or being sent out on forced retirement. Then the commandant of his own accord, without consulting me at all, or even informing me of the order, wrote back to the inspector general, the head of the police force in the state, that his assistant commandment was very popular in the force, so popular that he was afraid that if I was arrested there might be a rebellion. This was the Bihar military police. The IG then forwarded the note to the chief minister and the chief minister changed his order. Instead he had me sent out on forced retirement. Later on, that forced retirement was set aside by an inquiry commission. The Indira Gandhi government was responsible for many outrages and excesses during the emergency. When they lost power in the elections an inquiry commission headed up by a retired high court justice was instituted to look into all such cases. In my case the judge wrote in his decision that this officer has a very clean record of service and his forced retirement is not legal. He should be reinstated from the date of his forced retirement with all benefits. So after two years I was reinstated and given all my arrears in a lump sum.

Now I can't say what prompted my commandant to write to the IG as he did. Why should he go to so much trouble under what were then very difficult circumstances? But it was a fact that I was very popular among the men in the force because I always tried to see that justice was done.

Of course, sometimes you encounter opposition also. Once I was transferred to a place and my new boss was not a strong man when it came to morality. If a subordinate would offer him something he would accept it. He drank a lot. He used to use government property for his own purposes. He would use the government jeep for marketing, going to the cinema, driving his relatives around, and so on. Afterward he would get the controlling officer to doctor the logbook and sign it. As part of my new assignment I became the new controlling officer. Arms and ammunition, transport, training, discipline, and supplies were all controlled from my office. So at the end of the month the driver of that jeep brought the logbook to me and asked me to account for the mileage and sign it. He explained how my predecessor used to take care of it. Well I refused. I told him that I was not prepared to make any false entries. I had no idea how the jeep was used, so let my boss make the entries himself and sign it himself.

When my boss heard about this he became very displeased. He stopped talking to me or referring matters to me for some time. But after a few months passed, he gradually came to recognize my efficiency and my honesty. Whenever there were any difficulties with my subordinates I would always make sure that the matter ended in my office. He was relieved of much of the troubles that he had had to deal with previous to my arrival. So he gradually became very happy and he later wrote a very appreciative note about me to the higher authorities. Despite the fact that he was not a good man or a good officer so far as morality was concerned, he was still so impressed that one day he called me into his office to tell me that I had been right and that he had been wrong about the affair with the jeep. After that I never had any trouble with him.

Another time his superior officer got annoyed with me because he wanted something and I wouldn't agree to it since it went against the orders issued by the state chief. He wrote a very bad report against me but before any action could be taken on that report I was promoted and sent out to a place outside the state on central government deputation. After a few months of service under my new boss I received a very appreciative report and a copy was forwarded to the chief of Bihar. Then it came to light that the officer who had been annoyed with me had countermanded the order of the state chief, and he ended up incurring his wrath. As a result that bad report ceased to carry any weight.

Now I didn't do anything myself in any of these instances. It was managed by Providence. My promotion remained and no harm came to me. So I have met some setbacks but all of those setbacks ultimately went in my favor. They were set aside and I got my legitimate rights. Even my forced retirement was withdrawn. So I would advise everybody to be firm. Be strong and do your duty. People will respect you one day. They may be against you today, or tomorrow, or for the next six months, but ultimately they will appreciate you. They will have to appreciate you. And even if they don't appreciate you, don't worry about it. Providence will help you. I have that firm conviction because I have experienced it in my life. Providence has always helped in the end.

When I was stationed at Bhagalpur my boss was very strict and stern. He was so stern that people used to be afraid of him. This officer wouldn't even accept a glass of water when he would go to inspect a police station. He would carry his own water bottle with him. He never allowed his subordinates to meet him at his residence. Whosoever wanted to meet him had to meet him in his office. Now I wanted to go to Jamalpur every

Sunday to see Baba. Sunday is a holiday, the office is closed, but without permission one could not leave the headquarters. So I went to his office and requested permission to go to Jamalpur to see my spiritual guide. He gave me permission and after that he started calling me regularly to his residence. Whenever he had some instructions to give, he would phone me, even on holidays, and if it required some discussion then he would request me to come to his house to discuss the matter.

My co-workers saw this and they were surprised: "What is going on here? He visits him at his residence, he gets permission to go to Jamalpur every Sunday?" My colleagues and my friends used to ask me, "What kind of magic have you worked on this old man? He is so stern to us, yet he is so good to you." Well all I can say is that I was doing my duty efficiently and working very hard. That might have impressed him. And he was spared a lot of troubles and anxieties because I tried my best to deal with matters and set them right at my level. He felt very happy not to have to make minor decisions at every turn because of subordinates who were not taking enough responsibility.

So these are a few examples from my life. But in the end I would say, in short: Be honest, be hard-working and be efficient also—you must know your trade. But at the same time, be kind, be benevolent, be sympathetic. Both your superiors and your subordinates will respect you.

D: Dada, having spent a lot of time with people who weren't doing sadhana, did it ever have a negative effect on your spiritual practices?

C: No. I never had that experience—no negative effects. After my initiation I was always talking to people about sadhana. Whosoever came to me I told them about sadhana.

D: At work also?

C: No, not in the office. At my residence. In the office I used to concentrate on doing my job, the official work that was entrusted to me. I was always very keen in my own work to see that nothing was left for the next day. Whatever needs to be done today should be done today. Once I had finished everything, every chit, every piece of paper, every slip, I used to ask my subordinates if there was anything else left to be done. Of course, there were setbacks, as I said, but they always vanished and I had the satisfaction of a duty well done.

When I would get home there would always be two or three persons waiting for me. I would talk to them about sadhana, initiate them, give lessons and so on, so my mind was always engaged in spiritual ideation. Thus I never felt negative at any time, either in the office or at home.

So I would advise everybody: Be efficient, be honest, be hard-working. At the same time be sympathetic and be benevolent. In the beginning you may have to face some trouble but that will be temporary. When people get to know you, when they see your hard work and your passion for justice, they will begin to appreciate you.

D: When people are not at work they often like to spend time socializing, talking to their friends, and so on. One famous yogi once said that it's not good to spend much time socializing with other people, that it is detrimental to one's spiritual development. What is your opinion?

C: If I don't meet other people then how can I convince them about the value of sadhana? Unless I meet new people, who will I have to talk with about spiritual philosophy and spiritual practice? So I do not agree that one should not meet other people. I must meet other people. Let anyone come to me who wishes. I am happy to talk to them, whosoever they may be. They may not agree with me, or with what I have to say, but it is my duty to try to convince them about spirituality. Spirituality is the main thing in a person's life. No one can achieve perfection without becoming a perfect spiritualist, and how can anyone become a perfect spiritualist unless they first learn about spirituality? And if we don't talk to them, if we don't befriend them, then how can we convey to them the philosophy and practice of spirituality?

So, I don't think it is proper to avoid other people.

D: And you don't find it to be detrimental to one's sadhana?

C: Say a man has fallen into a well and you are a weak man. If you try to pull him up you may fall in yourself because you lack the necessary strength. But if you are a strong person, or if you know the proper method, then you can rescue that person without endangering yourself. You can bring a rope, for instance, tell him to tie it around his waist and then tie the other end around a nearby tree to eliminate the chance of your falling in. Then you go ahead and start pulling on the rope. Once that man comes out of the well he will be very grateful to you; he will pay respect to you.

Why then should I fall down? Let me make myself strong so that I can pull up the person who has fallen down into the well. Devise the necessary ways and means to pull him out. So this may be the view of that particular yogi but I don't like it. If I don't help people to climb out of their difficulties then how will they progress? And how can I help others if I don't meet with them? So, I must meet people, I must talk to them. If they don't listen to me, it doesn't matter. But this is not to say that I will allow myself to fall into bad company. I will not go to a place that is full of bad influences. There are many such places in the society and we are all familiar with them. Well, I won't go there. But if someone who has fallen victim to such bad influences seeks out my company then I will welcome them, talk to them, and try to convince them to become a good person. Why should this have any negative effect on me? Will I fall victim or prey to their bad habits? No, I will not. Go on doing your practices sincerely and regularly. You will not stumble; rather, you will pick others up and bring them along with you. This is my view.

D: So, Dada, a short while ago you gave some advice for a spiritualist to be successful at their job. Be honest; be hard-working and efficient; be benevolent and kind. Can you give some advice for family life? How can one develop a harmonious family life and a harmonious married life?

C: Now this is a practical question: how can one be successful in their married life?

D: Exactly. What are the important factors or secrets to achieving a harmonious married life?

C: Marriage means the joining of a man and a woman, and then their living together. Now, everyone has certain people that they are particularly close to. Suppose there are twenty young men in your neighborhood. You are not as good friends with all twenty of them as you are with one or two. So why are one or two of them particularly good friends, and the others less so? Because you accommodate them and they accommodate you. Your ways of thinking may be alike, your habits may be alike; you might like to do the same things. Because you think alike it has made it easy for you to accommodate one another, and that has made you both good friends.

When a man and a woman marry they come together to make a joint family. There are two persons in the beginning, the husband and the wife. Now the husband should think about the wife, and the wife should think about the husband. She should think about how to keep this man comfortable and happy, so that he doesn't have to face any worries or difficulties, and he should do the same. Each should think about the other. That is what I mean by being accommodating. Each should develop an accommodating nature, and each should try to take care of the other's troubles or difficulties or wants. Suppose you like to eat sweets, but your companion doesn't like it when you eat sweets and she expresses her dislike. "Huh! How many sweets did you eat? Why do you eat so many sweets? They're not good for you." Here she is not being accommodating and that will have its effect. You may not express it outwardly, but inwardly you will certainly feel hurt or unhappy because you have been scolded, or because you are not allowed to take as many sweets as you would like.

The next point is that one should also study the psychology of one's partner and try to please them in a psychological way. It's not a question of servility. One should not feel that they are being servile. No. The proper attitude is one of service and accommodation. That is the attitude of a good companion. The two of us are living together and I want us both to be happy. If I don't keep you happy, then I will also be unhappy, How can I remain happy if you are unhappy? So don't allow that situation to arise. Be accommodating, be helpful, and study the psychology of your partner. Always try to behave in such a manner, to talk in such a manner, that is psychologically sound.

So, accommodating nature, helpful attitude, psychological approach, and giving equal status to both partners. Many men have a superiority complex simply because they are men. This kind of attitude is not good. Give equal status to both. Let the wife know that she enjoys equal status. Likewise, suppose the wife comes from a rich family, or she is highly educated or better educated than her husband. If she thinks, "Oh, I am superior to this man; he comes from a poor family and he is not as educated as I am," then that is also wrong. One should give equal respect to the other, irrespective of any material factor.

So, respect for each other, accommodating nature, helpful attitude, always treating each other on an equal basis. All these, and at the same time—be faithful! In this modern society some husbands or some wives are not faithful to each other. One should always remain faithful to the other, otherwise it will ruin the family. It will cause a reaction in the mind of the other person that will completely disturb the family. If the husband is unfaithful, the wife may end up being unfaithful someday, not because it is in her nature, but simply out of reaction.

So these are the factors which make for a happy family life: accommodating nature; helpful attitude; psychological approach; giving equal status, equal respect, equal prestige, to each other; and faithfulness. Above all, if you develop an accommodating nature then everything will be set right. If there is something you like and she doesn't like, try to accommodate her; if there is something she likes and you don't like, she should try to accommodate you. If these qualities are developed in a family, then that family will be very happy.

In addition, there should be some common factor, some binding factor in the family. What do I mean by common factor? Well the most important is ideology. If both husband and wife follow the same ideology then that will be the binding force. Also, when the couple has children those children become a binding force. So that binding force, either of ideology or of offspring or both, is also very important in family life.

D: And what advice would you give to a family who wants to have children? How should parents raise their children so they grow up to be happy and spiritually inclined?

C: The first and foremost advice I would give is that they should never quarrel in the presence of their children. Don't ever allow the children to see or feel that their father and mother are quarreling, or are unhappy with each other, or don't like each other. Don't allow them to have this impression. Let the child see that their father and mother are very happy with each other, and are very respectful and accommodating to each other. This will help greatly to develop good qualities in the child.

And then there are other things that everyone is already familiar with. Giving the child a good education and dealing with the child in a very psychological way because when a child is very young their mind is not yet formed. It is in the process of formation, and in the process of formation all the best qualities should be presented before them so that the child doesn't deviate from the right path. These good qualities can be inculcated in the child through the manners and behaviors of the parents. If I am a gambler or a smoker or a drunkard, can I expect my children to be better than this? They may grow up to be better of their own accord. That is a different matter altogether. But I have no right to expect that they should be better.

So you have to mend yourself, and if you have some bad habits then you should try to conceal them. The best is not to have any bad habits. If you do, then please give them up. For the sake of your child, give them up. But if you can't, or if you need some time to do so, then keep whatever bad habits you have concealed from the child. Do not let the child know that their father or their mother is doing this or doing that. Your own actions will teach the child, and teaching through action has a much longer lasting effect than teaching through words. Even if you tell your child a hundred times — Don't smoke, it's bad for you. It causes throat cancer and lung cancer and emphysema — but you go ahead and smoke yourself, then your child will probably end up smoking. They might not smoke in your presence but they will smoke behind your back. Your words won't have any effect on their mind.

So parents should reform themselves, and they should behave in a proper way. This will have more effect on the child than simply telling them what to do and what not to do. The good relationship between the father and the mother, their own manners, behaviors, ways of dealing with people — all these will teach the child how to live. They will help the child to pick up good qualities.

And then schooling, of course, is very important. This is the age of mass education, so the child should be given the best education that the parents can manage.

One thing more I would add is: never beat the child. There is an old saying: "Spare the rod, spoil the child." Well, I don't agree with this. Never beat your children. Give them good instruction, teach them with kindness and sympathy, love them, show them your affection, and teach them through affection. Affection is always more effective than the rod or the stick. Baba has also said in one of his discourses that the fear complex blocks mental development. If you beat a child or threaten them, they will develop a fear complex and this will block their mental development. So no father, no mother should ever beat or threaten their child. Teach them through affection.

D: Dada, in India and in other traditional cultures the system of arranged marriage is still prevalent, where the father or the mother find a suitable bride for their son, or a suitable husband for their daughter. But in western countries there is no such system and people there find it difficult to understand. In the west people get married when they meet somebody with whom they feel a mutual attraction. What is your opinion regarding the difference between arranged marriages and ...

C: Baba has discussed this point in *Caryacarya*, in the chapter on marriage. He has said that it is the responsibility of the parents or the guardians to arrange for a good marriage for their children or wards. But if the son or the daughter want to marry according to their own choice then that is their prerogative. However, in that case the responsibility for the outcome of the marriage does not fall on the guardian. If it turns out to be a poor marriage you can't blame the guardian.

D: Do you have any opinion as to which is the better system?

C: No. Both are good. Take the case of my eldest son, Amarnathjii. One family acharya was looking for a husband for his daughter and Acharya Shraddhanandajii asked me whether or not I thought Amarnathjii would be interested. So I asked Amarnathjii first of all if he wanted to get married and he said yes. Then I told him about the proposal and suggested that if he liked, he could go and meet the girl. If he approved of her, and she approved of him, then I would make all the necessary arrangements for the marriage. Because in *Caryacarya* it stipulates that even if the parents arrange a marriage, the consent of both the boy and the girl is required, even in the system of arranged marriage. But Amarnathjii said, "I will not go. Ask my mother to go. If she approves, then I will marry the girl." My wife then persuaded me to go in her stead. So I went to the girl's house, met with her, talked with her, took food there, then came back to talk to my wife about it. I described the girl to her, what she looked like, her disposition, her nature, her education, and so on. My wife was satisfied. She said that since Acharya Shraddhanandajii has known the girl from her childhood and has a high opinion of her, and since I had gone there and formed a good opinion of her, then she was satisfied. "She is well-educated," she said, "well-mannered, good-looking, comes from a good family, she's a good singer and she cooks very nicely. What more do you want?" Then she went and told Amarnathjii that she approved of the marriage and he agreed. And now you see the family. He agreed without even seeing the girl and they have a very successful, very happy family.

So Baba has said that if the guardian arranges the marriage then the consent of the boy and the girl must be obtained, and the guardian is responsible for the success of the marriage. If the boy and the girl arrange the marriage themselves then the future responsibility is theirs, not the parents' or the guardians'. So both are good. Both can bring good results.

D: What exactly does Baba mean when he says that the responsibility belongs to the boy and the girl if they arrange the marriage themselves? Does that also refer to financial responsibility, for example, or ...?

C: Any kind of responsibility. Suppose I am the father and there is a quarrel between the two of you. You are not getting along. What can I do? It was your choice to marry this person. Suppose you have financial difficulty. You are not financially able to support a family. Again it was your choice. Or suppose the father-in-law is bad-natured or bad-tempered, and he is constantly interfering in your household affairs. Then again it is your responsibility. This doesn't mean that I won't help if help is needed; this is not a boycott. The guardian should help where and when they can, but the responsibility is not theirs.

D: But if it is an arranged marriage, then it becomes the responsibility of the guardian?

C: Yes, then at every step the guardian has a responsibility to see that there is no difficulty in the marriage. If they are bickering then the guardian has to find a way to solve the problem. If they are unable to meet their financial needs then the guardian has to step in and make up the deficit. If the father-in-law is creating difficulties then the guardian has to deal with him since it was the guardians' responsibility in the first place to carefully consider the merits of the family of their son or daughter's spouse. At every step they have to take responsibility and try to solve the problem.

D: Very interesting. One thing I have noticed here in India is that it seems that in the rural areas most marriages are arranged marriages, whereas in the cities there are less arranged marriages. Perhaps it is due to the greater western influence that is felt in the cities along with the effects of modernization. What do you think will happen in India in the future, as society changes?

C: As society changes more and more young people are living away from home, no longer living in the house of their parents. In this case the percentage of mutual marriage—I mean marriage through mutual understanding between the boy and the girl, as opposed to arranged marriage—that percentage will continue to increase. Suppose the father is living in Calcutta and his son is living in Bombay. Somebody else's son is living in London. The world has become smaller as life has sped up. Members of the same family are living at different places and they can marry wherever they are. So I think the percentage of marriage through mutual understanding will increase because the parents or guardians will not have the time or opportunity to arrange the marriage of their children.

And then there is the question of suitability also. Suppose a boy who is a skilled engineer lands a job in a company working outside India. Now if the parents arrange a marriage for the boy with a girl who will not fit in with the society in which he is living, then that boy will feel unhappy. Unhappy in the sense that wherever he goes he will see that his wife is not adjusting in that atmosphere or in that society. It will be a problem for him. It will make him feel uncomfortable. So why burden him with that problem? Let him find a suitable girl from that place.

Of course there are some young people who still prefer to have an arranged marriage, even under those conditions. My elder daughter's son is a computer engineer working in America. His other grandfather, Mangalbihari—you know him, I think?—so Mangalbihari wrote to him that he had a girl who he thought would make him a good wife. "She is highly educated, she comes from a good family, her grandfather and father both are doctors. She is quite good-looking also. Would you come to India on leave and meet her?" So he came to India on leave and went to visit the girl. After they met each other they both gave their consent. The marriage was celebrated, and now they have gone to America and are quite happy there.

So, it's like that. Marriage may be either arranged or through mutual understanding. The main thing is that both partners should be accommodating. Otherwise, if they are not accommodating, if they are not respectful to each other, if they don't try to understand each other, if they are not faithful, then the marriage will not turn out good, even if they were married through mutual understanding.

D: In India it is common for the sons to live with their parents after they are married, and sometimes other family members as well, such as uncles and aunts—what we call in English the extended family. In western countries, however, this is extremely rare. Most people live in the nuclear family—the husband, the wife and their children. Generally, as soon as the son or daughter reaches adulthood—twenty or twenty-one or so—they go and live independently, even before they are married. It is very rare for children to live with their parents after they are married. Now some people feel that the extended family is a better system, especially for the children, while others disagree. What is your opinion?

C: You see, in a society where everybody has their minimum requirements then it is quite fine for anyone to live wherever they like, whether it is in an extended family—what is called "joint family" here—or on their own. If the minimum necessities are assured, then it is all right. But in a poor country or society where the minimum necessities are not assured, the joint family becomes necessary, because if you fall into difficulty, I can help, and if I fall into difficulty, you can help.

Suppose there are two brothers. One has quite a good income while the other earns very little. Now if each is living on their own then the family of the second brother, his wife and children, will suffer. They will not get the same facilities as the family of the first brother. The children will be deprived of a good education because there is no guarantee or provision for education in this country—the government doesn't provide for it. If you are starving the government is not going to help you. Neither the society nor the government will come to your rescue. So here the first brother should come forward and ensure that his brother's family does not undergo any unnecessary suffering, not simply because he is his brother but because this is his responsibility as a member of the society, to help him if possible.

So in this case, if the second brother is living with the first brother, if they are living in a joint family, then no one will starve and the children will receive the same education. Their resources are pooled together. So in a backward society, or in an under-developed society, a joint family becomes very helpful. But if people are independent and have their minimum necessities assured, then they can live anywhere they please and in the manner they please. There is no need there for the extended family or joint family.

September 17

D: There is a phenomenon in western countries which is very popular these days where a person will enter into trance and some other being supposedly comes and speaks through them, usually bringing with them some kind of esoteric or spiritual knowledge that would ordinarily be inaccessible. Generally the person who goes into trance is not conscious of the other being who is speaking through them. In your experience, is it possible that a person can go into trance and then have another being come and speak through them?

C: Yes, it is possible. This kind of thing happens here also. It is an old art. There are people in the villages in India, often illiterate people, who practice something through which they can achieve this kind of temporary trance, and they are able to speak many things. So it is possible. The question is: how is it possible? There are two principle ways in which it happens. The first is that somebody who is capable of hypnotizing another person speaks through that subject. That person need not be nearby if they have the capacity to hypnotize from a distance. Once the subject is hypnotized, they will speak whatever the hypnotizer thinks or desires. The subject will have no knowledge or memory of what happened while they were under that person's control. So this is the first method. Somebody else is behind it.

What happens in the second case is that a person, due to their spiritual bent of mind, is sometimes able to go into a temporary trance; it is not the real trance, just a bit of the beginning of it. Now under normal conditions the conscious mind is functioning while the greater portion of mind, which we may call the unconscious mind, is not functioning. What happens in this case is that the conscious mind comes into limited contact with the unconscious mind for some period of time, and the unconscious mind is all-knowing. Suppose I am talking to you and only my conscious mind is functioning. At that moment in time my knowledge is limited. I am an ordinary person. But the moment my conscious mind comes into contact with my unconscious mind, the flow of knowledge that is in the unconscious mind enters my conscious mind and suddenly I can tell you all sorts of things that it would otherwise be impossible for me to know.

When Vivekananda first left India and went abroad he went to America and gave a talk in Chicago at the world parliament of religions. It was an important talk. You should be familiar with it. After that he traveled from place to place and while he was in England he gave a talk about the unconscious mind. He explained to the people in the audience that each and every person is all-knowing, but that they don't know they are all-knowing because they only work with their conscious mind. Their unconscious mind remains idle. But once their conscious mind gets linked to their unconscious mind they become all-knowing because the unconscious mind is already a part of the Cosmic Mind and the Cosmic Mind is the storehouse of all knowledge. Whatever knowledge exists in the Cosmic Mind can be yours through your unconscious mind. Now people in the audience were skeptical. So Vivekananda gave them an example from their own culture. Newton discovered that the earth has the power of gravitation, but how did he discover this? He didn't read it in any book; nobody taught it to him. What happened was that after seeing an apple fall he got to thinking: "Why are they falling? Why do they fall straight down instead of going in a different direction? What prevents them from going upward or sideways?" He kept on thinking and thinking until his mind became one-pointed, became concentrated, and he experienced a sort of momentary trance. As a result his conscious mind got linked to his unconscious mind, a momentary link, and the flow of knowledge came into his conscious mind. He realized that the earth was attracting the apple and he gave this knowledge to the world.

So it is possible. In one case someone else controls that person's mind through a kind of hypnosis and directs what they say; in the second case it is that person's own mind which is working, under the influence of their unconscious mind.

Let us return to the first case where someone is working from behind the screen. Many people do this as a kind of magic show or miracle show. When I was a student I was living in a hostel and a person from Orissa showed up one day who had this power to hypnotize. He was traveling on foot from place to place, using his powers to put on a kind of act.

From Orissa he went to Assam, then to Bengal, then he arrived in Bihar. He gathered a crowd of students around him and claimed that he could tell us many amazing things through somebody. Then he picked one boy from the hostel to be the subject. I was a senior student then, studying for matriculation in class eleven. The boy he picked was about four years younger than me. He was in class seven or eight. He hypnotized the boy and asked him to describe Robin Shaw College at Cuttack. We were in Muzzafarpur, in the north of Bihar, and Robin Shaw College is in Orissa. Moreover, it's in the south of Orissa, a very, very long distance away. That young student had never been to Cuttack but he described the college buildings and the college hostel there without any hesitation.

We all thought that this fellow was a miracle maker, but actually his subject had only been speaking out loud what that mesmerizer was thinking in his mind. He was from Orissa. He had been to Cuttack and he had been a student there. So he simply thought of the building and the grounds and the boy started describing them because the boy was under his control. It was not actually the boy who was speaking, although it appeared to be.

But this kind of thing, this playing from behind the screen, is bad for both parties. It weakens the heart and mind of the person who is hypnotized, especially if it is done repeatedly. And the person who does the hypnotizing eventually loses their mental strength and their memory if they keep it up. They become a sort of half-madman. So it is a harmful practice. But in the second case, where knowledge comes from the conscious mind to the unconscious mind, there is no harm if one cultivates this art. It is easy to cultivate through the practice of concentration and one should try to cultivate it. But if you put on a show of this once you have cultivated it and gained some control over it, then that is bad. Then further progress will be retarded or blocked, and after some years or many years that person may lose entirely their powers of concentration. So it is not good to practice it. It is good to have it, but not good to practice it.

D: In the first scenario, is it possible that the person behind the screen is a person without a body?

C: No. That person must have a body. They must be a human being. It is not possible for a bodiless mind to do this. Mental force cannot function or be active without a brain because the brain is the seat or the vehicle of the mind. However, it is possible for someone to attract a bodiless mind, that is, a mind which has left the body and not yet gotten another body, and to get something done with the help of that bodiless mind. During this period of transition a powerful spiritualist can attract that mind and put it to work.[1] But in this case it is that powerful spiritualist who is actually behind whatever takes place. Whatever happens, happens according to their desire, and they are able to do this because they have a body.

Now there are some people who gain access to their unconscious mind, but they are not aware of what they are doing. They don't even know that they are acting while they are in this state. This is a sort of semi-trance that occurs due to concentration. It is a trance but of inferior quality. This is quite common in the villages in India. There are certain people who practice this. They are called *ojah*. *Ojah* means a sort of priest, a priest with magical power. Generally such priests are half-educated or practically illiterate, but they have developed this art, which has been passed down orally from generation to generation. They learn it from other *ojah*s. These *ojah*s can tell you many things when they are in such a trance. If you have a headache, they can cure you of it. If you have a stomach ache, they give you a glass of water and it will cure you. These things are common in Indian villages but they are minor things and not beneficial. People think they are doing good but they are not doing good, neither to themselves nor to the person whom they think they are helping.

But when this connection between the conscious and unconscious minds is cultivated consciously then it is good. You can gain knowledge from the unconscious mind, and with this knowledge you can work for the good of the people. Use that knowledge to work for the welfare of others, but don't show it to them or let them know where you have gotten it from. Keep that knowledge to yourself and take advantage of it for guidance when you do service to others. It will be helpful to you, and you will be helpful to the society.

1 Here Dada is not referring to the phenomenon of channeling, as practiced in the west, but rather to the ability of great yogis or great Tantrics to be able to control a bodiless mind. Baba once gave a demonstration in 1956 where he temporarily stilled the life-force of one Margi and allowed his mind to separate from his body. Baba then commanded a bodiless mind to enter the body and that mind communicated various things, including information from the unconscious mind, to the people present. Then Baba told that mind to leave and commanded the original mind to return. That Margi returned to normal consciousness without any awareness of what had happened, nor did he suffer any ill effects from the demonstration.

D: I have heard of instances where a person goes into a trance and someone else comes into their body and answers questions. They say, "Oh, I am so-and-so; I lived two hundred years ago."

C: That may be hypocrisy, but it may be true also. True in the sense that that knowledge, those answers, come from the unconscious mind. If you have the capacity, consciously or unconsciously, to take your mind back three thousand five hundred years, or two thousand six hundred years, or one thousand years, or even two hundred years, then you can describe the scene as it was happening at that time. Once, in 1955, Baba gave a discourse in which he talked about the capacity of the mind to go forward or backward in time. It can be done but it depends on the capacity of the person who is practicing it. A person can take their mind two hundred years into the future and describe what is going to happen then. They can also take their mind two hundred years back and describe what they see. After the discourse Baba called a young sadhaka up to the front of the room to give us an example, to show us that it was possible. He told that sadhaka to sit down and begin doing sadhana. Then Baba asked him to concentrate his mind and take it back three thousand three hundred and some-odd years. "Take it to Vrindavan, to the bank of the Yamuna river, and tell us what you see there." He described a group of young boys at play, and among them was a boy who looked like their leader. There was a small herd of cows as well, grazing on the riverbank. The boy who looked like the leader was carrying a flute in his hand. Then Baba said, "Okay, open your eyes and be normal." He came back to normal consciousness and when he did he started sobbing and weeping. He wept for some time and eventually he was all right.

After Baba left the room, we asked this fellow why he had been weeping. "You should have felt very happy, very proud," we said, "to be able to see what you saw. None of us were able to see it. So why were you crying?"

"I didn't want to become normal", he replied. "I wanted to remain in that state because it was so pleasant. I was feeling so happy. When Baba ordered me to become normal, my mind came back to its normal condition without any effort on my part. Then I felt like crying because I had lost that state of joy."

So that was the demonstration. During his discourse Baba also talked about light and how nothing in this physical universe can be considered to be absolutely true or permanent. Suppose there is a planet, and due to its distance from the earth the reflected light rays from earth take three thousand five hundred years to reach that planet. Now if the people on that planet have a very powerful telescope and they look at earth through this telescope, what will they find? Well, the light that they are using to see the earth has taken three thousand five hundred years to reach there so they will see the Mahabharata. If it takes two thousand six hundred years to reach they will see Lord Buddha preaching. For you that is the past, three thousand five hundred years past, but for them it is present, and for another planet where the earth's light has yet to reach, it is future. So neither past, future or present is an absolute truth. It is all relative. Likewise, you can take the mind forward or backward, to the future or the past, and view what is going on. It becomes possible then to say many things. Of course, as I explained earlier, there are cases of semi-trance where the person is not even aware that their mind has gained access to a flow of knowledge from the unconscious.

D: There are bound to be some people who would like to learn the secret of how to send their minds forward or backward in time.

C: For us it is only possible through sadhana. When your mind advances spiritually, that power will come. It will come through concentration. What do we practice in sadhana? It is mainly concentration, spiritual concentration. The outward concentration that some people practice, such as concentration on some light or star can also bring some minor power, but the spiritual power is cultivated within through sadhana—through internal practice, not outward practice.

With this spiritual power a person can take their mind either forward or backward. It is a fact that there is no such thing as the present. The present is merely the conjunction of past and future. I have uttered these words. They are past. I am thinking of saying something. Those words are future. As soon as I utter them they become past. So it is just the connecting point of past and future. The mind remains either in the past or the future. Whatever we say or do or think immediately becomes past. Now anyone is capable of taking their mind back five hours or twenty hours. You can remember what you ate last night or the night before last. How do you remember it? By taking your mind back to that place with the help of impressions stored in your subconscious. In the same way, if you can take your mind back thirty-six hours or thirty six days or thirty-six years, then, with the help of your unconscious, you can take it back one hundred or two hundred years when you were somewhere else in some other form.

There is a well-known story in the Mahabharata where Gandhari narrates her previous one hundred lives. Gandhari was the mother of Duryodhana who fought the battle with the Pandavas. Was it possible for her to do this? Yes, it was possible. She had the capacity to take her mind back that far. To get this power one has to practice spirituality, and Gandhari was a great spiritualist. But it is not possible through normal efforts. No amount of study or gathering of knowledge can help you achieve it, only spirituality.

There are many people who can tell you about events in your future, but they do it through a process of calculation. This star, that planet, the time of your birth, the date of your birth. It is a valid art, but a spiritualist can get this knowledge directly from their own mind, without any study or calculation, without knowing any details about you. That is the real art, or real power I should say. The sadhaka who achieves this power can do whatever they like with their mind.

D: Dada can you explain a little bit about psychic phenomenon, like ghost possession and telepathy. How are these different from the occult powers?

C: They cannot be called occult power. They are a much simpler thing. You see it even with those who are not sadhakas. Sometimes you go someplace and you see that someone is very sad. An old man is very sad, sitting quietly on his verandah. When you ask him what the matter is he says, "I don't know. I feel like something is wrong, like something bad has happened. I don't know why, but I'm feeling very unhappy." And the next day he gets a telegram saying that his son is very sick and has been admitted to a hospital. This is a sort of telepathy. It's a very ordinary thing which happens even with non-sadhakas.

Somebody has a dream during the night and the next day that dream comes true. This is the play of the mind. The unconscious mind sometimes pushes something into your conscious mind and you get such feelings or see such dreams. It happens even to people who have no occult power or who are not sadhakas. But this is just natural telepathy. The person has not earned it. They have no command over it. They can't get such signals for anything and everything that will happen. No. Just now and then it so happens that they get such a signal. But for those who have occult powers, who have earned such power due to a high level of spirituality, it is completely different. They can know whatever they want at any moment, everything that will happen, if they so desire. Everything is possible for them.

You mentioned how Baba had once said that for doing certain things he would have to go into savikalpa samadhi. What does this mean? Savikalpa samadhi is a level of mind in spirituality. In the realm of spirituality there is a certain level of mind, a certain state, which is called savikalpa samadhi. There the mind becomes, for all intents and purposes, all-powerful. So a spiritualist goes into savikalpa samadhi to do certain things that require that power—to see a thing, to dictate a thing, to guide a thing. That is the perfection; occult power is simply an expression of that perfection. Savikalpa samadhi is the real perfection. But such kinds of psychic phenomenon, these signals, are just the play of the mind. It can happen to anyone, but not according to their will. Only one who has achieved savikalpa samadhi can do this when and wherever they like. Whatever they want to know, whatever they want to do, they will know it, they will do it.

These kinds of uncommon experiences generally happen to everyone at one time or another. Most people experience them at least three or four times in the course of their life. Most everyone, if they have lived a long life and if they think back deeply over their experiences, will tell you, "Yes, something like this happened to me about forty years ago. I felt some apprehension in my mind and it turned out to be true."

D: So when Baba would do certain things he would go into savikalpa samadhi …

C: Well for him savikalpa samadhi was a matter of one moment to the next. He would be sitting there with you and he would raise his mind, raise his serpentine power, in a single instant. You see, what is savikalpa samadhi? When the serpentine power or the kundalini rises from muladhara to ajina chakra. He could do this instantly while he was sitting there talking to us. Whenever he liked he could go into savikalpa samadhi—for as long or as short a time as he pleased.

D: So when Baba was sitting and talking, he would sometimes keep the kundalini down and sometimes up?

C: Normally the kundalini remains in its own place. But if he wanted to do something, say something, know something, then a moment's concentration and it rises to that point, to the ajina chakra. If he desired it, it would rise instantaneously to that point.

As far as the occult powers go, I will point out again that these things are milestones, and the milestones should not be given much importance. So let us keep moving ahead. If we want to reach the destination we should not let ourselves be sidetracked by the beautiful sights on the roadside—the beautiful gardens, beautiful houses, the museums of the material world. If one does not control one's mind and avoid wasting time, then one may have to face some delay before reaching the destination. Or one may fail to reach one's destination entirely. If a person gets stuck at some point on the road, they may never reach at all.

So these things are possible, but then one should not think of them, one should not care for them. One should try to keep moving in the right direction. And what is the right direction? Do sadhana and service, regularly and sincerely. The mere desire itself for powers will bring the mind down.

When Baba founded the organization, his first discourse, on the first of January 1955, was "the Gradual Evolution of Society." He quoted one Sanskrit *shloka* [verse] in that discourse: *sah bhavati daridra yasya asha vishala. Sah* means "he", *bhavati* means "becomes", *daridra* means "pauper", *asha* means "desires, aspirations", and *vishala* means "big." He who has big aspirations, great aspirations, great desires, is a pauper. *Sah bhavati daridra yasya asha vishala, manasi paritushte arthavan ko daridra. Manasi* means "mentally", *paritushte* means "fully satisfied", *arthavan ko daridra*—who is rich and who is a pauper? For one who is fully mentally satisfied, who is a pauper and who is rich? But those people who have many aspirations and desires—they are paupers. So nobody should desire power or try to acquire it through sadhana. It is just possible that the Cosmic Mind will not allow that person to gain that power. If a sadhaka desires power then their progress will be retarded, so the Cosmic Mind may not allow that person to gain power, simply because they desire it. Their goal is not to merge their mind in the Cosmic mind. It is to gain power and that is not a good thing.

A saint has said, *aur nahin kachu chahi mor he kevala nath amudra tor he.* "Oh Lord, I don't want anything else; I want you alone." Don't give me anything else, I don't want anything else; I want you alone. That should be the attitude of a sadhaka. So tell those brothers and sisters who are interested in this occult power that it is not good. If it comes of its own, well and good—let it come. But don't use it, don't feel proud of it, don't allow your ego to grow. Don't allow your ego to increase simply because you have gained something, some power. Forget about it. Let it be just like the milestones or beautiful scenes on the roadside that you pass by when you are moving ahead in a fast-moving vehicle toward your destination. Always keep your destination in mind and forget everything else. Otherwise, if you become charmed by these roadside attractions, you will never leave that place. You will go on wandering inside your beautiful garden and your destination will remain far, far away. Be like that saint who said, "Oh Lord, I want you alone; nothing else."

That is devotion and no one can be perfect without devotion. He can only be achieved through his grace, and I have already said that grace cannot be had by begging. You must have devotion, and you must do what he wants you to do. That is devotion. And he wants you to do sadhana and service. Even if the Lord himself appears before you and asks you, "What do you want?" tell him, "O Lord, I don't want anything, I want you alone."

D: Earlier you mentioned that it is possible to remember one's past lives. Dada, is it possible to retain consciousness after death? There is one book called *The Tibetan Book of the Dead*, and it details the different stages of awareness that the mind goes through after it leaves the body. I have read elsewhere that while it is not possible for an ordinary person to remain conscious, a highly developed person can remain conscious even after leaving the body. Is that really possible?

C: Yes, it is possible. There are certain stages of mind that one may experience—Baba has delineated them in one of his discourses—known as *yaksha, raksha, kinnar, gandharva, vidyadhar, videhilina*, and *siddha*. But in such a state the mind cannot act; it remembers but the person cannot act. If a very powerful person, a very good devotee, a very good sadhaka, has some desire when they die then they may pass into one of these states. "Oh, if I only would have gotten all these powers, I would have done so much good to the world." The person had a desire to acquire power. They wanted this power for doing good, but nevertheless it became their binding force, a sort of binding rope which prevented them from getting liberation. Since they do not get liberated, what happens? The mind remains in the atmosphere for some time until it gets another body, but during that period that mind remains conscious. It continues moving in the ether but it cannot do anything, because in order to act, the mind needs a body. It does have a sort of body, you can say, but that body consists of only three elements, three fundamental elements—ethereal, aerial and luminous. No action is possible with only these three. But the mind is conscious and during this period it experiences a sense of repentance. This condition is very painful for that mind. It is painful because of that one desire which has prevented the person from reaching the goal. Then, when that mind gets a new body, it again takes up sadhana and achieves liberation.

D: So this is a painful stage.

C: Yes. The mind could not get liberation because of that desire. So the desire is fulfilled but they are unable to do anything because they don't have a body. Because this period is painful such a mind is always roaming about, looking for good saints, good people, good sadhakas, and they remain near them. A very good sadhaka has the capacity to see them. They can see that so-and-so *siddha* has come, but they feel helpless to do anything for them. Nothing can be done until that *siddha* gets a new body. Once they get a body they become a sadhaka again because of their past samskara, their good thinking. They will again have the opportunity to do sadhana and get liberation.

A good sadhaka can see a body of light moving around nearby, but that sadhaka can't help them or ease their suffering because that bodiless mind is bound by their samskaras; they are under the bondage of the reactions of their own action. Unless and until those reactions are exhausted they can't get liberation. And to get liberation they will have to get another body. Now that repentance they feel will cause them to get a body, a suitable body, and once they do, they will again take up their spiritual practice, attain perfection, and get liberation after leaving that body. So it is possible to remain conscious. But this is an immaterial stage. You can't help them, nor can they help you. The utmost a bodiless mind can do is give you some hints, some guidance, that's all.

D: Then does an ordinary sadhaka, someone who has not reached such a high stage, who has not attained samadhi, lose consciousness completely as soon as they leave their body at the time of death?

C: Yes, unless they get another brain, a physical brain, they won't have any remembrance or be able to maintain consciousness. After getting a new brain some people may then remember their previous life, but that is also quite rare. If that particular person was a good sadhaka, then for some time after getting a new body the remembrance of the previous life remains in the mind, but gradually it is forgotten. As the person grows and gets mixed up in worldly affairs during childhood, they gradually lose those memories. But if the person starts doing sadhana again—and you can be sure that the person will get the opportunity to do sadhana in the next life—they will eventually remember their past life.

The ordinary person, the non-sadhaka, forgets everything when their mind leaves the body. They become a sort of energy without consciousness, like electricity. The ordinary mind after death is like that. It's an energy in the ether, just flowing about, moving about. Its movement is directed by nature. *Prakriti*, that is, nature, directs that mind to the proper field when it becomes available. Then the mind takes its new body. It gets the new body according to its samskara.

Samskara refers to one's reactions in potentiality. Suppose the reaction in potential form dictates that when the person reaches twelve years of age they will lose their body, they will die. In that case they will get a body which will die at twelve years of age. Both the mother and father have their own reactions in potentiality, or samskara, to lose their son when their son becomes twelve. Similar is the case with the samskaras of the brothers and sisters, relatives and friends. Suppose the boy has one very close friend and they remain inseparable from the age of six. At the age of twelve he will have to lose his close friend; his companion has to go. This is also the friend's samskara. So that is what is meant by "proper field." Is it clear? The mind will get such a field where everybody's samskara is interconnected.

This is the universal law of nature. It is nature that orchestrates the process. I told you what Krishna said to Arjuna. *Na kartrtwam na karmani lokasya srjati prabhuh, na karmaphala samyogam svabhavastu pravartate*. "I don't do anything. God doesn't do anything. Everything happens according to the law of nature." So this is the law of nature, that a particular mind with its reactions in potentiality gets a proper field where its reactions can find expression.

D: Dada, is it true that when we take our next body, the people we are associated with in the new life are the same people we have been associated with in previous lifetimes?

C: No, no. This is not true. I have just explained that the mind gets a body according to one's reactions in potentiality, and those reactions must correspond to one's associates' reactions in potentiality as well—father, brother, mother, sister, friends, spouse, children. All must have corresponding samskara. So a person may not get the old associates from their previous life because their reactions in potentiality may not accord. Everything is arranged according to the needs of one's reactions in potentiality. Otherwise how can the reactions manifest? How can that person reap the consequences of their actions in the form of reactions? So it is not true. Some acquaintances from the previous life may reappear in the new life. Some of them may not. But whether they do or not, the proper place, the proper field is given to that particular mind by nature, according to the law of nature.

D: There is a type of process that people have started to use in some western countries, a type of hypnotism that allows people to remember their previous lifetimes. The doctor will put people under a certain kind of hypnosis and …

C: It is possible if the conscious mind, for whatever reason, gets connected to the unconscious mind. There are so many different circumstances under which that connection can occur. The best way, the best process, is if one makes the connection oneself through sadhana. But it can happen to a normal person in other ways, through concentration, for example, as was the case with Newton. So it is possible, because that knowledge is there in the unconscious mind. Once the unconscious mind gets connected, either through the help of another person or through one's own efforts, then the person gets that knowledge; they can remember their past lives.

D: Previously you mentioned that it can be harmful if someone else hypnotizes you.

C: Yes, it is harmful. In the long run it is harmful. It may make both people invalid—the one who does it and the one on whom it is done. Both may have to suffer at a later stage if they do it repeatedly. If one does it once or twice, however, then it's all right, it should not cause any harm. But if the person is a spiritualist then their progress will definitely be retarded for some months or some years.

D: Dada, in this lifetime we have the good fortune to have Baba as our guru. But most of us will still have unfinished samskara when we die. We will have to come back; we will have to do sadhana again. Will we again get Baba as our guru, or is it possible that we will have a different guru in our next life?

C: Generally people get the same guru. Why? Why do they get the same guru? Because they have that reaction in potential form, that samskara. All along the mind has been working in that atmosphere, in that way, in that manner. This creates a certain type of reaction in potentiality. Therefore, the person generally gets a body that will give them the opportunity to have the same guru.

D: So if Baba doesn't come back to this planet for many thousands of years, we will also have to wait that long?

C: No, it's not necessary. You can liberate yourself through your own efforts. You can liberate yourself even in this lifetime.

D: But for those of us who have to come back again, maybe two, three more times ...

C: You may achieve liberation today. You may achieve it tomorrow or the day after. Who knows? Or, if you have that desire, then that becomes your reaction in potentiality. If you have the desire to come when he comes, then you will come again when he comes.

D: In Ananda Marga and many other spiritual organizations there are two main ways of life. One is that of the monk or renunciate, and the other is that of the family person. Can you say something about the proper interaction or relationship between the renunciates and family people? What is the primary role of the renunciate and what is the primary role of the family person? How should they work together, interact together? What is the proper balance?

C: In Christianity there is this system of monks and nuns, and everything is guided by them. Islam has the system of maulavii and mullah, but there are no monks or nuns. In Ananda Marga, Baba has made provisions for both, and both share the responsibility in the organization. Family people are also acharyas, family people are also Purodha,[2] family people are also Bhukti Pradhana.[3] So he has created an organization which consists of both

2 Purodha is a title that is conferred on certain select few members of Ananda Marga who then have a correspondingly greater organizational responsibility. It may be compared with the title or position of Cardinal in Catholicism, except that one need not be a renunciate to be Purodha.

3 The director of Ananda Marga activities in a particular district.

systems—the work is done through monks and nuns, and the work is done through family people. Now there should be full cooperation between the whole-time workers—"whole-time worker" refers to the monks and nuns—and family people. The whole-time workers have left their hearth and home to become monks and nuns. The family people are living in the family. But both are doing the same work. What work? Again we come to the same principle—sadhana and service.

Now the only difference between the two is that the whole-time worker has nothing else to do, so he or she can devote the entire twenty-four hours to sadhana and service—of course, after taking rest, bath and food. They don't have to waste time earning money. A family person, however, has a dual responsibility, the responsibility of the family and the responsibility of the Marga—the responsibility bestowed upon them by virtue of being a Margi, that is, sadhana and service. So they have to do sadhana and service, and look after the family as well. In order to look after the family properly they have to earn something. They have to pay for food, clothing, residence, medical aid and the education of the children. So the time they have at their disposal needs to be distributed to different categories; some time has to be devoted to earning money, and whatever time is left over should be spent on sadhana and service.

Now the ideology is common to both, the cult of sadhana or the spiritual practices are the same, the type of service is the same. There is no difference. The only difference is that of time. A family person has less time for doing service than a monk or nun. But at the same time a family person has more responsibilities. More responsibilities in what sense? More responsibilities in the sense that a family person has two families to look after. One is the personal family, and the other is society. A monk will go to serve in some area, but where will they get money? Where will they get blankets? Where will they get medicine? Who will supply them? It is the family person, the one who is earning who has to supply them. The monks will work, but the finances have to be arranged by the family person. So in the end we find that there is no real difference between the two. One gives all of their time, and the other also gives their full time in the sense that they part with some of their earnings for which they have devoted time. The renunciate gives their time for social service and the family person gives time as well as finance for social service.

So both have equal responsibility. The method or the manner of working is different, but both have equal responsibility. Baba once explained that he gave this dual system of monkhood and family life so that wherever the family member needs help, the renunciates will come forward; wherever the renunciates need help, the family people will come forward—whatever kind of difficulty it may be. Suppose for some reason the monk or nun becomes misguided. They go astray, or become lazy, or do something which needs rectification. The family person will help them. If they fall down, the family person will pick them up. And if the family person falls down, the renunciate will pick them up. If that family person is not treating their family members well, if they are neglecting their family or not making any efforts to do social service, then the monk or the nun will come and tell them, "Look brother, look sister, this is not right. You should look after your children. Your child is sick; you need to take them to the doctor."

Now both should work in close cooperation. I would like to stress this point, that we should all work in close cooperation. We should not feel that one is superior and the other inferior. No, it simply isn't so. The robes of the renunciate are like a uniform—the worker is the uniformed volunteer of the organization, and we are the financiers. Both have equal responsibility in my opinion. The family person gives their time and finance; the renunciate gives all their time. And, with a spirit of cooperation, each helps the other to rectify their failings. Therefore an avadhuta or avadhutika and a family person are equals. They have equal dignity and equal responsibility.

Now as to the matter of sadhana. There may be some family people who are very good in sadhana, who might have achieved good progress; there may be some monks who have not been able to achieve that height. So no one should think that by becoming a monk they will automatically become a good sadhaka, or that by remaining a family person one cannot be a good sadhaka. This is not the case. A monk may be a very good sadhaka; a family person may also be a very good sadhaka, Some family people may not be good sadhakas; some monks are also not good sadhakas—they may be good social workers but not good sadhakas. So as far as sadhana goes there is no difference between the two. Both are equal in sadhana, and both are equal in service also, with the only difference being that one gives their time and also finance, while the other gives only their time, but their whole time. Nobody should ever consider one path to be inferior or superior to the other.

D: In family life, the family person has to try to achieve some kind of balance between serving their personal family and serving the society.

C: Yes, they have dual responsibility.

D: Now, the question arises: How does one find or maintain this balance? For example, let's say someone sees some social service that needs to be done and wants to do something. They give a certain amount of money for that, but in the process their family suffers because they give too much.

C: No. You should not allow the family to suffer. You meet the needs of the family, and then whatever you set aside you can give to charity. Not at the cost of the family. Deprive your child of a proper education and then donate the money you've saved at the cost of their education? I would not appreciate this. This is your responsibility; it is your primary responsibility, your direct responsibility. Baba used the word "direct." The family is your direct responsibility, and social service is your indirect responsibility. So you should not neglect your direct responsibility. First take care of your direct responsibility, and whatever is saved or left over you can use for your indirect responsibility. Because, as regards your direct responsibility, no one else is going to do that for you. No one else is going to educate your children. It is your duty, your responsibility. But your indirect responsibility is shared among the members of the society. Suppose there are ten or fifteen people in your area. All will help, all will donate according to their means since all share that same responsibility. That is why Baba called it indirect responsibility. You donate for a certain cause, I will donate for that same cause, another person will donate, so many people will donate, but nobody will donate for the education of your child, or for the medical treatment of your child.

D: Does the same go for time? For example, the wife complains that the husband is always going out to do some social service and is not devoting sufficient time to the family. And the husband says, "No, I am doing service; you know how important this is."

C: Then such people should be advised to make adjustments. I have already said that the family should not be neglected. Give some time to them also. During times of emergency there are family people who also serve. There are soldiers who are family men and who go to the front lines? How so? Well they go with the consent or understanding of the family. So make your family such that you have clear understanding amongst yourselves, and if there is an emergency then decide with your family that so-and-so will be going for four days or five days, or for one week on this emergency duty. Let there be a clear understanding, and then go and do that social service. But neglecting the family on a daily basis on the pretext of social service is not good. You have accepted direct responsibility for the family, so you must attend to that also.

So you have to make adjustments—time, money, comforts, everything. And you have to look after your direct responsibility because nobody else will come forward to take care of it. Many people will come forward for that indirect responsibility and you will be one of them. So one's direct responsibility must always be fulfilled.

D: Dada, I have met a number of young people who have difficulty deciding which path is best for them. Some people think, "Well, I want to do good sadhana, so maybe it's better for me to become a monk; then I will have more time for sadhana." What advice would you give to a young person who is trying to decide whether they should become a renunciate or a family person?

C: First of all, I would say that if someone wants to become a sannyasi they must be mentally prepared to face all sorts of inconveniences, to forego any kind of worldly convenience or comfort. Only then should they opt to become a sannyasi. Because once you become a sannyasi you should remain firm in your decision. You should not return to family life. This sets a bad example for the society. If you are not completely sure that you have the fortitude to stick to the vows of sannyasi life then it is better that you get married, lead a family life, and do social service and sadhana. But once you accept the life of a sannyasi, remain a sannyasi.

Now the life of a sannyasi is often filled with inconvenience and humiliation. People may insult you. If you ask for food, somebody says, "Oh, go away. You have become a great sannyasi. Why did you become a sannyasi? Why don't you go and work? Why are you begging?" You have to be prepared to listen to such things and tolerate them. It may so happen that you have to stop in Patna but you don't know anyone there. You have no place to stay and no money for a room in a hotel. So you have to go to a *dharmasala*, a public inn. Is there such a system in America?

D: No, no such system. In fact, in America there is almost no system of sannyasa. There are some sannyasis but people are not familiar with the idea.

C: So you go to some *dharmasala*. *Sala* means "house" and *dharma* means "meant for good purposes." A place to stay for doing good. It is free for everyone. Anyone who doesn't have any shelter can go to a *dharmasala* and spend the night. So you go to a *dharmasala* and you find all kinds of people there. It's dirty. Somebody has just vacated the place and gone away without cleaning it. So you have to clean it before you can spread your blanket.

Furthermore, in any order of sannyasis there are seniors and juniors. Everywhere, whether it is this mission or that mission. Now the seniors are generally in the positions of command and the juniors are under them, so the juniors have to obey them. If the seniors have some work to be done they order the juniors to do it, and they have to do it.

So when a person has to face these sorts of inconveniences and difficulties they may feel demoralized and think about returning home, but that will be disgraceful. Whatever sort of inconveniences you have to face, face them. Or if you are not sure that you can face them, then wait until you develop the necessary strength of mind before becoming a sannyasi.

As far as the question of sadhana goes, both have equal status, equal opportunity in my eyes. I have just said that a family person can become a very good sadhaka, better than the sannyasi standing by their side. The sannyasi can be a very good sadhaka, better than the family person beside them. So the desire for doing good sadhana or making good spiritual progress should never enter into the question of becoming a sannyasi or becoming a family person. Anybody can be a good sadhaka. For that one need not become a monk. But if a person wants to devote all their time to social service, then it is better that they become a monk or a nun rather than a family person. A family person does not get as much time for social service. They have to devote time for the family because that is their direct responsibility. If a person is sure that they can shoulder the responsibility of the family, and that after shouldering the responsibility of the family, they can devote some time and some money for social service, then they can marry. But if the person feels that they will not be able to look after the family properly, and after taking care of the family also do some social service, then it is better for them to go and become a monk. No one should ever shirk their direct responsibility; the service they do elsewhere ends up being negated by the disservice they do to the family.

Then there are a few exceptions who neither become a sannyasi nor a family person. They have no direct responsibility, no family, but neither are they monks or nuns. They lead a bachelor life and prefer to remain that way. Now what about them? They should judge themselves carefully and be completely honest. They should see whether or not they can remain unmarried with honor, whether or not they can continue to uphold a high standard of morality. If they can, then okay. But if they are not sure that they have that mental strength, then it is better for them to marry.

Baba has given a clear mandate on this subject. He has said that unless one has a valid reason then one should get married. No one should remain a bachelor if they don't have a valid reason to do so. Why? Because the system of marriage preserves the chastity and purity of the society. This is what Baba has said, and I agree. These are the words of my teacher and I accept them, but from my own experience I can also say that I feel this to be correct.

Now suppose someone doesn't want to become a sannyasi, or renunciate, but nevertheless that person still wants to devote all their time, all the twenty-four hours to doing social service. Then in that case they may remain a bachelor. This becomes the valid reason, a dedicated life. That person knows that if they marry they won't be able to make their partner happy because they will always be out doing social service. Their partner will feel lonely; they won't feel satisfied. So such a person should not marry. This becomes a valid reason and this is what Baba meant to say. Unless you have some valid reason to remain a bachelor you should marry.

D: Are there other valid reasons, or is this the main one?

C: No, there are others. Someone who is diseased, physically unfit, or infirm should not marry. Also, if you are financially incapable of maintaining a family, then you should not marry until you become financially capable. You must have the wherewithal to maintain a family properly before undertaking the responsibility of marriage.

D: So ideally, one should complete one's education first and be financially independent.

C: Nowadays this is the general impression among people in the society. Formerly marriages in India were celebrated earlier. The boy would be married before he had even passed matriculation. Girls who had barely learned how to read would already be married. But nowadays, even in the villages, the impression is, "My son is still studying; I am not willing to arrange for his marriage until he completes his education." What people feel, and rightly so, is that if someone is married at the age of eighteen, while they are still pursuing their studies, then their mind will be diverted in two directions. They won't be able to concentrate properly on their studies. Age is also an important factor. The body should be fully matured; then and then only should a marriage be celebrated. And financial independence is necessary so that the family can be maintained without having to depend on any outside source. All these are the practical things that one should consider.

D: Dada, when we sing kirtan, or when we dance kirtan, we use many different tunes, different melodies and rhythms. Are there certain tunes and certain rhythms which are better for our spiritual ideation than others? And if so, how can we choose which melodies and rhythms are better for kirtan?

C: In kirtan the melody is not the main point; the important point is the meaning. You can sing *Baba Nam Kevalam* any way you like.[4] It need not be sung in any particular melody or rhythm—sing it any way you like. It is the custom nowadays in India that many singers are adjusting kirtan to the tunes of Prabhat Samgita, and that is also good.

D: In western countries people like to adapt kirtan to the style of music they are comfortable with, but occasionally some people raise the objection that some of these musical styles are not sentient enough, or not suitable for kirtan. This has on occasion sparked a bit of a debate since the people from those cultures feel that this is their natural style of singing. When they sing kirtan in that way they feel inspired. So they want to know, can they not sing kirtan in their natural ...?

C: Yes, yes, definitely. Sing whatever tune makes you feel happy. The only important thing is not to change the words. Simply that much—do not change the words. But whatever tune makes you feel happy, whatever tune attracts your mind more, sing the kirtan in that tune.

D: Dada, sometimes people wear certain stones or certain metals next to their skin because they are supposed to have certain beneficial effects. Some doctors, and some yogis also, prescribe these precious metals and stones as a kind of treatment, and they claim that they have some good effect on sadhana. Can certain types of metals and certain types of gemstones,

4 The mantra used for kirtan in Ananda Marga. It means "Divine Consciousness is all there is."

when worn next to the skin, actually affect our sadhana, and perhaps our samskara?

C: There is a traditional practice of using certain stones and some kinds of metals also in this way; one person prescribes copper, someone else prescribes iron, a third person prescribes a certain kind of gemstone or a certain color of gemstone. Well this is a part of *jyotisvidya*—astrology in English.

D: Yes. It's considered a branch of astrology.

C: So it is prescribed that if you are under the adverse effect of the moon, or if you are under the adverse effect of Saturn, then you should wear such-and-such stone and that will counter those adverse effects. This is the general import. Well, for a sadhaka who creates vibrations within themselves through sadhana, through incantation, through kirtan, these things are not important. I don't wear a ring. I don't have any stone. Of course, I wear a *pratika* but a *pratika* can be of any metal. A *pratika* is an emblem, something which reminds us of our ideology. If I always keep it with me then it serves as a continuous reminder. For example, if I think of doing something wrong, and if I put my hand here and feel it then immediately my ideology will flash in my mind. And when the ideology appears in my mind, the evil thought immediately vanishes. It is pushed out. It is not to protect me from any evil; it is just to remind me of my ideology. So I would say that such stones or rings or metals do not matter much in the life of a sadhaka.

D: One Dada told me that he read in one of Baba's books that when people do a lot of social service or a lot of social activity then their spiritual progress may be hampered. But this same intense activity contributes to a big leap in collective progress. Could you give some comment on this, especially given the fact that our ideology encourages us to do as much social service as possible?

C: This is why we should do sadhana along with social service. We should not neglect our sadhana. And if we do proper sadhana along with social service then our progress will not be retarded. It will not suffer. But if we completely neglect our sadhana, thinking that we should devote all our time to social service, then our progress will definitely suffer. That is why

Baba used to say that one should never neglect their sadhana. Do service, but do sadhana at the same time. You must find time to do your sadhana.

Whenever one goes out to do service, one has to make time for sadhana. Do some sadhana and then do some work, otherwise your spiritual progress will definitely be hampered. One should never develop the attitude that sadhana is unnecessary because one is doing so much social service. Other problems may arise. If someone is so busy doing social service that they don't get the time or opportunity to eat properly then they may become weak. They may spend so much money that their own pocket becomes empty. These things may happen, but their spiritual progress will never be hampered provided that they simultaneously give importance to sadhana as well.

D: What about a situation where a person is doing a lot of social service and doing their sadhana, but is working so hard that their body falls sick. Vivekananda, for example, died very young because he worked so hard that his body could not stand the stress.

C: He was a sannyasi. But this attitude, this philosophy, doesn't hold good for a family person. For a sannyasi it is all right, but no family person should ever emulate Vivekananda because they have a direct responsibility to shoulder. Vivekananda, as a sannyasi, was able to give up everything, to sacrifice everything for the people, but in his case the society was his direct responsibility. A family person is directly responsible for their own family. They cannot act in the same way as Vivekananda because it would amount to their neglecting their direct responsibility.

D: But if a sannyasi of Ananda Marga feels that way, then they can make that choice.

C: They can do so. Go on working till you die …

D: … and while you die, continue working.

C: Yes, while you are dying, continue working. Go on working till you die, and while dying, keep on working. Baba said this in 1958. He was addressing the acharyas. He said, "Never be idle. Go on working till you die, and even while dying, keep on working." This acharyajii [referring to his wife], she remembers it very well. She often quotes these lines from

Baba: *kam karte karte maro, marte marte bhi kam karte raho.* You understand Hindi. He spoke in Hindi. Go on working till you die, and while dying, keep on working.

September 18

D: Dada, is it possible that in some of the healing professions the doctor or healer may be susceptible to taking on some of the samskaras of the patient during the healing process?

C: No. This is their profession. They are professionally competent to treat the patient, so they are simply doing their job. The teacher imparts knowledge to the student—why should they take on the samskara of the student? They are teaching them good things, helping them to become a scientist, a mathematician, a historian. Why should they take the samskara of the child? On this earth everybody has to take up some profession. This is simply the practice of a respectable profession—teaching people, healing the sick.

A person takes up the profession of selling goods and in the process they mix in something which doesn't belong. They are practicing adulteration. Instead of selling pure ghee, or pure butter, or pure oil, they are selling something adulterated. They are mixing the oil with an inferior quality oil and selling it as the high-grade product. They are also practicing a profession but they are practicing it badly or dishonestly. So everybody has some sort of profession on this earth.

Now when you act in a professional capacity you don't take on anybody's samskara, but when you do something wrong in your profession, if you cheat, if you act treacherously, whether you are a teacher, scientist, seller or trader, doctor, whatever, then you earn bad samskara as a result of your actions. The reaction to those actions will be very painful. If a person practices a profession in a wrong way they don't take on samskara from other people, but they do earn the bad samskara from their own actions.

D: Are there other kinds of situations where we may run the risk of taking on samskara from other people?

C: That is possible. If you are not professionally competent to do something and you do it, let us say, with the help of your mental power, then you will definitely take on samskara. If you cure someone from disease with your mental power then you are not practicing a profession. That is not the normal way of doing things. Suppose you have earned some sort of mental power through your sadhana, or through your practice of concentration. If you use that mental power to cure someone's disease, or if you help a lady to conceive a child—she wants to be a mother but she is not able to conceive so she becomes very unhappy—if you use your mental power to help these people, then you will definitely have to suffer a part of that person's samskara. Because that is not your profession, and that is not the right method of doing things. You have not done sadhana to be able to cure diseases. That is not the purpose of sadhana. So in this case one definitely takes on some of the samskara of that suffering person.

D: In the case of guru it is said that sometimes the guru will take on the samskaras of the disciple. Could you explain the circumstances under which this happens?

C: Yes, gurus will take on their disciple's samskara, but since the guru has the capacity to erase such reactions, they can do it. But only the sadguru can do it, only a guru who is capable of erasing the samskaras. Suppose I do this; I will not be spared. They alone can do it.

D: Baba also is said to have done this sometimes.

C: He must have done it many times, but for us it is an improper thing to do. We should guide the people, help them, show them what to do, but we should not use our power which we have earned through sadhana to help them. Never. We should help through our ordinary effort, through out human effort, not with spiritual powers. You can help them in sadhana, however. In this case you can use your spiritual power.

D: That is okay?

C: That's okay because you are professionally allowed to do so. When an acharya gives a person initiation they don't take on their samskaras, because this is their profession. They have been authorized to do so. They are just helping their brother or sister to do sadhana, to follow the right path, the path of virtue. They do not earn any samskaras doing this. But if you are not professionally authorized to do so, and you use your spiritual power to do something, good or bad, then you will definitely be responsible for the reactions.

D: I think this must be a big temptation for many sadhakas.

C: It is a temptation. When people get power they feel tempted to use it. Therefore it is strictly prohibited, both by the gurus and in the scriptures as well. The gurus have been very strict about this.

Before I went to Baba and got my initiation, I knew one man, one gentleman from my village, who was a good sadhaka, a spiritual practitioner. I have already told you about him. He, in my opinion, had attained some height on this path. He had a guru and his guru was a *muktapurush*, a realized soul. This man was practicing what the guru taught him and after he gained some power he started displaying it. When somebody was sick he used to give them a flower to put by the side of their bed and the next day they would be cured. When somebody was suffering from headaches he would give them a flower to smell and the headaches would be cured.

Now one day his teacher came to visit him. His teacher was very old by then, nearing one hundred years of age. When he saw his disciple doing this, he said, "What are you doing, my child? This is wrong; if you do not discontinue this thing you will end up being a pauper." What he meant was that his power would be spent and he would become an ordinary man, even lower than what he had been before he had attained that power. He would fall to the lowest level in his life as a sadhaka.

The disciple, this mahatma, stopped that practice immediately. The guru stayed with him for two or three days more and then returned to his own place, but the disciple never again used that power as long as he lived. That was the instruction of his guru—you will become a pauper one day soon if you continue to do this. So nobody should use ever use their spiritual power on the pretext that they are doing good to others.

D: Dada in your own life have you ever felt tempted to …

C: In the beginning a person gets tempted; it is but natural that everybody gets tempted. But when you have such a strict guru, such a strict disciplinarian, then you are under his control also. That is why the physical presence of the guru is also of great importance. In his absence, the only way out is through your Dhyana.

Now, since we are on this subject I must tell you one thing. A sadhaka should attach a great deal of importance to the practice of Dhyana. This practice transmits the vibration of the guru's physical presence. Many of the benefits which one gets through physical contact with the guru can be gotten through Dhyana. So Dhyana is very important—a sadhaka should pay more attention to Dhyana. One should do all the practices, no practice should be neglected, but one should pay more attention to Dhyana. Dhyana is very valuable. It is, I should say, superior among the processes of sadhana. Anyway, we are deviating.

D: This is an important deviation! Yesterday, while you were discussing a different topic—I think it was life and death—you mentioned inborn samskara and earned samskara. The samskara that we bring into this life, and that which we earn during this life. But I have read that there is also imposed samskara.

C: Imposed and earned—they amount to the same thing. What I meant by earned samskara is the same as imposed samskara—the samskara which you earn or accumulate after birth by living in a particular set of circumstances, by getting a particular kind of education, by living in a particular society or in a particular family. Those are the conditions in which you earn samskaras.

D: So it is what we get from our situation?

C: From the situation and from our actions also. Suppose the house of your next door neighbor catches fire and you think to yourself, "Oh, this is his samskara. He has done some bad actions in the past, and due to these bad actions his house has caught fire and all his belongings are burning up."

So with this excuse you don't go and help him, you don't help to extinguish the fire. You remain at home thinking that he is suffering from his own samskara. Now this inaction of yours is also an action. You have been put in a particular situation according to your samskara and you have decided to act in a particular way. So the situation is there and the action is also there. In this case your action is deciding not to go and help. Now because this is an action, it will incur a reaction. He is suffering as a result of his own samskara, true enough, but you are also earning samskara by not going to help him. Your duty was to go and help a man in distress, a man in trouble, a man in difficulty. That should have been your duty, but here you used your philosophy to avoid that responsibility. That action of yours will create an unpleasant reaction because you have failed in your duty. So this is imposed or earned samskara.

D: I read recently that while we are suffering the reactions of previous actions, we don't earn any new samskara—we only earn new samskara when we do an original action.

C: No. You make some decisions, you will have to act also, so definitely you will incur new reactions.

D: But if we're just suffering the reactions ...?

C: Suppose you are suffering because of your past actions and you have become penniless as a result. Now you start thinking that since you are penniless and that man has lots of rupees, why not steal some of his surplus money? So in order to feed yourself or clothe yourself, that is, in response to your situation, you steal or rob. This is a new action. While undergoing the reaction of your past action you are acting and those are new actions. Will you not suffer the reactions of this action? Of course you will. If you deprive someone of their money by theft then you will create an adverse reaction for yourself which will only increase your future suffering. While you are suffering you should have the determination, "Oh, never mind; I will try to earn my bread through honest means. And if I can't earn what I need then I will accept the suffering. I will take only one meal a day."

In this case as well you are both suffering the reactions of your past actions, and at the same time you are doing new actions. But here your actions are morally correct. Due to your strong determination you are following the right path. So the reactions you create will be quite helpful to you, quite good to you. And it is just possible that after completing the prescribed period of suffering you will have good days ahead, no new difficulties. So it is not correct to say that while suffering we do not earn new samskara. Whatever action we do while we are suffering will cause its own reaction as well.

D: I have heard some people say, "Well, I only did it because my samskara made me do it."

C: Your samskara is telling you to do this? I see. But you can earn good samskara for yourself by setting aside that mental desire. That is also within your capacity. Many people have some desire and then they think, "No, this is not good. I should not do this." And they give up that idea. The past samskara may goad a person to steal, it may give rise to that desire or impulse. But the person is free to decide, "No, I should not do this. This is a bad thing." Instead they can go and earn an honest living. Each action is a new decision, because man is independent.

You see, in the course of evolution, the human being is the creature with the most developed brain and the most developed mind. So much so that the human mind has become independent; it is not guided or controlled by nature. The course of evolution proceeds from less developed forms such as plant life and insect life, through animal life, to the most developed creatures like apes and so on, until it finally reaches the level of human beings. Now up to the level of human beings the mind is carried forward by the law of nature. But when the mind attains a human body it becomes independent. People can think independently and act independently. And when you think independently and act independently, then the reaction is yours as well, because that action is due to your independent thinking. That is why human beings earn the reaction of their actions—because they are capable of acting independently.

So if somebody says that they were goaded into doing some wrong action by their past samskara, then that excuse simply will not do. It is correct to say that because of the past samskara your mind wanted to do something wrong, but you have this thinking capacity. You are a human being, not an animal. I have the capacity to think, so let me consider whether what my mind is goading me to do is correct or incorrect. And to help me in my decision I take recourse to the spiritual teachings. The sages have said certain things. The saints have prohibited certain things. The scriptures have given certain guidance. If you keep on thinking and ultimately avoid that wrong action, then you save yourself. But if you simply allow yourself to run after those desires then you will create new and painful reactions.

So it is not correct to say that since I am being goaded by my past samskara, I don't earn any new samskara. You will definitely earn new samskara because you are a human being with the capacity to think and take a decision. You know what is right and what is wrong. You have a mind which can read, write, learn, and listen to other people's talks, and you have a mind that can think deeply on subjects. So take a decision and don't offer the excuse that my samskara made me do so. No one can escape the reaction of their actions on such a pretext.

D: At the same time Baba says that not even a blade of grass can move except by the will of God. So it seems, at least on an intellectual level, that there is some contradiction. We are independent, but at the same time everything happens according to the will of God.

C: Yes, correct.

D: Then how does one reconcile the two?

C: I will tell you how the two can be reconciled. You say that not even a blade of grass can move without his will. All right, this is correct, but if you accept this then you must accept this fully. Let us say, for instance, that someone verbally abuses you and you slap him. Now, why did you slap him? If he has abused you, think that God has done this, God has abused me? Why should you get angry and slap him?

D: Somebody may say, "I slapped him because it was the will of God that I slapped him."

C: But first he abused you. So before you slapped him why didn't you accept that abuse as the will of God? You didn't take it in that way, therefore you have slapped him. Your slapping him was a later action. His action was completed first. So why did you not take that prior action to be God's will? If you say that not even a blade of grass can move without his will, then stick to this principle everywhere. That is complete surrender, something which is very difficult for the common person to do.

If you go deep into this sentiment you will find that there is no contradiction. If you truly think that not a single blade of grass, not a single leaf can move without his will, that there can be no stir, no movement, no action if he doesn't will it so, then you will have resolved that apparent contradiction. But then you have to extend this to every action of yours and to every action of everyone else, and that means complete surrender. Simply parroting this intellectually will not do. And accepting it in one situation and forgetting it somewhere else will also not do. You do something wrong or something unpleasant happens and you say it was his will, but then you achieve something and there you forget that this was also his will. Then you think, "Oh, I have done this, I have earned this, this success has come because of my efforts," even if you do not admit it.

Suppose there is a very good soldier. He goes to battle and during the fighting he captures the place that he set out to capture. Then he thinks, "This is my skill, this is my determination, this is my strength." He forgets that this was the will of God. But when the table turns on him, he says, "Oh, this was the will of God."

So it is not right to say that everything happens according to the will of God unless you have the mental inclination of one hundred-percent surrender. If you have that sense, that inclination of mind, that complete surrender to God, then you have the right to say that everything moves as per his will. But if someone follows this philosophy in one place and then forgets it someplace else, then they don't have the right to make this claim. This philosophy means hundred-percent surrender to him—every moment, every action. This is extremely difficult. It is very easy to say but very difficult to follow.

D: Then as long as we haven't developed that total surrender, we must accept our independence and take responsibility for our actions.

C: Yes. And that is why we practice sadhana, why we cultivate proper thinking, why we study spiritual philosophy. These are the means to mend the mind, to help the mind to mend itself.

D: I have a further question about samskara. There are some people who believe or teach that when a person is in the first two or three decades of life, or when they are not so spiritually developed, then they are mostly just suffering reactions to their previous actions and not creating so much new samskara. But when a person becomes older, or becomes elevated in sadhana, then most or all of their actions become independent actions, rather than just reactions. In other words, they believe that when we are young we are mostly exhausting old samskaras, and when we mature then we really start acting independently.

C: Even a child acts independently. They may not be able to think as much or as deeply as you can, but they think and they act accordingly. Say a schoolboy is going to school during the rainy season and the road is flooded with water. There are pits in the road which are hidden under the water. Now this schoolboy of nine years or ten years of age has been taking the same path to school every day. He can't see those pits but he remembers where they are due to his previous experience and he steers clear of them by keeping to the other side of the road. What is this if not his independent thinking? So how can we say that that schoolboy has no independent thinking? There may be a difference between his way of thinking and that of a grown man. He may not think as deeply. But this doesn't mean that a child doesn't think independently. Avoiding the pit by keeping to the other side of the road, looking around while crossing the road to see whether a vehicle is coming or not—this is all independent thinking.

D: So then even very young children, say three or four …

C: Of course, they are acting according to their old samskara, but at the same time they are being guided by the imposed samskara as well. The family, the society, the neighborhood, the school, the teachers—whatever that child is hearing or watching is casting some influence on their mind. It influences them to think in a certain way. The child knows that if you fall in a pit you will be injured. How have they learned this? It is imposed samskara. The child has learned it in this life by hearing it, either from their teacher, their mother or from somebody else. According to this imposed samskara the child thinks, "No, no, I should avoid this pit," and acts on that thought. So the imposed samskara goes side by side with the samskara inherited from previous lives.

D: Then even from a very young age the child starts to earn new samskaras?

C: Yes, definitely. Now it may so happen that the child with the better samskara from the past may supersede the child with the less favorable samskara. I told you about Devavrata. He sat for the merit test examination and was one of only six students to receive the scholarship that goes with the exam. Thousands of students appeared in the exam but only six received the scholarship. Why? The imposed samskara is similar for everyone. Everybody is studying the same subjects in the same school system, living in the same culture, enjoying the same facilities and training. But in spite of that, only six among several thousand got the merit scholarship. Definitely there is something in his past samskara which enabled him to compete successfully in this exam.

So the past samskara and the imposed samskara combine together to give the result in this life. They go side by side, intricately intertwined.

D: I read a story once by a western writer. The main character in the story was a young boy who remembered his previous lives. In his previous lifetime he had been a yogi in India, but he had gotten involved with a woman and stopped doing sadhana. So in the story the boy was telling some people that as a punishment he was born in America, because in America it is nearly impossible to do proper sadhana. And there are many people who feel like this, that being born in western countries is not a good samskara, because one doesn't get the benefit of a spiritual environment.

C: No, no, I don't accept this, I don't accept this at all. The environment may not be very helpful but I don't accept that people with good samskaras cannot be born there. You see, if you are born in America you live in a very neat and clean place where everything is very systematic—the telephone system, the means of transport, the roads, the restaurants, the shops—everything is in better condition in America than in India. So if you get such facilities there, how can you say it is a bad samskara? Rather I would say that it is because of your good samskara that you are born there. Because there you have so many facilities all around you and we do not have those facilities here. On the contrary, you see the place where I am living. Full of mud and water. Eh? Nor is that water being purified to prevent the spread of infection. Is it not the responsibility of the government of the society to do so? But nothing is being done. Had it been in America it would have been cleaned immediately. Something would have been done.

D: There would be no need because there's a proper drainage system everywhere.

C: So how can we say that people with bad samskaras get born there?

D: The popular conception is that all the gurus have been born in India, and therefore ...

C: That is something else. You see, Lord Shiva took birth here and he created a spiritual atmosphere. He infused the place with a spiritual vibration. And when that spiritual vibration started declining Lord Krishna came. In the meantime so many other saints were coming who were not as powerful as Lord Shiva or Lord Krishna, but who were saints nonetheless. They took the help of that vibrational force. When something is available in a certain place then you go to that place to get it, and since that vibrational force is here the saints have taken birth here.

If you want fruit, you go to a fruit-seller. If you want flowers, you go to a flower-seller. If you want fish, you go to a fishmonger. You go to the place where things are available if you want them. Now there was no history of spirituality before Lord Shiva. Earth's spiritual history begins with Lord Shiva. He created a vibration, an atmosphere, and people came to him to learn, and they kept on coming. Many of them became saints in their own right, and after Shiva left people continued coming to them to learn, and it continued on in this way. But this doesn't mean that people with good samskaras are only born in India. A beggar is born in India and he remains a beggar lifelong. Even a poor person in America is better off than a middle class person in India—I mean according to worldly standards of living. So why should I not say that you were born in America because of your good samskara?

D: But sometimes we feel, those of us who want to learn sadhana, that we have to come to India. We had to come to India to see Baba, for example, because Baba was in India.

C: That is why I said that if the fruit-seller is here, then you have to come here to go to the fruit-seller's shop. If you want to buy fruit, you can't go to a clothing shop. So because the spiritual teacher is here you come here. And because you live in an affluent place you have the means to do so. You climb aboard a plane and you come, just as you have done. But suppose you want something that is not available in India—good food, clothes, a nice place to live—then you can go to a place where it is available. The people here don't have that opportunity. So if anybody says that people with good samskaras are born in India, and people with bad samskaras are born in western countries, then they are wrong. Rather I could say that people with good samskaras are born in Europe, and people with bad samskaras are born here, because the people here have to suffer a lot. But this is also not the correct way of thinking.

Anyhow, these conditions are always changing. You talked about that story, the story of the Vedic saint or scholar who hated Muslims and therefore was born as a Muslim in his next life. So it is like that. Suppose someone has done a lot of good in their life, they have practiced sadhana sincerely, but they had the desire to live very nicely, in a very neat and clean place with a comfortable living standard. So in the next life they will be born in a place where all these things are available to them. People are born according to their samskaras, no doubt, but more specifically according to the desires they have. That man's desire took the form of an aversion, an aversion to Muslims, so he was born in the same category which he hated.

Now in the story which you mentioned, the boy was a good sadhaka. He was a good sadhaka but he made some mistake. He had a desire and he went astray due to that desire. First came the desire. Earlier we talked about how the root of every action is in the mind, and its outward manifestation becomes action. So that young man did some wrong because he had some desire. The idea had been born in his mind to enjoy that kind of life. And he acted on that desire. He was a good sadhaka, he had good samskaras, but he also had this desire. So in his next life he was born in a country conducive to those desires.

So it is not correct to say that one is born in a particular country, or in a particular family, or in a particular culture, because of good samskaras or bad samskaras.

D: Dada, you mentioned that if you create a desire then that may determine your next birth. Is it useful, do you think, under certain circumstances, to do this consciously. Let us say we have a desire to enjoy Baba's physical presence because we didn't get the opportunity to spend sufficient time with him in this life. Is it worthwhile to cultivate that desire in order to influence the circumstances of our next life?

C: Well that depends on the person, what that person wants. If it makes you happy to come again and do service to the people, to the society, either on this earth or if required on some other planet, then this is your personal choice. You can desire this if you wish. Or you may think, "No, I don't want to do any more work. I want to get salvation now." This is up to the independent thinking of the person. In India there have been two kinds of philosophy regarding this. Many people say: *cini hote cai na re man, cini khete bhalobasi*. You know Bengali. "I don't want to be sugar …

D: I want to eat sugar.

C: I want to eat sugar, because I feel pleasure eating sugar. So it's like that. *Cini hote* [to be sugar] means "salvation", *cini khete bhalobasi* means …

D: Coming to this world …

C: Coming to this world and enjoying what is pleasant. It is for the person to decide, to think and decide independently. Whether one says *cini hote cai na re man, cini khete bhalobasi*, or one says, "No, no, I don't want to eat sugar, I don't say *cini khete bhalobasi*. Let me have salvation, let me become sugar. I will become sugar instead of eating sugar." So this saying is just an example to illustrate the philosophy. Many people want to come again and again to do service, and others don't want to come anymore. They want to get away, to get salvation.

D: And the Lord will grant that desire if you have that desire?

C: But for the fulfillment of that desire, the desire for salvation, you must exhaust your samskara. Desire alone won't do; the samskara, the binding force is there. You may have the desire for salvation, but if you are bound by so many ropes over the whole of your life, then how can you get salvation? You have to do something for salvation. Once you deserve salvation, once you become a deserving candidate for salvation, then you will get whatever you desire: if you want to be sugar or if you want to eat sugar.

D: But first you must reach that position.

C: Definitely. And for that we come to the same old principle—sadhana and seva, sadhana and service.

D: It occurs to me that part of the reason we put so much emphasis on service is because it also helps to exhaust our samskara.

C: Yes, there is a definite process at work. It is a balancing process. Suppose you have some bad samskaras and through your spiritual progress you earn good samskaras. They become the balancing force.

D: They cancel each other out?

C: Oh, definitely. You see, here is a tap. On one side there is a pipe for the water to flow out, and on the other side a pipe for the water to flow in. Life is like that. You are earning, you are losing; you are earning, you are losing. That is the balancing force. If you earn good samskaras you will definitely neutralize your bad samskaras.

D: Dada, it is said that while we are doing sadhana we are actually burning samskaras. How does this process work?

C: I have already explained it. The root of all action is in the mind. You may or may not manifest it outwardly, in the external world, but the action exists already. Suppose the idea comes to you, "I must do my meditation", but you don't do it. What will the result be? You had a good idea, the idea to perform a good action, and that idea itself is also an action. So that action is complete. The consequence of that action in its outward manifestation, which is the actual sitting in meditation, did not take place so you do not get the benefit of the meditation, but you will definitely get the benefit of that good idea. And what is the principle benefit of that idea? That the idea will come again and one day you will sit down in meditation due to that idea. So the idea itself is also an action.

Now suppose you think of stealing something, but you didn't get an opportunity to steal it. The actual stealing, the outward manifestation of that thought, didn't happen, so your action is not completed physically in the external world. But in the mental world, in your mental arena, your action is complete. You thought of stealing and that thought will definitely bring you a bad reaction. So the mental action is also an action.

D: Let us say that we sit for sadhana and for forty-five minutes we perform Ishvara Pranidhana. During that forty-five minutes do we exhaust some of our samskaras, that is, during that actual process of going through the shuddhis and reciting Ista Mantra?

C: Yes, certainly. You see, even from the point of view of sheer effort, you are going through some strain. You are practicing asanas, you are doing meditation, you are sitting for an hour or for two hours, devoting time to your practice, and in the process you are giving up so many other pursuits, you are sacrificing so many pleasures. So all this effort and devotion of time exhausts your past bad samskaras. To put it in a crude way, you are giving yourself a kind of self-inflicted punishment and that in itself becomes the requital of those accumulated samskaras. You have already completed the punishment and now you are a free man. You have stolen this book and the judge sentences you to six months imprisonment. You do your six months imprisonment and then you are free. So all these sacrifices in the life of a sadhaka are, in the most mundane sense, a self-inflicted punishment. You yourself arrange to pay the penalty so you will be free from paying any future penalty. So take it in this way, as a kind of self-inflicted punishment or requital of past reactions. And it so happens that in the life of a sadhaka most of the samskaras are exhausted during the actual sadhana period.

D: So there is an acceleration of this process of exhausting the samskara while we're actually doing sadhana?

C: Everyday, for so many years of your practice, you are adjusting the quantity of samskara that is held in store for you. In time, most or all of your bad reactions finish and only the good remain. So those reactions no longer serve as your binding force. You are a free man in respect to your bad reactions and thus your mind will be freer. And what will happen? Your progress will accelerate because the binding force is defeated. From then on you progress more and more rapidly. That is why a sadhaka's speed gradually increases, and you will generally observe that when a sadhaka becomes a good sadhaka in time, then their speed becomes extremely rapid.

D: Because they don't have so many samskaras to hold them back?

C: Exactly. Because the binding forces are gradually being exhausted. There is less resistance. That is why a sadhaka begins to progress very rapidly after they have done sadhana for a long period of time. They begin to move very quickly, they achieve what they want to achieve very quickly, because they now have the capacity for that rapid movement in the absence of the old binding forces which have finally been spent.

D: Is it still possible to achieve samadhi even if a sadhaka still has a lot of samskara to exhaust? Or can samadhi only be achieved when most of one's samskaras have already been spent?

C: No, no. Samadhi can be achieved and the samskaras will be adjusted accordingly. The sadhaka may still have samskara to suffer. They may have bad reactions which will have to be suffered through, and good reactions are also a binding force. It is said: *Avasyameva bhutavyam krtam karma shubhashubham. Shubha* means "good" and *ashubha* means "bad." A human being is responsible for all their actions, and therefore they will have to bear all the reactions, whether they are good or bad. Suppose you have done very good things and as a result you are born into a good family, into a rich family in a good environment where you are enjoying your life. It is your samskara which has brought you there. But then, while you are enjoying this life you are still in bondage, because you are still acting and creating new samskara, and moreover you are acting in a very crude way, that is, you are enjoying life through your senses, through the opportunities that this good samskara has brought you. These actions of yours, this enjoyment is born out of a desire to enjoy life through the senses, and again you are creating bindings and bondage for yourself. Either in this life or in the next, what you are doing now will rebound on you as reactions to your actions.

Suppose a man is born in a multi-millionaire's family, and he lives his entire life in a lavish, carefree way, always enjoying life and not caring to replenish his wealth, not fulfilling that responsibility. Now, suppose that man reaches sixty years of age and he finds that he has exhausted all his wealth. He has exhausted that good samskara without replenishing it and for the rest of the life he will have to remain a poor man. So while acting you are earning. And who will bear the fruit of that reaction? The person who has acted.

The point is that while a person is reaping their good samskara or bad samskara, they don't remain inactive. They react to their situation and create new samskara. A poor man or a suffering man or a sick man is reaping the fruits of his previous actions. A very rich man, a man living luxuriantly and comfortably, is also reaping the fruits of his previous actions. But both will exhaust those fruits one day. So try to earn good reactions through good actions, and then, when you get good fruits or good reactions, don't remain satisfied with them. Don't simply enjoy them. Try to escape from the bondage of those good fruits as well.

D: That is the hard part.

C: Undoubtedly, but since a person is independent, they can think independently and act independently. I remember when I was a student studying for matriculation I used to read the newspapers everyday. One day the news came that the King of England had abdicated the throne. I thought to myself, "What kind of man is he that he has abdicated the throne of the biggest empire on Earth." People used to say that the sun never set on the British Empire—this was about 1936 or 1937—and this man has abdicated! For the next several days articles were being published about the abdication. It came out that the Prince of Wales, as he was commonly called, wanted to marry a certain lady who was divorced and the rules didn't allow him to remain king and also marry her. The alternative was given him to either marry someone else who fit the proper criteria or else abdicate the throne. Lady Simpson was her name, I believe. So he chose to abdicate the throne and his younger brother became king. He became King Edward VIII for a short time after his father died, and after his abdication his younger brother became George VI. Elizabeth is most probably the daughter of George VI, Edward VIII's niece.

So this was his independent thinking. He didn't feel happy being the king of this great empire, the British Empire, if he couldn't marry according to his choice. He decided that he would rather live the life of an ordinary man than give up his freedom of choice. So he married and became some kind of Lord instead. These things are all due to the power of independent decision. One thinks independently, takes a decision, and acts accordingly. In his case he preferred a happy married life to being king of an entire empire. Somebody else has a desire to be born in a rich family so they can enjoy life. Another person desires to be born in a priest's family so they can worship all the time. Yet another person thinks, "I should be born in India where I will get a spiritual teacher easily." So I have already said that in the process of evolution the human being has become independent-minded. They can think independently, take a decision independently and therefore they will have to reap the fruits of that independent thinking and independent action.

At this point we broke for noon meditation and lunch. During lunch the conversation turned to the spiritual history of India and when we moved to the sitting room for our afternoon session we picked it up there.

D: India has a very strong spiritual tradition. Has Baba ever said anything, either in your presence or that you know of, about the spiritual tradition of other places? For example, did Baba ever say anything to your knowledge about China? Though China doesn't have a spiritual culture like India, they do have a tradition of spirituality.

C: No, Baba never talked specifically of other countries to my knowledge. That includes China. He always talked about human beings, human society, never referring to any country. In the early days, before Ananda Marga began, there was ample time for us to be with Baba. We were often alone, Baba and I, for hours together, and I never heard him talk about any country. Whatever he said, he said about humanity, about human beings. He never talked about China, or about India, or about Australia. When we asked him about the division of mankind into different races, he explained the early history of the human race, about the migrations of the Aryans, the Mongolians, the Red Indians, the Negroes. He answered us in a general way, but he never mentioned any country.

D: Many Margis all over the world, and many other people as well, are seriously concerned about predictions of a worldwide crisis in the near future. People are expecting a depression, natural disasters, possibly a third world war. What is your opinion about what can or may happen in the near future? And how should we prepare, both internally and externally, for what we may have to face?

C: You see, there is no doubt that we are facing bad days, not only in one country but all over the world. Such a condition is already prevailing practically everywhere on this earth, and there is every likelihood of this bad becoming worse in the near future. Now, how should we prepare to meet such an eventuality? Nothing can be accomplished without spirituality, without the spread of spirituality. By this I mean that spirituality should be passed on to the maximum number of human beings. They should be helped to turn toward spirituality. That is the only way to save ourselves from devastation and destruction.

But at the same time, since we are living in a society we have to make certain temporary arrangements also, such as united defense projects, wherever and in whichever manner it is necessary, because the same formula may not hold good everywhere. Such things will have to be done on a temporary basis. But on a permanent basis the spread of spirituality is necessary, very necessary, to save us from the bloodshed and anarchy that is gradually taking hold all over the world.

Now if you think about the different countries, the condition they were in thirty years ago or fifty years ago, and then look at how things are today, you will realize that the disturbance is increasing everywhere and for a few years more it may go on increasing. Under such circumstances our principle duty is to try to convince people to take to the path of spirituality so that all human beings on this earth can benefit thereby. And that is what we are striving to do. We are trying to convince people, to explain to them the philosophy as well as the practical side of spirituality. And then, during adverse circumstances we are trying to help a particular country, or a particular race, or a particular area, or a particular society through social service work. This is what AMURT is trying to do.[1] It is a group of people who have gotten together to do good to other people, to people who are suffering, because a lot of people are suffering nowadays. And it is expected that in the coming few years the amount of suffering will go up rather than come down.

Of course I am an old man and I think I'll be fortunate enough not to see those days, but you are a young man. You will see those days. So it is better that you young people work hard to spread spirituality. Those people who will take up the study of spirituality and practice spirituality will definitely not like this practice of creating troubles for other people, or this creation of machinery of mass destruction. Even a person with a minimal interest in spirituality will not like it. So try to mold the human society in a spiritual way.

Since these disturbances are on the rise, we should all try to safeguard ourselves and our future by making efforts to spread spirituality. But at the same time temporary arrangements have to be made. Whatever you think best for America, organize the people there and do accordingly. Each in their own place and community. Spirituality will not reach door to door in the immediate future. And even if you carry it to that door, who is to say whether it will be accepted or not? That you do not know. You may be rejected at one door and welcomed at another. People have different mentalities. Some will welcome you; some will dislike you. But irrespective of this, it is our duty to go on spreading spirituality. We don't know how long it will take. Therefore, I say that some temporary defense arrangements, food and water, supplies, etc. are needed. People should organize in each village, in each locality, in each area, in each country, according to the prevailing circumstances.

1 Ananda Marga Universal Relief Team. It is an internationally recognized organization dedicated both to disaster relief and developmental projects.

D: People are naturally worried about what may take place over the next few years and some people think, "Well, I shouldn't have children now because of the kind of world they will have to grow up in." Other people think, "Well, why should I bother studying now; in three or four years the universities may be closed." What attitude would you advise people to adopt if they have these anxieties?

C: You see, the principle should be: Do good works thinking that you are immortal, and avoid bad deeds thinking that you may not be present in the next moment. If you want to rob somebody, or burglarize some house, then think, "Why should I commit this robbery? I may not be here tomorrow. Why should I go to all this unnecessary trouble when I won't have an opportunity to benefit from it?" So while doing a bad thing one should think that one may not be alive the next moment, that life is transitory. But if you go to an area, to a disturbed area, to do service to the suffering humanity, then think, "I am immortal." And thinking that you are immortal go on helping the people. You have plenty of time to do other things later. That is the principle. Do good, thinking that you are immortal; avoid bad deeds, thinking that your life is transitory and you may not be alive the next moment.

This is the advice I would give everyone. While acquiring good qualities, while doing good works, while doing sadhana, while doing service, you should not think about tomorrow. Do not worry whether or not the world will survive, or whether or not there will be anybody left alive on the earth tomorrow. Do not think at all about these things. Act in the present, in the living present, heart within and God overhead. Approach the present moment with courage and confidence and faith in him.

D: So there is no need to worry for what …

C: No need to worry. Act in the present; forget the future. Come what may, I am alive at this moment. That much is definite. No one can say that I am not surviving, that I am dead. You are speaking, you are talking, you are eating, you are moving, you are here in the present moment—so act in the present moment. According to the present circumstances, according to the present need. Act. That is the reason I quoted those lines of poetry. Act in the living present, heart within and God overhead. That poet has given us a very good piece of advice. Lord Sadashiva said *varttamanesu vartteta*. That means, "act in the present." Don't keep on pondering over the past, and don't go on thinking about the future. Face the present situation and act.

So again I will repeat this advice to all my brothers and sisters. Come what may, act in the present. Look at what is happening today and decide how to act in that situation, under those circumstances.

D: Then some people feel, "Oh, maybe the depression will come. Maybe I should take some steps to safeguard my money."

C: Money? Let us say you have one thousand rupees in your pocket and the cost of one plate of food is fifty rupees. Fine. But what if food is not available in your area, in the locality, in this town. What good will your money do you then? You can accumulate millions of rupees but you can't eat rupees. You go to all that trouble to put away a treasure for the future and then tomorrow you don't have any drinking water. You will die for want of drinking water. Of what use will your gold and silver be then? So forget all those things and first see that the minimum requirements are available, the minimum necessities. Make arrangements for that. Food, clothes, residence, medical facilities, and arrangements for the education of the children. You must have a place to live in, something to eat, water to drink, clothes to cover yourself, medicine and somebody to advise you what to do when you are sick. The children have their whole future lying ahead of them. It should not be wasted, so we should make proper arrangements for their education. These are the minimum requirements in a human society. Don't waste your time trying to amass treasure for the future. You cannot eat or drink gold and silver and the circumstances tomorrow may be such that your treasure becomes useless. First let us think about providing for the minimum necessities.

There are many things you can do to prepare practically for the future while concentrating on the present. In rural areas you can dig wells and construct dams so that there is an adequate water supply for drinking and irrigation. You can also make arrangements for bartering important materials. Suppose you produce surplus clothes and I produce surplus grain. We can exchange our surplus keeping in mind that everyone should at least have their minimum requirements. If you live in a very cold country and I live in a warm country then you will need some woolen garments while I can make do with a simple vest. This sort of attitude will help a great deal. People should be ready to see that everyone has what they need. If I keep ten blankets stored in the basement of my house while people are dying of cold in another part of the country, or in another part of the world, it will be a crime. So this needs to be thought over collectively and then action should be taken.

The general principle should be that we should make efforts to see that everyone has their minimum requirements. And let us work with the idea that whatever I am doing today, at this moment, will do good to others in times to come. Forget what is going to happen tomorrow, let us work in the present, but let us work with this in mind—that everyone should be provided with their minimum requirements, what they need for a healthy and happy existence.

If a student thinks, "Why should I continue studying if the earth is facing devastation?" then that student will remain uneducated. They won't gain the knowledge they need to live successfully in this age. A person must keep up with the necessities of the age they live in, but if a person doesn't educate themselves as best they can then what will they do when the devastation is over? No matter how bad it gets, it is only a temporary phase. If that person is educated then they will be able to do many things, and they can teach others as well. The society will flourish again. But if they remain a fool then they will be of little service, either to themselves or to others when the crisis passes. No matter how difficult things get, no one should ever lose hope. We should work with the spirit that we are going to survive those bad days. Make yourself a strong moralist. Do sadhana regularly and always be ready to do service to the needy people. Those who think like this will definitely survive, and not only will they survive, they will become the leaders of the future. The people themselves will recognize them and approach them for advice.

D: Dada, you were just saying that over the past few decades things have been getting worse and worse. But everything is guided by the Cosmic Mind. So what is the purpose, the cosmic purpose behind this downward slide that society is experiencing?

C: The Cosmic Mind has said through its great saints: "I am not doing anything; I am not giving anybody their reactions to make them suffer. Everything is happening according to the law of nature." There is a law and everything happens according to that law. The Cosmic Mind has nothing to do with it. I am responsible and you are responsible. Let us improve ourselves and the society will improve. If we allow ourselves to deteriorate then the society will deteriorate. We will create our own hell on earth if we allow the society, through our actions, to deteriorate. If we act in a way that the society is elevated then we will create a heaven. We are responsible for what we have.

Look at this country. The parliament itself has become filled with criminals and they are discussing what to do about it in that same parliament. The politicians, leaders, bureaucrats, and high officials everywhere are corrupt, and everyone is aware of it. Finally the government is admitting as much and discussing how they can improve the situation. We have been striving for this all along, working for so many years to improve matters, to make people spiritually inclined, to persuade them to follow the path of spirituality so that matters may improve.

D: I was reading an article in a magazine outside India, it was either *Time* or *Newsweek*, which listed the number of parliamentary and governmental officials in India charged with crimes. It amazed me to see how big the list was.

C: Yes, they were listed here also, and now you see the reaction, a good reaction. The problem is being recognized. Now they are anxious to improve matters, but when we said the same thing thirty years ago they didn't listen to us. They branded us as enemies. They tried to disband us. They tried to destroy our organization, to wipe out our organization. But now they are trying to do the same thing that we were calling for thirty or thirty-five years ago. This is the law of nature at work. As per the law, if you commit the crime then you must face the reactions, one day or another. You will have to reap what you have sown. So these corrupt officials, these criminals in the guise of political leaders, are now gradually beginning to face bad times.

So again I will say the same thing: Act in the living present, heart within and God overhead. Let us work with confidence and courage, always keeping him as our pole star, as our *dhruvatara*. If you can always keep the pole star in sight, you will never lose your way. When you find yourself in the dead of night, and you don't know in which direction you are headed, look to the pole star and you will find your way. He is the pole star. Do your sadhana, serve the people, act in the present, and have courage and confidence and faith in him. Let tomorrow take care of itself. Be good and do good. Work with this spirit.

D: Granted, we human beings have created this situation, but what happens if things become too much for us, if we cannot stop it, if it keeps on getting worse and worse?

C: Try to intervene, try to stop it, and if you fail, it doesn't matter. I am doing my duty. I am responsible for my duty. In the Lord's eye, I am guilty only if I do not make the effort to do my duty. But if I try and I fail, then I am not guilty, because I have done my duty. I am not responsible for the outcome. That is his business, his responsibility. "Lord, it is your business to see to the results. I am doing as per your dictates. I am striving hard and making efforts. I won't worry about the results. I am trying to make things better, but if I fail please take care of it. I have limited power, limited scope; you are infinite, you are omnipotent. Please take care." Hand the responsibility over to him, but do not fail to act. Leave the results to him, but don't sit idle. Go on working and things will improve. If you are sitting idle and then say, "O Lord, this is your responsibility, please look to it!" then he will not listen. You must strive, and if you meet with failure, then offer it to him.

At this point the batteries cut out on my tape recorder, although I didn't realize it until it was time to leave. As a result the last hour or so of our discussion was recorded only in the Cosmic Mind, where it is destined to remain, at least until I can make the journey from conscious to unconscious and back again. When I got back to my hotel that evening, however, I jotted down in my diary what I remembered from Dada's answer to my final question.

As Dada was talking during that last hour he was reclining on his side, very relaxed. I had abandoned my list and I was feeling my way more and more into the conversation, rather than just stringing together a list of disjointed questions. At one point, while he was talking about service and becoming an ideal human being, he raised his fist and made a downward motion several times without actually striking the cot, to emphasize his point. There was a powerful vibration behind his words and I was feeling it deep inside. Internally my mind was shouting out, "Yes, I want to be like that," as I followed his words, following the images my mind was creating of what it would be like to lead that sort of life, to actually live with that kind of noble, elevated outlook. I could feel the inspiration growing as the light changed. Twilight was just coming on as we got to the question about the *kosas*,[2] and as Dada answered I could see his mood changing. When he got to the highest kosa and went on from there to talk about savikalpa and nirvikalpa samadhi, he half closed his eyes and I could literally feel his mind climbing into the regions he was describing. It was a magical feeling, and his words were full of that same magic. I was really sorry later on when I discovered that those words were lost, because there is no way that I can do justice to what he said. It was not only what he said, but how he said it—the words he used and the vibration behind them. It was such a perfect end to the session that I didn't want to ask any more questions, even though he was ready to go on for some time more. It felt so perfect, and resonated so much inside, that I knew I had to stop.

From here I have no choice but to let my memory take over and hope that it doesn't leave out any of the main points he made.

The *kosas*, Dada began, are just the different stages of mind as one rises in subtlety. The crude mind, or *kamamaya kosa*, is primarily concerned with the pleasures of the body. When a person's mind is at this level the person is thinking about their sensual comforts and desires, pleasures or pain. Eating, drinking, sleeping, trying to make themselves comfortable and enjoying the sensory pleasures as best they can. Here the person is mostly concerned with their own well-being, and not so much with others. When the mind rises higher it comes to the pure mental body, the *manomaya kosa*. Here is where most of the usual mental activities take place, and here is where the person realizes that they are not alone. A sense of social responsibility comes into play, doing something for others, being aware of society, of what to do and what not to do. When the mind rises even higher it reaches the supra-mental body, or *atimanasa kosa*. At this stage the mind becomes even more detached from the world of the senses. Very little attachment is left. The mind is dominated by subtle thoughts of art, philosophy, concern about the world situation in a universal sense, and such things. Here, especially, the person starts thinking that they must do sadhana and that others should also do sadhana. Here arises the desire and action of sadhana. One thinks about doing sadhana, and one practices it as well. Then comes the *vijinanamaya kosa* which is the highest level of the conscious functioning of the mind. At this level the mind becomes almost completely selfless. Only very elevated sadhakas reach this stage. Here the only thoughts that arise in the mind are thoughts of sadhana and service.

2 The *kosas* are the different layers of the mind, five in all, the crude mind (sometimes called "conscious mind"), the subtle mind (also called "subconscious"), and three layers of the superconscious.

"Let me know Consciousness and let me serve him." No other thought comes. It is a very pure state of mind, extremely detached. When the mind climbs even higher it gets to the *hiranamaya kosa*, which is the highest state of mind. Here the mind becomes completely detached from the world. If someone walks by, you won't hear them, you won't see them. The mind becomes completely engrossed in the inner world, though a subtle sense of duality still exists. I am he. Both I and he are still there, but you realize your oneness with him.

Then Dada half closed his eyes and leaned back, completely absorbed in his inner mood. But there is another state, he continued, beyond the *hiranamaya kosa* where the mind completely disappears. That is the state of nirvikalpa samadhi where the mind dissolves in him and all duality is lost. This state cannot be described because there is no mind there to experience it. When you come out of savikalpa samadhi you can describe what it was like because your mind was there, but when you come out of nirvikalpa you cannot say anything because you were not there to experience it. Only he was there. Then Dada quoted a Sanskrit shloka and translated it. "Beyond the *hiranamaya* is the unmanifest entity."

He said a few more words about that state, his eyes still half closed, looking completely withdrawn, and then he fell silent for a few moments. Just when I was wondering if he would come back at all, he started talking again—then the mind comes out of the unmanifest and back into savikalpa samadhi, and then it comes down still further into *vijinanamaya*—and as he was talking he came out of his mood, opened his eyes, and started becoming animated again. Finally the mind comes down to its original stance, to the *manomaya kosa*, and then you are a common man again. Now he was beaming from ear to ear. But you should never let your mind come down below *manomaya kosa*. A sadhaka should never let their mind go below this level. The light was fading, the divine magic glowing everywhere in the room, and I knew that I didn't want to ask any more questions. After a few minutes I asked Dada if a good sadhaka would keep their mind in *vijinanamaya kosa* all the time. He said that sometimes you have to come down to the lower *kosas* if you have some work that needs to be done in those lower *kosas*. I asked if one would need to come down to *atimanasa* to talk about philosophy or art. No, he replied. This can be done in *vijinanamaya kosa*. But if you have to go to the store to make some purchases then you have to walk there, you have to look at the different items, compare the prices, and for that you have to come down to *manomaya*, but never lower.

What if someone comes to you with questions, I asked? Let us say they have a tape recorder. What *kosa* do you stay in? Dada replied that it depends on the question also. With some questions the mind goes up, and with other questions you have to come down to answer them. One person asks you questions and you don't even want to answer those questions. It's a feeling that comes in the mind. Who can say why, but it comes. But then another person asks you questions and you feel very happy. You want to answer those questions. You find your mind naturally going up when you think about the questions. There the questioner has to stop you from going into samadhi. They will have to pull you back and say, "No, don't go into samadhi, otherwise how will you be able to answer any more questions?" Especially when the question is about sadhana or guru. Then the mind goes up very quickly.

I told Dada that I hoped that he had enjoyed the questions I'd brought him. He smiled and said that he had enjoyed my questions very much. "If a better sadhaka had been sitting before you then he certainly would have gone into samadhi with these questions." We both laughed. I knew, of course, that Dada had the control not to go into samadhi when he was answering questions or spending time with people.

And then I remembered reading about Ramakrishna and the times he would go into samadhi when he would listen to devotional singing, and what I wouldn't have given for an opportunity to be there in the room with him, oh so long ago. Now here I was sitting before another Indian saint, and while I perhaps could not fully appreciate the great fortune I had to be in the position I was in, I understood enough to feel humbled by the experience. Chandranath, and the sadhakas throughout history like him, are the inspiration that keeps us climbing. When we see God manifest in another human being then we feel that there is hope for us yet. That here is an example of what we would like to become one day, and may yet become.

GLOSSARY

Acharya: Spiritual teacher. Literally, "one who teaches by example."
Ananda: Bliss.
Ananda Marga: The path of bliss. The spiritual organization founded in 1955 by Shrii Shrii Anandamurti for the propagation of his spiritual teachings and for establishing social service projects.
Anandamurti: The guru of Ananda Marga. b. 1922, d. 1990.
Asana: Literally, "seat"; yoga posture.
Ashram: Spiritual center or community.
Astaunga yoga: Astaunga means "eight-limbed." This is the name given by Patanjali to his systemization of the discipline of yoga. The eight limbs or practices are yama, niyama, asana, pranayama, pratyahara, dharana, dhyana and samadhi.
Atman: Unit consciousness or soul.
Avadhuta or Avadhutika (f): Literally, "one who is thoroughly cleansed mentally and spiritually"; a monk or a nun of an order close to the tradition of Shaeva Tantra.
Baba: Etymologically, "beloved"; colloquially, "father." It is a common form of address for one's guru in India if one's guru is male.
Chakra: Literally, "circle." It refers to psycho-spiritual energy centers located within the spinal column that are used as points of concentration for meditation.
Dada: Elder brother; a common form of address in north India. It denotes respect.
Dharma: Spirituality; essential nature of any entity; the path of righteousness in social affairs.
Dhyana: Literally, "meditation." The sixth lesson of Ananda Marga sadhana is called Dhyana.

Didi: Elder sister. A common form of address in north India. It denotes respect.
Guna: Quality or binding principle.
Guru: Literally, "dispeller of darkness"; spiritual teacher or spiritual master.
Guru Shakash: A meditation technique practiced in Ananda Marga in the morning immediately upon waking.
Ishvara: Literally, "controller of controllers"; God.
Ishvara Pranidhana: Literally, "to focus all one's propensities toward the Supreme"; the name of the first lesson of Ananda Marga sadhana.
Ista: Goal; one's personal conception of God or one's spiritual goal.
Ista Chakra: The point of concentration used in the practice of Ishvara Pranidhana; it varies from person to person.
Ista Mantra: The mantra used in Ishvara Pranidhana; different mantras are given to different people according to their individual mental vibration.
Japa: The repetition of one's mantra.
Kirtan: The chanting of mantra, usually accompanied by the Lalita Marmika dance.
Kundalini or kulakundalini: Literally, "coiled serpentine." It refers to the dormant spiritual energy of the individual, which resides at the base of the spine and can be aroused through spiritual practice.
Mantra: Incantation; a sound or collection of sounds that, when meditated upon, leads to spiritual liberation.
Maya: Illusion; the creative principle, Prakriti, in her phase of creation.
Moksha: Salvation; when the mind merges into Supreme Consciousness at the time of death.
Mukti: Liberation; when the mind attains union with the Cosmic Mind at the time of death.
Nirvikalpa Samadhi: The trance of indeterminate absorption, where the mind of the aspirant merges into pure Consciousness and the feeling of "I" disappears. It is the ultimate goal of yogic practice.
Patanjali: An ancient yogic master and author of the first systematic and comprehensive treatise on yogic practice to which he gave the name *Yoga Sutras*.
Prakriti: Cosmic Operative Principle.
Sadguru: True guru.
Sadhaka: Spiritual aspirant or practitioner.
Sadhana: Literally, "effort to complete." In common parlance it means "spiritual practice", or more simply, "meditation."
Sahasrara: The seventh chakra located at the top of the cranium.

Samadhi: Yogic trance; the state of union with God; the eighth limb of astaunga yoga.
Samskara: Reaction in potentiality; the sum total of an individual's pending reactions; character.
Satsaunga: Literally, "keeping company with the truth"; generally refers to keeping company with spiritual people.
Savikalpa Samadhi: The trance of determinate absorption, where the unit mind attains union with the Cosmic Mind.
Seva: Service.
Shloka: Sanskrit verse.
Tantra: A spiritual tradition that originated in India in prehistoric times, first systematized by Shiva. It emphasizes the development of human vigor, both through meditation and through the confrontation of difficult external situations so as to overcome all fears and weaknesses; also, a scripture expounding that tradition.
Yama and Niyama: The ten moral principles of yogic sadhana and the first two limbs of astaunga yoga.
Yoga: Literally, "union"; a spiritual practice or discipline which leads to union between the individual and the Divine.

ACKNOWLEDGMENTS

I would like to thank Ramesh Bjonnes who took time out from his own writing to read this manuscript and give some very helpful feedback.

The epigraph is taken from *Ananda Sutram*, Ananda Marga Publications.

CPSIA information can be obtained at www.ICGtesting.com
Printed in the USA
LVOW040232061112

305943LV00001BA/19/P

9 781881 717010